Talk about the ironies of life . . . I had ordered the red beanbag chair for Riann for Valentine's Day. Not that her parents couldn't afford it. Not that she'd get a lot of use out of it. But simply because it was *doing* something to make her happy, to add a little bit . . .

But it didn't come. And it didn't come. The saleslady had casually promised delivery in "five days." That would have been February 4. . . . On April 5 someone called. "Your red beanbag chair is in! Shall we deliver it? By the way, the card reads, 'Happy Valentine's Day.' Should we change it to 'Happy Easter?' "

I almost didn't have it sent. But what the heck. It wasn't Riann's fault she was dying.

The tickled look on her face that Wednesday was enough. She had enjoyed it. It was all hers, her very own.

But I wanted to wring someone's neck at that department store.

You can't buy it, can you? . . . Time. . .

Also by Nina Herrmann Donnelley:

I NEVER KNOW WHAT TO SAY

GO OUT IN JOY!

Nina Herrmann Donnelley

BALLANTINE BOOKS • NEW YORK

Library of Congress Catalog Card Number: 76-44972

ISBN 0-345-36054-0

Manufactured in the United States of America

First Ballantine Books Edition: March 1990

to my parents
with abiding love

INTRODUCTION

When I wrote "Not the End" on the last page of *Go Out In Joy!* fifteen years ago I did not intend its meaning to include republication of the book, nor the addition of an epilogue. When I wrote those words I simply meant that it was not the end to the love and influence of the lives of those children within its pages. But the statement was to prove prophetic for the book itself notwithstanding.

I was frankly pleased when Ballantine Books asked for permission to republish *Go Out In Joy!* I had received numerous inquiries for copies of the book over the years since publication had ceased, and I was glad to be able to tell people it soon would be in print again.

At the same time, it crossed my mind that I had maintained contact over the years with at least three families about whom I had written in *Go Out In Joy!* "Perhaps you would like me to add a short epilogue about what has happened to some of the families involved," I innocently suggested to Toni Simmons, my editor at Ballantine/Epiphany.

"Sure," she replied.

I say "innocently" because I had no idea at that moment that I would find such a wealth and diversity of information, feelings and advice in my follow-up interviews with the members of the Miles, Felini and Collins families. At the end of exhaustive, and emotionally exhausting, interviews I had what some people pointed out was almost enough material for another book. Perhaps they were right. But another book is not the goal.

The goal is to republish, virtually in its original form, the true story, *Go Out In Joy!*; then to supplement that story with three epilogues which tell, *in the families' own words*, how the deaths of Riann Miles and Alex Felini and the disability of Joey Collins have affected them over the last fifteen years.

I have made *no* attempt to analyze the material presented in the epilogues. This is not a research study. The epilogues stand as they are: The memories, thoughts, feelings and perceptions of the people involved.

I commend each person who speaks in the epilogues for his or her raw courage in sharing with me and with you that which is, at times, *extremely personal and extremely painful*. Each person did this solely as an effort to help any reader who needs such help to understand what it *can* be like for those involved, years down the road, after a child dies or is born with a handicap. Their experiences and feelings are in no way universal. But neither are they unique.

The information presented in the three epilogues came from interviews that were completely unrehearsed. It is material that comes from love which, in each situation, most certainly was "Not the End."

Nina Herrmann Donnelley
Hilton Head, S.C. 1989

ACKNOWLEDGMENTS

This book was not written to be a book. It was written to tell my divinity school professors what it was like to be an embryo hospital chaplain who had never faced suffering and death. It was to fulfill a requirement . . . but mostly it was the paper-and-pencil process of one person trying to unscramble a compression of feelings, thoughts, reactions, and questions.

That it evolved, basically in its original form, into a book is the result of Dr. Martin E. Marty of the University of Chicago: my adviser, good friend—and agent! To him my deep thanks, not only for his literary encouragement but for his support and kindness throughout my divinity school days and beyond.

Many thanks, too, to Dr. Martin Maloney of Northwestern University, who, by giving me *freedom* of pen and mind in my undergraduate days, helped me discover the *fun* of writing.

To watch your child die or struggle daily with a physical or mental handicap is a pain that is not describable. But each of us has a neighbor somewhere who is either sinking or swimming within this pain. If these writings do nothing else, perhaps they will contribute to the sensitivity of the persons who read them— the sensitivity that encourages one to reach out and touch, life to life, another person who may be terminally ill or physically or mentally handicapped or have a child who is.

The people in this book are real. Care has been taken to protect their identities and privacy. But they need no apologies. They are truly valiant people—children, parents, nurses, doctors, relatives, and friends—who endured. To them I give my unspeakably deep appreciation always. For this book is *their* gift to you.

. . . Their gift, and the gift of Dr. Elam Davies, Pastor Emeritus of the Fourth Presbyterian Church in Chicago, who—though consistently warning me of the "hazards" of ministry—has given me my greatest spiritual and personal strength and support throughout. His theology is uniquely uplifting and worthy. It is neither panacea nor condemnation. It is affirmative of the worth of personhood . . . it is inclusive rather than exclusive . . . and it reminds—at times when one is at the brink of despair—that God's love is unconditional and everlasting and will conquer all in the end. To him I owe whatever good I have been or am able to be as minister, no matter how far the journey takes me.

Nina Herrmann
Chicago, 1976

for you shall go out in joy,
and be led forth in peace;
the mountains and the hills before you
shall break forth into singing,
and all the trees of the field
  shall clap their hands.

ISAIAH 55:12

PROLOGUE

THERE'S AN INTERIM now, a lull before the storm, a waiting for the other shoe to drop . . . what you will.

Nine-year-old Riann Miles is going to die, probably before summer. No one can be sure. But she has begun her final descent. There is no way back.

Right now she is still "with it." She still laughs and smiles and wrinkles up her nose, and giggles, and plays little jokes, and complains when she has to take her afternoon "rest." She still hugs and kisses and gives back love.

I want to remember her this way. Desperately I want to remember her this way. But it won't happen. The slides that stack up in my mind and play back at random years after their scenes were live will include pictures of Riann breathing beyond laughter and love. I know now the slides will be there. But I do not know what they will look like. And that's what frightens me.

Yes, I have seen other children die—both in the moment and in the months. So why is Riann different? I'm not sure. Maybe it's because I have known her long enough and well enough that my love for her is being returned beyond just a moment of sharing . . . And that forebodes the difference between sympathetic loss and personal loss when the days beyond love returned come.

But let me tell you the story from the beginning. I did not keep a diary. A good journalist would have kept a diary.

But I have not lived these months as a journalist. So you will have only my random slides reached for. Perhaps some will not return. Perhaps that is a kindness.

1

IT WAS A wet day in October and I was in bed with a box of Kleenex and a bottle of cold pills.

One month earlier I had resigned from my job, to take effect December 31. I was a reporter for a large Midwest television station. It was a goal I had had since my last year in college. For the first two years after the goal had been reached, I was ecstatic. I loved every moment of my work: the people I met, the conversations I had, the places I saw. I touched many forms of living, of existing. I was allowed to be creative, to reach into the emotions, the pain, the joy—the humanness beyond the "hard" news.

Then all that stopped: new management, save money, new approach . . . Sellout; that's what I saw happening, anyway. It wasn't the same. Now I was simply taking home a paycheck—a *big* paycheck, but only that.

Maybe I saw it coming. I don't know. But for some reason or another two autumns earlier I had enrolled in divinity school. For two years and one quarter I both went to school and worked, never sure why I was going to school. I think I chose ministry because I admire my minister, Dr. Elam Davies. Maybe if I had admired a physician I'd have studied medicine, or an attorney I'd have studied law. Maybe that's all there was to it. I've always been impressionable.

Be that as it may, as I sat in bed that wet October day with

3

my box of Kleenex I was trying to decide what to do with myself after my television news job ended in December.

The coursework for my master's degree in divinity was out of the way, or would be if I passed the two courses I was taking that fall. So after December I wouldn't have to attend classes and I also wouldn't have to work. I had saved enough money to live for five months without a job. I'd be "free" until June.

Sometime during those five months I did want to finish my master's paper and take my oral exam so I could get my degree. But I really had no plans to take up a form of ministry beyond that. Besides, that was too far away. The immediate problem was January through May.

I debated spending a month at home with my parents. But I decided we'd drive each other crazy. It was too long. They love me and I them. But they were too upset that at twenty-eight I was quitting my "well-paying" reporting job. They wanted things in my life settled—like marriage, security, children. Especially since I'm an only child; all their eggs in one basket, that kind of thing. I wanted that too, mind you. But it hadn't happened, and I now spent only a moderate amount of time worrying about it.

No, home for more than two weeks at Christmas was out.

Europe? Yes, that was for sure. But I don't ski, so springtime was best. I didn't want to spend all five months over there; too expensive. No, I'd just do Europe in April and May, maybe get my master's paper written on some hills in Switzerland. That sounded nice!

So what about January through March? Blank. I blew my nose and was about to give up the heavy pondering and take a nap. Clinical Pastoral Education! That was a possibility, a good possibility. Somewhere I had the pamphlet. I threw off the covers.

Part of my divinity school training required one quarter of Clinical Pastoral Education (C.P.E.). This, at best, is a full-time job, five days a week, working in a hospital as a student chaplain . . . for twelve weeks. That's what I would do between January and March! Get my Clinical Pastoral Education out of the way.

I found the folder under my bed in a box. There were a number of hospitals in the area offering C.P.E. I decided to look for one within reasonable distance of my apartment, and offering a stipend. Why not? Better money than no money. That certainly narrowed the choice—to one: University Adult and Children's Hospital Center, a combined program working both with adults and children.

I telephoned. Today was the last day for applications, I was told. The tone of the voice implied "sorry."

"I'm in bed with a cold," I pleaded. "But I won't breathe on the chaplain if he'll just see me for an interview."

"Wait a minute, please."

I waited.

"OK," said the voice. "But don't come in today. He'll extend the time and see you in two days."

"Thank you very much," I said. "Good-bye."

Somehow I figured his secretary had put in a good word for me, though I wasn't sure why. She had. " 'Cause you're a girl," she explained later. "I figured they needed some more girls in the chaplain program!"

Her "good word" was to change my life for a time . . .

Maybe it was because I looked different—so different from the average student chaplain that I figured the chaplin-director's curiosity would beat the odds against me. But whatever the reason, right then on that wet October afternoon I figured he'd accept me. It wasn't being sure of myself. It was just knowing how people had reacted to me in the past.

I was right. He accepted me. I received the letter November first.

So it was decided: Clinical Pastoral Education from January through March, Europe from April until June, some job or another after that . . .

I didn't think anything more about it, just saved my money.

2

I HAD NEVER seen anyone die, never been around death or serious illness. I wasn't afraid of it, but I didn't really know for sure what to be afraid of.

When I would tell people what I was going to do in January I'd mouth the words "be a hospital chaplain." But I didn't feel anything like fear of death and dying. I had no associations I could make.

As I was dressing on the morning of my first day, January 2, I had a feeling of unreality, of dissociation. It was as if I was watching a stranger dress, tell the cab driver "University Hospital Center," and walk up those stairs to the second floor rooms of the Clinical Pastoral Education office.

"This isn't for real," I wanted to say to someone. "It surely isn't television news reporting; and that's all I've lived since college."

The C.P.E. offices were in an old building several doors away from Children's and about two blocks away from Adult. There were several small rooms, all somewhat dilapidated. I had seen them when I came for my interview. But now they belonged to my life; my inspection was closer. I was actually going to come to these offices and have seminars with other students and the advisor every weekday for the next twelve weeks? Me? Who had never spent more than two hours in the same place on any workday in the last four years? Who had interviewed presidents and senators and movie stars and business leaders and authors and

6

crooked politicians and honest politicians . . . Yes, and protesters and fire victims and welfare recipients and unionists and murderers and thieves . . . And almost every other kind of person I had figured one time over coffee. Me? Here? For three months?

Did I feel like it was a game?

No; but it's hard to say all that and leave you with the real feeling I had in the moments I walked up these stairs and into those rooms. It wasn't one of haughty incredulity, though that's how my words may sound. And it wasn't one of wanting to turn back. Never, not once, have I had that feeling. It was just one of blank-association: I had a hat, but it just didn't seem to match my outfit and I couldn't visualize a nail to hang it on. I was ready, but for what I didn't know.

As it turned out, I was early. It was 9 A.M. and I should have been there at 9:30. The chaplain, Craig Hatfield, was there. "We usually have coffee," he said, "but I can't find the grounds." He had brown curly hair and corduroy clothes. He sat sort of rumpled.

"Is there a coffee shop nearby?" I offered. "I'll get some."

"Yeah, 'cross the street."

I went. Returned with four cups, two extra. "Gotta stop spending my money," I reminded myself. "It's only going out now!"

Homer Lowden, another student, was there when I returned. He was from the Methodist seminary down the street. He was average-looking, moustache, blond hair, glasses. He seemed friendly.

A few minutes later three more men came in. Terry Greer, skinny, medium height, black hair, southern accent. Al O'Connor, tall, good-looking, young, brown hair, light complexion, steel-rimmed glasses. And Ted Marshall, shorter, dark hair, jutting chin, good-looking. All three were Catholic seminarians.

We did the usual "getting to know you" things. I didn't feel uncomfortable. I didn't feel anything particular. It was still too new.

That afternoon we toured the hospitals. Children's first, then Adult. It's a good bit for one day but it goes too fast to guarantee the validity of impressions. The only thing I remembered about

Children's was that I hoped I would get assigned to a new wing—I always liked things clean and fresh—and that I would get a floor with older children on it so I wouldn't have to talk with parents as much. One floor in the old wing seemed to have nothing but babies. I didn't want that!

Children's seemed more threatening; Adult more like things I had already seen in my life. An old lady I used to visit for my church had died in April. They seemed to take good care of her.

We ended our day in a machine lunchroom at Adult, just to have some coffee and talk.

Wednesday we met some social workers at Adult and talked among ourselves. It seems like we may have seen a movie, but I don't remember for sure. Funny how being new at something strips you of everyday securities, like knowing where the ladies' room is and where to be alone for a minute . . . and who to trust. You just have to avoid drinking a lot of liquids and punt, I guess.

Thursday afternoon we got our floor assignments. I got a new wing at Adult; I think it was the same floor my old lady friend had died on. But at Children's I got the old wing with all the babies—just the one I didn't want! You can't win them all, I guess.

I went to Adult first that Friday. It seemed safer. And it was nearly three-thirty by the time I braved Children's. I looked for the head nurse, Mary Cooke, and introduced myself as the new student chaplain.

"I heard we were going to have a woman," she said; "Good! You came at the right time, too," she added. "I'm about ready to give report so I can't talk with you now. But the doctors are making rounds. Why don't I introduce you to them and you can go along. That will give you a fast picture of the whole floor."

I can't tell you how *new* all this was! I didn't know what "rounds" were, or what "report" was. I had the gut feeling that I'd really rather *not* see the whole floor at once. But I had no choice, I figured.

Mrs. Cooke and I entered a large room with four cribs. At the far end of the room on the right side stood about six doctors in hospital coats. One was washing his hands, another was raising the side of a crib.

Mrs. Cooke waited for a between-sentences, interrupted to

introduce me, and left. The doctors looked, nodded, gave professional half-smiles. The one washing his hands made a slight oriental bow. I thought it was a bit weird. Then they went on with their rounds. Mrs. Cooke had introduced two or three doctors by name, but I didn't remember.

The patients were all babies or toddlers. All! Not one I could really talk with. I followed the doctors in and out of rooms. Most had four beds, most were filled with patients.

I heard medical language. I saw children with bandages wrapped around their heads. Some had tubes implanted. Two babies were lying on their stomachs on boards. One had a big bandage on his back. The other had a big open wound—like an oozing mountain—on her back. It wasn't easy to look. I didn't. I had no idea what was wrong with the baby.

Sometimes the doctors would walk by a crib and not stop. Why, I wondered? They took off bandages and looked at wounds. They talked and talked and talked. I was trying to keep my head above water. I didn't understand any of it. No one was there to explain. I just stood back out of everyone's way, trying to fade into the wall and look interested at the same time.

But I could barely look at all. When they'd uncover a wound, I'd look in that direction, but I would blur my eyes so I really couldn't see. My feet hurt, too.

One baby had four scars on her head—one in each "corner." She had been beaten by one of her parents somebody said. Why four symmetrical scars, I wondered? Was it the beating, or an operation? Would I have to talk with those parents?

On and on went the doctors. I followed and waited and half-watched and listened to words I didn't understand. It was getting hotter and hotter. I didn't know if it was me or the ward.

It was me. We had been in a lot of rooms. This was Bobby's room. He had a bandage on his head. They unwrapped it and unwrapped it, like a turban. Bobby was really cute, about one year old. He had four scars on his head. Just like the other baby. They thought one of his parents had beaten him, too. Was that the kind of operation they did on children who were beaten? Four scars?

The room started to spin. I got big black and yellow spots in front of my eyes. I knew what that meant: Fainting.

I was very hot. I turned and quietly left Bobby's room. I was

operating by radar, fighting like mad to keep my faculties long
enough to find a ladies' room. That's the misery of being "new."
Where's the ladies' room? I didn't have enough stamina to ask;
I was almost gone. The hall was spinning faster and faster.

There it was: "Ladies." I went in. It was a self-contained
little room. Thank goodness! I locked the door, threw down the
toilet seat, sat, put my head way down, and held on. I know I
didn't move for five minutes.

But I didn't faint.

Finally, I put up my head, and sat and sat and sat. I didn't
think. I didn't feel. I just breathed.

At last I got up, splashed cold water on my face, opened the
door and walked back down the hall. I wasn't exactly sure I was
going in the right direction. But I came to Bobby's room, and
the doctors were still there! (As I said, they took a long time
with each patient.) I slipped in quietly, trying not to be noticed.

The last thing I remember about that day was the doctor who
had given me the little bow of greeting earlier. He looked up at
me now over the tops of his half-glasses as if to say, "Well, look
who came back. I wondered if you would." It was brief. He
didn't say a word. But it made me feel good. I guess I knew
then that I wouldn't quit.

3

TERRY GREER HAD volunteered to be the student chaplain on call that first weekend. So I and the rest of the students had Saturday and Sunday off. I decided Saturday morning that since I was going to *have* to talk with parents—because there seemed to be only "babies" on my floor at Children's—as well as talk with adult patients at Adult, I had better get something to make people take me seriously, something to make them recognize me as a chaplain, something like . . . a clerical collar.

I got out the yellow pages. I didn't know much about clerical garb. I finally found a store that was open on Saturday, but I didn't know how to get to it on public transportation. And there was no way I was going to pay for a cab any more!

David, good old David and his Mercedes! I had been dating David off and on for nearly five years. He was forty-four, had never married, and likely wouldn't until he needed a nurse. He dated as many girls as he could. But I was the only one he had dated for any length of time. I was still a challenge, they weren't.

I had figured David out a long time ago. He knew I dated other men, too. But he was *sure* none of them could be as wealthy or desirable as he!

Anyway, David had a blue Mercedes convertible. He let me drive it. It wasn't that new, but I loved it, especially the eight-track stereo with four speakers.

It was raining when I arrived at the clerical goods store on North Hamilton. It reminded me of a dry goods store my grand-

11

father had owned. I fancied that I heard a bell jingle as I opened the door.

Inside were long rows of wooden and glass cases, shelves piled high with books and boxes, and a row of hanging choir and clerical robes on the far side of the room.

Two gray-haired salesladies were chatting behind an old-fashioned metal cash register. "May I help you?" asked the shorter one.

"Yes, thank you. I'd like a clerical collar."

"What size?"

"I don't know. I guess you'll have to measure."

Silence.

"Is it for you?"

"Yes."

"Oh, I see. Well, I don't know if we have one that small. They only make them in men's sizes." Pause. "I don't know why, with more women coming into the ministry these days. But I guess that's just the way it is."

She pulled the tape measure from around my neck. "Thirteen and a half. We don't have one that small. Are you going to wear it with a robe? If so, maybe one of our white lace choir robe collars would do?"

"No, I'm going to wear it with a dress."

"Oh. Well, we just don't have one that small. We could order it, but it would take about four weeks. We do have a fourteen, maybe a half inch wouldn't make that much difference."

"All right. May I try that?"

"It looks all right. You really can't tell, I mean about the half inch. How does it feel?"

That little old lady had no way of knowing what feelings and unfeelings were going through me then. I had never put on a clerical collar before. It was the kind of thing I hadn't planned to do until I was ordained. But at the same time, it was something I had wanted to do ever since I had started divinity school.

I suppose to anyone else—to the little old ladies, perhaps—the collar really looked weird. But to me, it was me. I wasn't a character in a play. I wasn't acting a role. I didn't look weird to me.

"It feels fine. A bit loose, but that's all right. I need it now."

"Do you want me to order a thirteen and a half?"

"No, thank you. I'll only need it for twelve weeks."

"Oh, I see."

She didn't see. I suddenly realized that. I must have been quite a mystery to the two old ladies. I hadn't really thought of that.

"If you'll tell me the name of the church where you work we can give you a ten percent clerical discount. But I must have the name of the church . . ."

"Well, I'm really not affiliated in that way with a church."

Looks exchanged between the two old ladies.

"I'm a student chaplain at University Children's and Adult Hospitals. I started this week and I'll be there through March."

"Oh! That must be interesting!" Fluttered relief, not a "Jesus freak" after all.

"I guess so. I'm still sort of new."

"Do you have trouble . . . I mean, being a woman?"

"Not so far, but that's why I want the collar: Identity." (A crutch I wondered?)

"Yes, I guess that would be a problem. Well, good luck. Enjoy your collar. If you want a thirteen and a half, just call, we'll order it."

"Thank you."

Jingle. Jingle. Back to the Mercedes. Back to David.

"Well, let's see. Man, that's weird. Don't wear it when we go out, you'll ruin my reputation! Grief! Giving up a glamor job like yours to run around in that thing and take care of sick kids. You'll be sorry! Why couldn't you just have volunteered on Saturdays?"

It was the same speech I had heard before and before and would hear again and again. David's bark is always worse than his bite. I can count on him in a pinch, and that's what matters.

Barbecued ribs and martinis. The collar stayed in its box.

Later, alone, at home, I tried on the collar with every hairdo and outfit I could think of at the moment. Who would know? I'm still a woman, after all.

4

MONDAY MORNING WE talked about the weekend. Terry Greer waxed eloquent, sort of. He had had a weekend of saved souls, and on top of that, no one had died.

They all seemed so young, the other students. I hadn't done much "group" work. I can remember when first at divinity school I thought a "T" group was a gathering in which people sat around drinking tea and eating cookies! Groups had never been my thing. And after all was said and done, they still weren't to be.

I don't remember much of Monday afternoon. I guess I went over to Adult for a while. I was "on call" that evening. I wore my collar for the first time that day. Maybe it was getting used to it that made me forget everything else . . .

Until ten-thirty that night, that is.

We had been told by Craig Hatfield that when we were on call we should check with the nursing stations on each floor before going home, to see if there were any serious situations for which we might be called back. I did, and there weren't any until I reached the last station—six-center, Intensive Care—at Children's.

"There's a baby who will die within the next two hours," I was told. "She's a newborn, brought here from Plainfield at noon, lung problems. Her father and grandmother are in the waiting room. Her name is Tracy Marks."

"You're *sure* she's going to die? Tonight?"

14

"I'm sure."

The nurse was nice. She sensed I was new.

It had all been OK until now. Now it wasn't OK any more. A baby was going to die. She wouldn't wait until morning.

(Can't you keep her alive until tomorrow, until Ted Marshall, whose floor this is, gets here. I don't want to hear what you're saying. Let's just pretend you didn't . . .)

But she wouldn't wait until morning. She was going to die now. I had to talk with her father. The nurse was watching. She would know if I ran away home. I had to.

I didn't even know these people.

It seems like I took the long way around to the six-center waiting room. Maybe I didn't, because I wouldn't have known the long way then. Maybe I just walked slowly. Whatever . . . I finally got there.

They were over in the far right corner. Huddled. Much later I was to realize that parents of dying children always sit huddled. Maybe it's to keep themselves from exploding. Maybe it's to shelter against the blow. Maybe it's because their stomachs are too knotted for them to sit straight.

When I saw their faces I realized the negative effect a clerical collar can have in a situation like that. They thought the infant already had died, and I was sent to tell the news.

"I'm the chaplain on call," I explained, still standing. "I was just passing. Would you like to talk?"

"Oh, then you don't know anything," said the young man sitting on an orange vinyl stool.

I shook my head.

"He didn't mean it the way it sounded," said the lady. "It's just that his little daughter—newborn—is in the Intensive Care room and she's not doing too good. He saw you and thought . . ."

"I'm sorry," I said. "I didn't mean to frighten you. I'm afraid I don't have any news about your daughter," I lied.

"Won't you have a seat?" asked the lady. "I'm Sylvia Carson and this is my son-in-law, Tony Marks."

The young man stood briefly and nodded as I sat down and introduced myself.

"You see," said the woman, "Tony and his wife, Mary, they

had another little girl die at birth two years ago, some of these same symptoms. The doctors said it wasn't genetic . . . wouldn't happen again . . .''

I don't remember whether I mentioned praying first or they did. But I think it was me. And that's what we did next. I knew the baby was going to die. They didn't. They had been waiting since noon. They wanted to hear words of hope, of life . . .

I had never lived through anything like this before. Never. The collar, the title chaplain, the whole bag full of symbols. Entering the lives of strangers—total strangers—at the close personal moment of death. It isn't a very real thing . . . at first.

In the moment I had to decide what was central. Was it me, the reverend figure, the holy intercessor? Was it the parents, frightened, separated by distance, suffering in a time set aside for rejoicing? Was it the baby, the little bundle of warmth soon to turn cold; the baby I hadn't even seen? One day I would discover it isn't any of these. And yet it is all of these.

That night I opted for "b"—the parents. As for "a"—me, even if I wanted to play the role, I didn't know how. I felt powerless to effect the change these people wanted. And it never entered my mind that the doctors could be wrong, to pray for a miracle, that the child had a chance to live. Was I just too rational a being, having already been told the answer was death? Had I "too little faith"? As for "c"—the child, there was nothing I could do to save her medically. And nothing within me was *afraid* to let her die, afraid that she would be alone, unloved.

But then, I never carried her, never bore her.

"Dear God . . ."

I don't remember what I said. I could make up something. I won't. I do know I didn't give up hope. I do know I prayed that little Tracy would live. But I also know that I prayed for acceptance in the face of God's greater knowledge and love that wants what's best for each of us, regardless of our own lack of understanding.

I also know that the corn on the little toe of my left foot hurt viciously the whole way through the prayer. When I look back on that night, the pain in that little toe is one of the vivid memories. Maybe because it was the only thing that seemed real, the

only thing that I had experienced before, that I could latch
onto . . .

But my most vivid memory is that of Tony Marks crying when
he was told Tracy had died.

He had gotten up to pace, to be alone, to remind himself that
he was alive.

It was hard for me to be sure they wanted me to stay. But they
had kept talking, initiating sentences.

When Tony Marks was out of earshot and I was getting up to
leave for a bit, the older woman beckoned me closer. "I know
what's bothering Tony," she said. "He hasn't been going to
church much lately, and he thinks this is God's way of punishing
him."

How can people think God is like that, I thought to myself.
And then I remembered a time when I had believed God was
exactly like that!

"Under the circumstances," I said, "I can understand him
feeling that way. But the God I believe in isn't like that. If God
went around punishing everyone in exact measure for his sins,
there wouldn't be any happiness or love in the world at all."

"I agree with you," said the woman. "And I've told Tony
that. But maybe it would help if you told him. I mean, being a
chaplain and all . . ."

That was the first time I realized anyone could take more
seriously what I say because I wear a reversed collar and carry
a title. It made me worry a lot more about the validity of what
I say. It still does.

I never had a chance to talk with Tony Marks about his fears.
While he was pacing, the doctor told him Tracy had died.

I remember his eyes as he walked back toward us. But no
words will describe them. Then he wept . . . trying not to.

"She just didn't make it. She just didn't have the strength.
Her little lungs were too weak," he repeated and repeated and
repeated, choking. Would I pray again, please? This time he
asked.

"Dear God . . ."

He sobbed. From the first words of the prayer throughout. It
all burst out on the brown carpet and orange vinyl chairs. It was
too personal for me to see.

From that night on, I have held those moments of raping grief at death in the highest respect and awe—as the total awareness of finitude. For never, never are we more human.

That was the climax, for me at least. I couldn't deal with anything more. More happened, and I remember participating in it, but not as something lived through, only as something watched.

Would I go with them to see the baby? To say goodbye, they asked.

Yes.

She was in an incubator. The top was tilted back. She was like a sleeping doll. They looked a long time. The father kissed her and stroked her little cheek . . . and wept. The grandmother wept. I stood there. She's asleep, that's all. I knew better. But she didn't look dead, just asleep. I had seen a sleeping baby before. I hadn't seen a dead baby before.

The doctor asked for permission for an autopsy, "to help future children and parents." They all say that. They have to say something. And it's important, the autopsy. But there's no way to wrap the words in cotton.

Would I take them to "admitting"—how funny the name sounded under the circumstances—to sign the "body release" papers, asked the nurse.

Yes.

It was after midnight. There was a young girl behind a small desk and this was probably all the excitement she would get all night. Or maybe it was an interruption in her daydreaming. Or maybe she was just uptight in the situation, too. Whatever it was, she didn't sound very sympathetic. She flew questions like darts: "Child's full name, parents' names, date of birth, time of birth, brothers' and sisters' names, name of funeral home to which the body is to be released . . ."

That last one got Tony Marks. He turned absolutely white. They discussed, he and his mother-in-law, and gave a name.

"If you change your mind on that," said the insipid girl, "call. That's all. Thank you."

I'm sorry. She didn't even say "I'm sorry." Maybe Tony Marks and his mother-in-law didn't notice, wouldn't have heard if she did say it.

But I needed it.

"Thank you," they said to me. "Thank you for staying."

"I'm sorry," I said. "Will you be all right getting home?"

"Yes . . ."

"She lived twelve hours," said Tony Marks, not to anyone particular. "That's two hours longer than her sister. We've had twenty-two hours' worth of babies . . . almost a full day . . ."

They walked out the Emergency Room double doors. The cold air blasted in. They didn't turn back.

I think I went somewhere and sat down. But I don't remember.

5

TUESDAY I TOLD "the group" about Tracy Marks. They sympathized appropriately. But I couldn't tell it well. I felt uncomfortable force-dissecting an experience that personal, that new. It's difficult even now. Then it was impossible.

Craig Hatfield had wanted me to say what I felt when I still was having trouble comprehending feeling itself. Perhaps people can't say what they feel when they're in shock. And I guess I still was, though I didn't know it then.

Early Tuesday evening I found Lindsay Grice. I had thought she was a boy. Not because her name was Lindsay, but because she had a crew cut.

Three-north, I was discovering, was the neuro-surgery floor—that's brain surgery. And that's why most of the patients had bandages on their heads, all over their heads. And underneath the bandages was . . . no hair.

Mrs. Cooke had suggested that I play with Lindsay. "She's been in and out so many times in her four years that she needs as much love and cuddling as she can get."

When I saw Lindsay I was apprehensive . . . for about two minutes. On the left side of her head, a little toward the back, was a square bandage. On the right side of her head, showing through the crew cut, was a snakelike scar. I had never seen one like it. It seemed to wind round and round. It had healed, so it couldn't have been done recently, I reasoned. Her eyes were crossed and she was skinny, skinny, and she couldn't stand up.

But she won. She beat out all the "stuff" that was wrong with her. From the moment I moved toward her crib she let it be known that she wanted to be picked up so badly that no scars, no bandages, no crew cut, nothing, would have stood in my way . . . or yours, had you been there. Lindsay Grice had won. I didn't even have a chance. She was that way with everyone.

I had been given permission—gladly by the busy nurses—to hold babies and give milk and cereal where medically approved, and even change diapers! Lindsay was my first diaper change in ten years. It must have given her a good laugh!

I have never received such rewards simply by holding a child. Her joy and contentment were almost pathetic. But then the need had been acute: fifty operations in four years; lots of time in medical isolation, flat on her back, rarely able to be held . . . No wonder her need was acute.

We rocked and rocked and rocked. She played with my hair. She explored my watch. But mostly, she just held on . . . and smiled. And I unwound.

We must have sat that way for an hour. And I was planning to do so for hours more. I was on my "own time." I could do what I wanted.

"Chaplain, dial 4123." It was the speaker page, heard all over the hospital.

I wasn't on call that night; Al O'Connor was. He would have to answer. Craig Hatfield had been strict about that. "When the chaplain is paged, unless by name, only the person on call should answer," he had instructed.

"That's all right," I said to Lindsay. "I'm not on call tonight." She didn't care, of course, as long as I didn't move. But some parents in the room may have wondered. I had said it for their benefit, to get me "off the hook."

"Chaplain, dial 4123."

I got a bit uncomfortable. This time I didn't say anything. But I didn't answer the call, either. Craig had been very definite, I reminded myself. I didn't worry about the *reason* behind the call because I wouldn't let myself admit there was any possibility I'd answer it in the first place.

"Chaplain, dial 4123."

I put Lindsay down in her crib. She screamed. She had the right. I wanted to scream, too.

I went to the nurses' station. "May I use the phone?"

"Sure. It was 4123."

I didn't want to. I didn't want to hear the nurse say, "Please come to four-north right away." I didn't want to walk the L-shaped hall to the elevator and walk the L-shaped hall back to four-north, right above three-north. (Now I know there is a stairway that would have gotten me there in an eighth the time.) I didn't want to talk with the nursing supervisor in the starched white uniform with the starched white face.

I didn't want to. It wasn't fair. I wasn't on call.

A little girl, five years old, mongoloid, brought in for some tests, dropped dead while her parents were getting her undressed, the doctors don't know why, no idea . . . the nursing supervisor reported. "The parents are behind the curtain in the doctors' chart room, very upset, their names are Stone, Mr. and Mrs. James Stone, the little girl's name was Ethel."

She stopped. She waited. "Well, move!" said her eyes.

I moved. I didn't want to.

It was dark in the cubbyhole behind the curtain. There was a window. A street lamp cast a blue glow over the two huddled figures. The mother wore a purple wool pantsuit. Her hair was dyed black. The father, slightly balding, was holding a furry pink child's coat in his left arm. They were sitting on plexiglass chairs. And the only sound was of the plexiglass chairs . . . shaking.

"I'm a chaplain," I said. "Would you like to pray for Ethel?"

"Yes. Please . . ."

I've always wanted to thank those parents for what they gave me that moment. If it mattered that I was a woman, if it mattered that I was young, if it mattered that I didn't look like a chaplain, their faces didn't show it. There wasn't room for nitpicking, for stereotypes, I guess. In that moment of crisis I discovered that as long as a human being is there to offer support, to offer faith, she could have two heads. It wouldn't matter. And that fact never has changed.

"Dear God . . . We don't understand what has happened. It was so unexpected. We cannot comprehend . . .

"Dear God, please be with these parents now. Hold them up. Give them strength. Let them realize that there are some things in life that we, as human beings, can never understand. But that when these things happen we must rely upon your wisdom, dear God. For though we are told that your ways are not always our ways, we trust in your everlasting love for all of us.

"But one thing we do know amid the suffering in this room, dear God . . . We know, without doubt, that right now in this very moment you are holding little Ethel in your arms, next to your heart.

"Keep these parents there, too, dear God, in spirit. Renew their faith and let them understand that 'love never ends.' "

I don't know if it was a "good" prayer or not. I do know I didn't say it. Oh, the words came out, but I've never been sure from where. Though my mind tried to race ahead to form the thoughts, it didn't always get there in time. But the words kept coming out, one after another, in order. And that has happened more than once since.

I was awfully glad when it was over—the prayer. It happened too fast. My mind had barely left the aimless, drifting joy of holding Lindsay.

I had crouched down in front of the Stones to pray. It seemed closer that way. She had taken my hands. He had put his hand on my shoulder.

But after the prayer, I didn't know what to do next. I didn't have to know. The mother grabbed my arms, buried her head on my right shoulder, and sobbed. (Two hours later the patch of wool on my yellow sweater still was damp.)

I held onto her as best I could, crouched down in that dark cubbyhole. The father put his hand on her shoulder. He was fighting back the tears. He was succeeding. But the rims of his eyes were like blood.

She said Ethel was their only child.

She said she couldn't believe it happened.

He said the doctors had only promised one year. They had had five . . .

She said she couldn't believe it happened.

"Excuse me . . ."

I hadn't heard her come in. It was a doctor in a light blue coat. Her red hair was tied back and she wore horn-rimmed glasses that kept slipping down on her nose.

"Excuse me. I wonder if you would agree to an autopsy?"

"Yes."

"We don't know yet what happened and that way we can determine whether it was the blood or the heart or the brain . . ."

"Yes."

"Thank you."

Uncomfortable. What to do? The doctor kept standing there. The mourning had been brought to an unnatural end.

So had the child.

The father got up. I got up. My knees hurt. The leg muscles pulled taut. Mascara had made a map of the mother's face. She fumbled for a Kleenex in a deep, junky brown purse. Someone, the doctor, opened the curtain wider. The light hurt.

"I'm sorry," said the doctor. She made a fumbling gesture to put her hand on the father's shoulder.

Too late, I thought. You interrupted. You blew it. Your timing was wrong. They weren't finished . . .

I wasn't finished. I haven't put it all together, inside me. Dammit. Doctors are supposed to be perfect.

A very young nurse handed the father a brown paper bag. She helped him stuff the size five furry pink coat into the brown paper bag that already contained a size five dress, shoes and socks and underthings. He nestled it in his arms, the brown paper bag, like a child. Only it wasn't.

I may never forget that.

I never saw Ethel Stone.

I went back to three-north. I needed Lindsay's rewards. I needed to hold a live child. I needed.

Lindsay stuffed me full of love. I was too limp, too drained to respond. But that didn't matter to Lindsay. All she needed was to be held. She did all the rest.

We rocked, I don't know how long. She fell asleep in my arms, I don't know how long. I didn't move.

Somehow, sometime, I got home. I wanted to go to sleep. But when I sat down on my bed something inside me clicked, like a grenade pin pulled. Nothing more could be put inside me before something was let out. There hadn't been time to sort, to digest . . . Not enough time.

I barely had the presence left to dial the telephone. I knew what was happening and I needed someone for it to happen on.

There was only one person I trusted completely, trusted to understand: Dr. Davies, my minister, teacher, counselor, and friend for years. When he answered, it was like a button pushed, an explosion. A gusher of words and tears fell down all around me in piles on the furry bedspread.

I guess Dr. Davies understood the words. I know he understood their meaning. He gave me room to breathe and time to cry and showed the worth of silent presence.

I told about Tracy Marks.

I told about Ethel Stone.

I told about the brown paper bag. *The brown paper bag.*

"Why? Why?"

He got angry! At God.

At God? No, I was misinterpreting, I was too upset. It wasn't what I expected. It lashed out, his voice, at an unbound evil . . . and at God. At God? No.

Now I know. Now, one year and deaths and deaths later. Now I know. Now I begin to know.

But then? It wasn't what I expected. But he was there. He listened. He gave back. He was my friend, unfailing, as always.

I went to sleep, I guess.

6

THE NEXT AFTERNOON I was waiting for an elevator at Children's. A doctor in a gray coat walked up with another doctor in a gray coat. The first man was the one who had been washing his hands, who had made the strange bow to me, who had given me the look when I returned to Bobby's room the first day—one week before!—it seemed like months.

"You're our chaplain," he asked in a statement.

"Yes . . . I'm assigned to three-north."

"I know. That's my floor. I'm Dr. Verdi, chairman of neurosurgery. This is my colleague, Dr. Praeder. You really ought to come on rounds with us. Do you like it?"

Pause. Whew!

"Yes, so far. I don't understand many of the medical terms, though."

"That's why you should join us on rounds. We're going right now. Come with us."

"All right." I figured I didn't have much choice.

Other doctors joined us on rounds. Some wore blue coats, some white jackets, some gray coats. I didn't know the difference. I didn't understand any of it. But I didn't faint.

I knew some of the parents, some of the children . . . like Gary Larson. How everybody loved Gary Larson! He was three. I had trouble looking at his head at first. But he didn't give up on me. He had hydrocephalus.

* * *

Hydrocephalic babies are referred to by laymen as "water-head" babies. I hate the term, but it's the best way to understand it, I guess.

We all have four cavities—cavities called ventricles—in our brain system: two lateral ventricles, left and right sides; a third ventricle; and a fourth ventricle. We also have a clear fluid, cerebrospinal fluid (CSF), that circulates within our spinal columns, ventricles, and brain.

When there is an increase in the amount of CSF, and an increase in the size and pressure in the ventricles, then a person may have hydrocephalus.

This increase in CSF and in intraventricular size and pressure—to try to explain the whole thing in lay language—can be caused by any of a number of different things: a congenital abnormality, an obstruction, a constriction, a birth defect called myelomeningocele (spinabifida), a tumor, a cyst . . .

If this hydrocephalus is not corrected, the baby's head can get bigger and bigger and bigger. And the baby can die.

To correct the effect of hydrocephalus—not cure it, unfortunately—a tube called a "shunt" is implanted inside the head into one of the ventricles. Then the tube, the "shunt" (which looks like a transparent, very thin, hollow string of spaghetti), is pulled just under the skin from the ventricle down the neck and, usually, into the stomach. And it stays that way. A tube, draining excess CSF from the ventricle into the stomach cavity, where it is absorbed naturally.

Sound grotesque? Have you ever seen a person with untreated hydrocephalus? Shunts are beautiful.

Gary Larson had a shunt. About twelve shunts in all while I was there. Sometimes shunts get blocked. Not usually that often. But when they do, they have to be unblocked, or replaced. That's an operation, each time.

Gary had the longest head I had ever seen. It just went back and back, emphasized by the fact that his head had been shaved for surgery. Usually, if you notice the head of a hydrocephalic child at all, it looks bigger in front, at the forehead. But not Gary. His looked like someone had stretched it backwards.

I looked away fast the first time I saw the back of Gary's head.

He was cute, face on. Maybe that's why I looked away. I didn't want to admit the rest of his head.

"What's your name?" he had asked that first time.

"Nina."

He repeated, "What's your name?"

"Nina." But I wouldn't give. I wouldn't say, "What's *your* name?" or "Can you say 'Ni-na'?" I moved on, to another bed. Gary had looked a bit puzzled.

Gary was there that first night when we made rounds, sitting up in his crib in his blue bathrobe and blue slippers. I waited at the door, looking up at the ceiling light.

"Hi, Gary!"

"Hi, Dr. Verdi. Hi, Dr. Praeder. Hi, Dr. McMahan. Hi, Dr. Craig. Hi, Dr. Suter."

I stopped looking at the ceiling light.

"You missed one, Gary. Who's this?"

"Uh . . . what's your name?"

"That's Dr. Mills, Gary."

"Hi, Dr. Mills!"

"Will you remember?"

"Hi, Dr. Mills!"

"How do you feel, Gary?"

"Fine."

"Does your heart hurt?"

"No."

"Good boy! See you tomorrow. Bye."

"Bye! . . . Hi, Dr. Mills!"

"That kid remembers everyone's name. Don't know how he does it. We must have tickled something with all those shunts!"

Gary Larson had shown me! Another lesson. The more I knew Gary the less I saw his head. That happens a lot on three-north.

Thursday afternoons we had a staff floor meeting: the two head nurses, two social workers, physical therapy, recreational therapy, occupational therapy, home nursing coordinator, chaplain, and various other drop-ins.

I liked the meetings. At first I felt like an observer. They soon kicked me into participating. It was better that way. That's what made the meetings work; that and having central problems familiar to all.

Ostensibly, the purpose of the meetings was to discuss the current status of each child on the floor, physically, emotionally, educationally, etc., and the status of his or her family. That's what happened, too—total care, not just words.

But more than that happened at those meetings. They reminded us that we weren't alone, that each of us was getting knocked down by our emotions every now and then, and that maybe it would hurt less when we talked about it in a group once a week. Two can hurt as cheaply as one? In the chaplain group the children were different and the specialty was central; in this group the specialties were different and the child was central. I guess I just functioned better in the second type than the first.

It was right after such a meeting on Thursday afternoon that Mrs. Cooke asked me if I knew Mrs. Salvador.

"Yes, Jason's mother."

"Well, she's taking that baby home. She just gave me the discharge slip. She shouldn't, you know. He needs surgery. The doctors think he has hydrocephalus and needs a shunt . . . though it was a difficult diagnosis as I understand it. Anyway, I guess his mother is scared. She's leaving with Jason . . ."

"Do you want me to talk with her?"

"Please. But I don't know if it will make any difference now. Good luck."

"I'm leaving. I don't know what else to do. That doctor didn't make any sense. I came here for medical answers, and suddenly I have to make all the decisions. I can't decide something like that, so I'm leaving."

"What did the doctor say?"

"I don't believe it. I still don't believe it. But I know I heard him right. He said Jason *may* have hydrocephalus—*may* have. Now, he says he can operate and Jason will get better, or he can operate and Jason won't get better, or he can *not* operate and Jason will get better, or he can *not* operate and Jason won't get better. And he says my husband and I have to decide what to do! Can you beat that? *We* have to decide. He's the doctor!"

"Did he make a recommendation?"

''No, none. If he would have I probably would have gone along, either way. After all, this hospital is supposed to be the best. But no, he said he couldn't make a recommendation at all. *We* have to decide. Well, I can't and my husband can't and we're going home.''

''Which doctor told you this?''

''Dr. Verdi.''

''The one with gray hair?''

''Yeah, in a gray coat; that's him. Do you know him?''

''Yes, I think I do.'' He had seemed straightforward, if he was the same doctor who had asked me to go on rounds—I was still having trouble getting all the names together—and I was surprised he would tell a parent something like that. I had never heard of a doctor not being able to recommend a course of treatment.

''Would you talk with him? Maybe I didn't hear right after all. Maybe you'll understand something I didn't.''

''I'll try. Will you wait until I see if I can find him now?''

''Yeah. OK.''

I went back to the nursing station. ''Does that gray-haired doctor, his name begins with a 'V' . . . ?''

''Dr. Verdi?''

''Yes. Does he have an office here?''

''Yes. On the ground level.''

''How do I get there?''

''Take the elevator to 'G,' then turn right. It's the first door after the lab. It says 'neurosurgery' on the glass.''

''Thanks.''

''You're going to try to see him about Mrs. Salvador?''

''Yes.'' I didn't even think to question the ominous tone in her voice.

I almost burst into the neurosurgery office. There was Dr. Verdi putting on his topcoat.

''I *have* to see you for a moment. It's important. Do you have time?''

''Well, I was just going downtown''—he assessed my face and manner—''but yes, I have a few minutes. Go into my office.''

It was small, but well appointed: a large desk, two leather

chairs, two walls of X-ray lights, a bath off to the side, books and shelves, small table with ashtray, leather beanbag chair.

"I tell my secretaries the only time they can sit in the beanbag chair is when they wear miniskirts."

I smiled, but chose another place to sit. "I just talked with Mrs. Salvador. She's leaving."

"Mrs. who?"

"Mrs. Salvador, Jason's mother."

"Oh, yes. I talked with her earlier."

"I know. That's why she's leaving."

"Oh."

"She says you told her you could operate on Jason and he would get better, you could operate on him and he wouldn't get better, or you could not operate on him and he would get better, or you could not operate on him and he wouldn't get better; and that she and her husband had to decide for or against surgery. Now, maybe she didn't hear you correctly . . ." (I would be diplomatic.)

"She heard exactly correctly. That's exactly what I said."

My tone was even. "How could you? How can they decide? You're the surgeon." (Those last words scared me for a moment. Maybe he wasn't a surgeon. Maybe he just represented the surgeon. I still didn't know much about the medical staff hierarchy even though I had gone on rounds a few nights.)

"Yes, I'm the surgeon. But Jason is their child. All I can do is give them the results of the tests. How long are you going to be here?"

"Until the end of March."

He was very calm, sitting back in his chair, smiling. He had swung the chair around so he faced me directly.

"Good. That's not nearly long enough, but you may as well learn something while you're here. And since you're on my floor, I suppose I'm your teacher.

"Mrs. Salvador—and you—both would have a right to be upset with me if I had held something back, not given all I could. It wouldn't have been fair and it wouldn't have been medically ethical. Unfortunately, Jason's case is a difficult one. With some children I know the diagnosis is hydrocephalus before we even take the tests, just by touching the head, just by looking. That comes from experience. We take the angiograms to be sure, to have proof in black and white, and to determine the type of hydrocephalus, etc. But many times, the minute I see the child I know the diagnosis. I can recommend immediately to insert a shunt. Do you know what that is?''

"What Gary Larson has?''

"Right. And I know that ninety times out of a hundred surgery will have an immediate, positive effect.

"But with Jason Salvador it's different. He has, for want of a better term, what we call 'normal or low pressure' hydrocephalus. I can't diagnose that at a glance. So we took a lot of tests and we're still not sure. We've ruled out a cyst and a tumor and neurological damage, so we're left with this, with normal or low pressure hydrocephalus. And we *don't* know whether inserting a shunt will make any difference.

"There's obviously something wrong with the child. At this time—he's nearly ten months old—he's way behind in his milestones. He can't roll over or hold up his head. But I honestly can't recommend surgery as a 'cure' or a correction of the problem. Because I don't know if it *will* cure or correct the problem. Do you see?''

It was months later until I really understood medically what Dr. Verdi had said. But I got the gist of it.

"Yes, I think so. And I appreciate the problem. But still, as a doctor, isn't it your responsibility to recommend a form of treatment? How can the parents decide?''

"They *have* to . . . in this case. Jason's their child. I wish I could recommend treatment. I wish the decision was clear-cut. It isn't. And I can't assume the role of parent. Suppose I'm wrong?''

"Suppose they're wrong?''

"They're the parents. Their decision will be based on love, and on the knowledge that they'll be responsible for caring for the child no matter what. They *have* to make the ultimate decision.

"Now, mind you,'' he continued, "if the reverse were true, I'd fight like hell. In other words, if I were sure surgery was necessary, was the only way the child's life could be saved, or be meaningful, and the parents refused, I'd have them hauled into court before you could say your rosary. Oh, you're obviously not Catholic.''

"Presbyterian."

"Too bad." He winked. "With a name like Verdi, I'm not Jewish. Anyway, there I'd *know* my decision, *know* my diagnosis, *know* the odds, *know* what was necessary. There would be an operation no matter what." (I was to see this happen several times.)

"I agree with that. But what about Jason?"

"His mommy and daddy *have* to decide."

"What would you do if Jason were *your* child?"

"That's not a fair question. You're a good debater, and obviously concerned about this—I wouldn't be here talking with you if I didn't see that in you—but it's still not a fair question."

"Thank you. Why not?"

"Because I have an obvious prejudice. I'm a neurosurgeon, so naturally I would want to apply my skill, that for which I've trained my whole life, to try to save my child. I'd be looking at it with a different prejudice, a different set of values than Jason's parents. Yes, I'd operate if Jason were my child. But I can't tell Jason's parents that because it would be a personal prejudice rather than a medical opinion. Do you see?"

"Yes, but what if you were to say to them exactly what you just said to me; explain it just that way?"

Pause.

"All right, you win. Yes, I suppose I could do that. But it wouldn't be a medical recommendation. They'll have to understand that. They'll still have to decide.

"I don't like this case either, you know. They don't come that often, thank goodness. I like to be able to be definite. But if it's not this, it's something else, I guess.

"Parents of children with tumors want to know *before* surgery if the tumor is malignant, if we can get it all, if there will be damage. Once a terminal diagnosis is made, they want to know how long the child has, what type of decline, how much pain.

"They're all fair questions; it's just that usually they're unanswerable. We don't know. Sometimes we can guess pretty close from experience. But if we were to tell the parents, they usually couldn't take it all at once anyway. And if it proved different from our guess, they'd be angry with us. People can hear only so much at a time. So I only give them so much at a time in most cases.

"I told Mrs. Salvador *why* I couldn't give a recommendation for treatment. I explained about the difficulties in diagnosis, about the difficulties in recommending treatment for normal or low pressure hydrocephalus. But all she heard was what she repeated to you, and that's why she was confused. She just couldn't hear it all and comprehend it all at once. That's normal. I understand that. It's hard.

"Tell you what," he continued, "I'll have a chance to see Mrs. Salvador at 11:30 tomorrow morning—if she's still here. It's up to her. But if she is, I'll tell her what you want me to tell her, and explain the whole thing again. And you'll see, she still won't hear everything. OK?"

"Yes, thank you. And thanks for your time."

"That's OK, I'm just late for a speech I didn't want to give anyway."

He probably was, too.

Mrs. Salvador was thirty-three; her husband was forty-two. He was a quiet man with slightly graying hair and an earnest expression. He was Croatian and foreign-born. Mrs. Salvador was slender, taller by a few inches than her husband, and had short brown hair. Jason was a handsome baby with big blue eyes, dark brown hair and a happy smile. But he couldn't lift his head, couldn't roll over, couldn't do other things that normal nine-month-old babies do. He was small for nine months, too.

They had room 384, a private room at the other end of the hall from the nursing station. It was next to the small waiting room where parents—and the chaplain—could smoke. (I've since given it up . . . several times!) I met a lot of parents that way, in that little waiting room, without all the formal introducing of "Hello, I'm your friendly neighborhood chaplain." I would just sit there, have coffee and a cigarette, and conversation would come naturally, uninhibited, even with the clerical collar.

Mr. and Mrs. Salvador both were sitting in the small waiting room when I returned.

"Did you see him?"

"Yes. He said if you're still here tomorrow morning, he'll see you at 11:30 in Jason's room. But it's up to you whether or not you stay."

"Did I hear him right?"

"Yes, as far as the part about operating. Yes, he said you heard him exactly right."

"But how *can* we decide?" asked Jason's father. "I am not a doctor. I am not trained in medicine. I am a worker in a factory. I do a good job. I make decent living. I wait many years to find just right woman and to have a baby. I want a son very much. Jason, he is my son, my firstborn. I am very proud. And now this. I cannot sleep. I cannot eat. I cannot do my work with properness. My child, something is the matter with my child. I *cannot* decide. How can I decide?"

He was nearly in tears.

"Come," he got up, "we go into the room. Do you see?" he asked, sitting in an orange vinyl chair. "How can I decide?"

"Did he say anything more?" asked Jason's mother. "Anything that would help?"

"I think so. But I don't want to speak for him. He'll have to explain the situation and his thinking to you himself. I wouldn't want to risk misinterpreting anything medical."

"But you think we should stay?"

"If it were me, I'd at least stay until tomorrow and talk with him again. I don't think one more day could hurt. But that's your decision."

"Yes, she is right," Mr. Salvador said to his wife. "We will stay one more day, and listen again. This time I will be here, too. It is very important. It is our son. Too important to take chances."

The baby was asleep. Mr. Salvador got up and walked over to the crib. "He look so normal to me. I not know about 'milestones'—what Jason should do by age nine months. No one tell us. We think he have the flu. Bring him to doctor. Doctor say 'something more,' say Jason not meet 'milestones.' Suddenly Jason in hospital with many tests. I don't know. I don't know. He look so normal, so beautiful to me. Jason . . . Jason . . ."

He folded his arms on the crib railing and buried his head. It wasn't my time to be there. I nodded to his wife and started to leave.

"We'll stay. Tell Dr. Verdi we'll see him tomorrow, please," she said quietly as I left.

I felt he already knew that.

The surgery went well. But it would take months to know

if it had made any difference, if it had been the "right" decision . . .

(I saw Jason Salvador last week, about a year after his surgery. He's holding up his head and rolling over and sitting up and walking and talking and getting into the general mischief that all normal twenty-one-month-old babies get into. He's right up with his milestones.

The decision was "right." The surgery worked. Or would Jason have been this way without the shunt? We'll never know. His parents will never care.)

7

I HADN'T LEARNED how to read medical charts yet—or even realized that I was allowed to read them without someone slapping my hands. And even if I could have read them, I probably wouldn't have understood many of the diagnoses. But maybe reading Pat Allen's chart would have answered at least one question.

When I look back, I can't believe how naive I was. There she lay, in a coma, her eyes rolled back, steam to help her breathe more comfortably. And I didn't know what was wrong with her.

I'd try to talk with her . . . in a coma . . .

She was six.

One day I saw a lady sitting beside Pat's bed. I stopped at the doorway. "Hello, I'm Nina Herrmann. I'm the chaplain on three-north."

"Hello, I'm Karen Allen, Pat's mother. Want to come in?"

"All right."

Visiting Pat Allen was not an easy task. She was in isolation. One had to put on a blue gown, a paper mask, and rubber gloves. (The same thing you had to do anytime you went into Room 380, the eight-bed Neurosurgery-Neurology Constant Care room next to the nursing station.

(That used to get me on rounds. It would always be a race to see whether the doctors could finish before I felt as if I were going to faint, all wrapped up in the mask and gown and gloves.

I never actually fainted. But the close calls came out about fifty-fifty.)

Inside Pat Allen's room I sat on an orange vinyl stool. Pat's mother was sitting on a daybed. It was a private room. Mrs. Allen was rubbing the little girl's arm. Pat had a crew cut—hair growing out from an earlier operation? With her name and her hair, it wasn't until her mother referred to Pat as "she" that I was sure she was a girl.

I said a few words to Pat. So did her mother, maybe to make me feel more comfortable. "We don't know whether she can hear us any more or not. Sometimes I think she can and sometimes I think she can't. But I try anyway, just in case."

I should have realized right then. But I didn't. It wasn't that the thought entered my mind and I chose to push it out, to not accept it. The thought simply did not enter my mind, period. Looking back, I can hardly believe that.

But that was all Mrs. Allen wanted to say about Pat's condition. "But anyway," she went on, "what denomination are you?"

We discussed that, and talked about her family, and then I discovered that her husband was from England. A few falls ago I had spent five days driving through the English countryside. That was it. We had common ground to lessen the tension, though she was very pleasant all along.

She and her husband had taken their children to the British Isles the previous summer for a month. But Pat had been too ill to go. She told about the trip, the sights, the beauty, meeting her husband's relatives, how the other children had missed Pat, what they would write to her on their postcards, what she would write back.

It was a good story. She was happy and sad—and alone—in telling it. There was no way I could have appreciated or even vicariously participated in all the family love that went into that story.

The student chaplain who had been there before me could have. He had known Pat. He had been there for the diagnosis, for the surgery. He had been there through it all.

And now they had a chaplain who didn't even realize that Pat Allen was dying.

* * *

Less than two weeks later, she did.

I finally found out she was going to in one of our Thursday afternoon staff floor meetings.

In previous meetings when they had come to Pat's name they had said, "Just the same; no change. Her parents are OK," and gone on. But this particular week there was a guest social worker. When they came to Pat's name during the meeting someone commented that Dr. Craig had said that morning on rounds that "we should close the door and open the window" in Pat's room. It was explained to the visiting social worker that opening the window and closing the door was a frustrated wish that the *terminal* child could catch pneumonia and die more quickly.

(It sounds heartless, perhaps. But no one who said it or understood it was heartless. They just could do nothing more to save Pat Allen. And to watch her lying there, helpless, day after day, made the strain and suffering of her parents—and of the staff—greater and greater. To talk of opening the window and closing the door was "caring" about Pat Allen . . . caring about the dignity that is life in the face of the depersonalization that was her dying.)

"Terminal child . . ." The words stuck. I ventured to interrupt. "You mean Pat is going to die?" Everyone looked at me in utter amazement. They had forgotten what it was like to be so new, so unschooled in anything medical.

"Yes. Didn't you know?" asked Mary Cooke. But I guess she could tell by my face that I hadn't known. She was kind: "I'm sorry, I should have told you. I just thought you knew."

"I should have, I guess," I said quietly. And they went on.

The duty nurse called in a staff social worker when Pat died the following Monday morning. I don't blame her. I would have too. The social worker, Mary Lannen, had known the family from the beginning, just like the student chaplain who had preceded me. But Mary was still there. The student chaplain wasn't.

The staff social worker could be there when it counted—from beginning to end. But not the chaplain; a new one every three months, like a tube of toothpaste, a disposable lighter.

I would have called Mary Lannen too, had I been the duty nurse.

It was the first time I sensed—for a floor like three-north, at least—that there may be something wrong with the Children's chaplain program. Not everybody finds it convenient to get sick and die within premeasured three-month periods. Some take longer.

Which comes first, the student chaplain or the patient?

8

WITH MARILEE JOHNSON I was there from beginning to end. It made a difference, to me anyway.

Marilee was in a crib in the far right corner of a four-bed room, 391. Katharine Hanley was in the adult bed in the near left corner of the same room. Marilee was three. Katharine was twelve. They were hospital friends. Both were beautiful little girls.

Marilee would sit in her crib eating potato chips—always, it seemed—and plead "walk, walk" to everyone who entered.

She was the first black child I had ever held in my life. I was twenty-nine. To say it didn't feel any different would not be quite true. The mere fact that I thought about it—realized it as I picked her up—made it different.

Marilee pulled my hair; she played with my watch; the difference disappeared. It has never returned.

I walked with Marilee seated in the crook of my arm for hours, literally. She stayed unusually still for a three-year-old, and carried on ladylike little conversations. She was the most dainty three-year-old I have ever seen. That seemed to be everyone's word to describe Marilee—"dainty."

There were pictures of animals on a farm in the corridor between three-north and three-south, the orthopedics unit. We would stop by the pictures each time we walked and she would pick out each animal, repeating its name with perfect enunciation and pointing with a delicately arched finger.

41

Then there was the water fountain . . . always. "Drink, drink." (Have you ever tried to hold a child in one hand and adjust a water fountain with the other so the child's mouth and the stream of water meet? Well, try it!)

It seemed like the doctors were never going to get all the tests on Marilee they needed. It was a combination of "just one more test," and "we had to postpone the test until tomorrow."

That's how I met Marilee's mother, that and a prayer.

I had begun to stay at Children's later and later in the evenings, even when I wasn't on call. One evening I decided to take Marilee for a walk. When I went into her room an older lady was standing by her crib. I had on my collar. I said "hi" to Marilee and introduced myself to the lady.

"Oh, you know Marilee?"

"Yes, we take walks every now and then. I hope that's all right?"

"Oh, yes. It's perfectly all right. Marilee love to walk. I'm Marilee's grandmother, Mrs. Harris. I'm so happy to meet you."

"Thank you. I'm glad to meet you, too. I haven't had the opportunity to meet Marilee's mother yet."

"She be here when she can. She work funny hours. But she be here. I do wish the doctor hurry up and decide what he gonna do to Marilee, though. This waitin' is hard. Would you say a prayer for Marilee?"

"Yes."

She cried during the prayer, the grandmother. Not out loud, just running tears. I felt strange. I don't know why. Maybe it was her profuse gratitude at the end. That still makes me feel strange, uncomfortable.

The next evening I met Marilee's mother. But it was nearly two weeks and a number of conversations later that Mrs. Johnson began to let down her defenses, to talk comfortably.

It had been easier to talk about Marilee. The little girl had headaches and would lose her balance while walking so often that she was afraid to try any more. "Walk" to Marilee meant "in your arms." The neurosurgeons had tried a number of tests, and now they were asking to do just one more. Mrs. Johnson had about had it.

But it might have been less tense if she hadn't been worried about something else—her marriage. Her husband was a successful merchandiser. For a long time she talked as if nothing was wrong, he was just "away on business." He was.

But they were getting a divorce, too.

That came out one day when I wasn't expecting it. The two of us were sitting talking in the little waiting room. No one else was there. Mrs. Johnson had just been told that Marilee's final test was being postponed until the next day. All of a sudden I heard the whole story.

"Now I have to do all this alone; make all the decisions myself. She is *his* child, too. His own flesh and blood. You'd think he'd care.

"But I've been alone before; I can be again. I'm not going to fall apart like a shrinking violet, no sir. If he doesn't give a damn that's his business. He'll have to live with it."

I didn't have to say anything. She wasn't asking for that. Just my ears. It had taken a long time even for that, I realized. She continued the story for fifteen minutes, at least.

The next afternoon she asked me to pray for Marilee before her test. It was the first time.

Surgery was scheduled for the next morning. The test had finally shown that Marilee had a cyst in the lower back of her head. Cyst means "likely not malignant"; means they should be able to get it all. But check the statistics on posterior fossa cysts.

I remember seeing Dr. Verdi drive by in his little red Maserati about eight the morning of Marilee's surgery as I was walking the one block from Children's to Adult. He honked and I waved. "He'll be operating on Marilee in the next hour or so," I thought to myself. "I wonder how he feels, knowing that."

I had already been up to the sixth floor surgery waiting room to talk with Marilee's mother and grandmother before surgery. I promised to return later. It was my first experience with major surgery.

Dr. Verdi was good to parents during surgery. He would send someone out one or twice to give a progress report. Things like "surgery has begun," "they've approached the lesion" (cyst, tumor—the foreign area), "they're closing." It's good. It makes the parents and friends feel a little less in the dark, a little less helpless.

But one of the reports can be frustrating if it's not explained: the report about "closing." That makes the parents think the child will be in the recovery room momentarily. "Closing" to the parents means scalp sutures; "closing" to the neurosurgeon means hours of backtracking away from the lesion, being just as cautious as when they approached it. "Closing" means "from the lesion" not "of the scalp" in neurosurgery. It's a matter of hours versus a matter of minutes. A parent who doesn't realize this thinks something major has gone wrong, thinks the child has died.

They told Mrs. Johnson they were "closing" on Marilee at one o'clock. It was nearly three before we saw a surgeon. I arrived at about one-thirty. I could draw an exact picture of the face of that waiting room clock today, especially the minute hand. It was the hard way to learn what "closing" means neurosurgically. It helped the next time around. Then I could explain to the parents. But it didn't help Marilee's mother, because I didn't know what was going on then either. I was silently afraid she might have died, too.

The surgeon told Mrs. Johnson that Marilee was all right. It had been "delicate surgery" and she would have to be watched closely. But she was all right.

It's different from the movies, watching someone in real life relax after a terrible pressure has been lifted. It's as if they're a crumpled piece of paper being smoothed out, slowly, carefully, completely. There is no sudden sigh of relief like on the silver screen. It's quiet, subtle, unshareable.

Marilee's mother was the first person I had seen go through it. Mrs. Harris was more vocal. "Praise the Lord! Hallelujah! Praise the Lord God Almighty! Thank you Jesus!" It was a different world. It was an education, watching Mrs. Harris. But it was just as genuine.

Mrs. Johnson wanted to go to the chapel. There's a pretty children's chapel at Children's Hospital. There are services there on Sunday. We went there, the three of us. I remember my prayer was too profuse in thanks, like Mrs. Harris had been to me after my first prayer for Marilee. Maybe God was "uncomfortable" too, especially since he knew what was coming.

Or maybe that's why I remember my prayer as being too profuse. Maybe I wouldn't have remembered it at all if Marilee hadn't gone back to surgery at four that afternoon. Something had gone wrong.

I was down on three-north having a cigarette and talking with some nurses in the little room behind the nursing station. I had just recently been brave enough to venture in there. No one kicked me out. It was a very small area for nurses and doctors to relax without leaving the floor.

Someone stuck his head in and asked if I had heard that they took Marilee Johnson back to surgery.

"No! Why?"

"Something went wrong, I guess."

I went up to the sixth floor waiting room. There were Marilee's mother and grandmother huddled in the orange vinyl chairs. "Something went wrong. Something went wrong. I knew it couldn't last. I knew it was too good to be true."

We prayed. It seemed more "the thing to do" than anything else. We were too stunned to believe what we were saying.

I sat there, from four-fifteen on. I didn't leave. I didn't even know for sure if they wanted me to stay. But I had to. I had become involved. I had a vested interest. How dare God let me say a prayer of such profuse "thanks" and then let this happen. It was embarrassing.

It was about six-thirty. I was sitting on an orange vinyl stool. Mrs. Johnson was sitting on a similar one opposite me, knee to knee. Her mother was on a chair to my right. Her mother looked up toward the doorway. She stood and put out her arms. I looked up. I didn't believe what I saw.

There stood a large, stately black woman in a long white and silver evening gown with long sleeves and a high neck. She was wearing a large medallion and silver cross and she had a tiara in her hair. (I looked for a wand with a star on the end.)

Mrs. Harris and the glittering lady embraced. We were introduced. The glittering lady was a minister. She joined us and said a prayer. I don't remember a word of it.

I had decided I should leave. The glittering lady obviously was a family minister, I reasoned. I don't know if my feelings were hurt or not. I don't think they had room to be yet.

I slid my stool back away from Marilee's mother in a move to make a gracious exit. But before I could get up I felt a hand on my knee. "Don't go," whispered Mrs. Johnson. "Please;

she's very nice, but she's my mother's minister, not mine. Please stay.''

I stayed. Things worked themselves out. The glittering lady minister was very nice, and very aware of the situation. She did her "thing" and I did mine. But I sure watched a lot! I had never seen anything like it.

The clock became the focal point again, as if it were responsible, as if it could do something, as if it were holding back. No one ate. No one drank coffee. Soon, no one said anything.

Mrs. Johnson would take walks in the hall, each time either asking me not to leave or to come along. But she didn't talk much, just paced.

About eight that evening all four of us had gathered near the surgery doors. It just couldn't be much longer. Marilee's mother was sure Marilee would be dead. I was afraid she was right.

A doctor came out, motioned Mrs. Johnson over. They talked briefly.

"She's alive! She's alive!" She turned to us. Tears were streaking her face. "She's alive!" She almost staggered toward us. Her mother and the glittering lady minister rushed toward her, embraced her.

But she broke away. She came toward me and collapsed on my shoulder and sobbed.

I'm still sorting all the thoughts and feelings that raced through me then. But I think in that indescribable moment I wanted my father to see how color doesn't matter; I wanted a young minister at my church to see how gender doesn't matter; I wanted someone to see how tradition doesn't matter.

And I wanted not to be thinking about any of those things.

But I was two people, one participating and one watching. It would be easier to admit only the first.

The doctors knew then that Marilee very likely was going to die. I don't think her mother did. I know I didn't. I didn't know the signs. I didn't know the language. I didn't know the connotation of "respirator" in this case.

When I walked into Intensive Care a few minutes later they were trying to keep Marilee off one—a respirator. As chaplain I was allowed to go into Intensive Care anytime. Parents were allowed in for fifteen minutes at the beginning of every other hour.

Doctors and nurses were surrounding Marilee's bed; the doctors still dressed in green surgery scrub suits and white surgery shoes. Their shoes were spattered with blood and brownish-red sterile wash.

Dr. Verdi was bending over Marilee's bed, talking to her as if no one else was there. "Come on, Marilee, honey. Come on little girl. You're not cooperating, Marilee. You have to cooperate. Come on, Marilee, honey. This isn't good. It isn't good at all."

He went on and on.

He had a different look on his face. One I had never seen, and was rarely to see again. I remembered his smile of twelve hours earlier. It was no more.

He didn't notice me for a long time. I squeezed into a corner trying to be out of the way. I was mesmerized.

"Chris [Dr. Verdi's first name was Christian], Chris, we're going to have to hook her up," said a doctor I didn't know. "I don't see any other way. But we may lose her in the process."

"I know. I hate to do it. Come on, Marilee, honey. Please cooperate, please honey."

People were doing things to Marilee all the while. I don't know what. But everyone was moving.

Dr. Verdi saw me. He shook his head. His eyes dropped to the floor. "It's bad, Nina, honey," he said. "You better do your thing."

He turned away slightly and put his arms on the cabinet ledge by the window and looked out. It seemed like a long time. Then he went back to Marilee's bed. They were hooking her to a respirator.

It was the sound of her breathing and the multicolored blood pressure cuff and her shaven head that I remember.

Her breathing was a small whining, gasping, moan—a sound I had not heard before, and haven't since. At first I thought she was crying. After the respirator was in place I realized it had been breathing.

For adults, gray blood pressure cuffs are used. But in Intensive Care at Children's they had multicolored blood pressure cuffs. Anything for cheer. They used it so often on Marilee, I

guess, that they just left it there that evening. It reminded me
that she was a three-year-old child and children like bright colored things. Except she didn't see it. Ever.

Her head was shaved. The operation had been in the back but
they had shaved her entire head. She didn't look like the little
girl who said, "Walk, walk . . ."

I went downstairs to three-north. I'm sure I rocked a baby,
but I don't remember which one.

I decided to take one last look at Marilee before I went home.
I found Dr. Praeder in Intensive Care. "We have to operate
again."

I hadn't known Dr. Praeder very well before then. He had
been the one with Dr. Verdi the day I was first asked to go on
rounds. Maxmillian Praeder spoke with an accent, sometimes
very heavy, but understandable. He was shorter than Dr. Verdi,
a bit younger, and had black wavy hair. He was an "attending"
physician. So was Dr. Verdi; only Dr. Verdi was chief of the
service.

(I finally was beginning to figure out those things. Attending
physicians wore gray coats. In neurosurgery they were Dr. Verdi,
Dr. Praeder, and Dr. Len Craig, who I barely knew. Then there
were resident physicians. They wore blue coats. There were
several of them. I didn't know any that well yet. And finally
there were medical students. They wore short white jackets and
changed faces every few weeks. I never knew any of them well.)

Dr. Praeder was soft-spoken, a bit the opposite of Dr. Verdi,
who always exuded a commanding, assured aura.

"I thought you went home."

"I was going to. Another surgery tonight?"

"Yes, I am afraid so. There is some bleeding."

"Is she going to be all right?"

"We do not know that yet. We just do not know."

We walked out of Intensive Care and sat on a window ledge.
I was to have some major conversations on various window
ledges in that hospital. This was the first.

"How does it look to you?"

"I cannot predict. But you must not get so involved. It is bad.
You must be concerned, but not involved."

"It's my job to get involved, where I'm asked."

"But that is not good. You cannot perform at your best when you are emotionally involved."

"But I don't have to perform. I have to care. That's being emotionally involved at times. I can't just slip in, never having seen the parents before, and pray, and walk out. Not if I have the option. That's like 'put in a quarter, get your weight and a prayer.' Our jobs are different."

"I do not think so. If I become emotionally involved it is bad. It hurts my work."

Slowly I wondered if it were me or himself he was trying harder to convince. "But you do, don't you?" I ventured.

"No, I cannot. It is not good. Look, it is not good for you, either. You are pale and tired and upset. I'll bet you did not eat dinner."

"No. Did you?"

Pause. "No."

"And now you're going back to surgery again, right?"

"Right."

"And it's all routine. No feelings. Just a lump of clay."

"This conversation is supposed to be about you."

I would think clearer thoughts about a physicians's emotional involvement. And I would change my thinking on its importance several times. But that was the first time I had thought about it. Both Dr. Praeder and I were to remember this conversation later—in May and June. But then we didn't mention it.

I went home, making Dr. Praeder promise to call me when the surgery was over to let me know the results.

Marilee lived. For three more days. If you call being on a respirator living.

She died Saturday morning. I was there. It wasn't like it had been with Tracy Marks. I knew Marilee was dead. She looked dead.

I didn't see her die. Her mother did.

Mrs. Johnson had just talked with Dr. Verdi about a half hour earlier. He had painted a dark picture.

She went in to see Marilee.

I had come up the back way from three-north. It was late morning. Things were always quieter on Saturdays, no surgery but emergency and only morning rounds.

I ran into Dr. McMahan. He was Dr. Verdi's "best resident." Dr. Verdi had told me that. He hadn't told Dr. McMahan.

Patrick McMahan was in his early thirties, brown hair, medium build, Irish, married with five children—all the same size! He had merged professionalism with compassion in a way almost no other surgeon I have met has been able to do.

But I didn't know that yet. I only knew he was friendly, willing to talk and explain things to me.

I bumped into Dr. McMahan by the back elevator on the sixth floor. "Hi, Rev. Coming to see Marilee? She's not doing too well. I don't think she'll hang on much longer. We won't let her, anyway. It's hopeless."

"Really?" That was the first time any of the neurosurgeons had put it into words for me. Dr. McMahan always would.

"What do you mean you 'won't let her'?"

"We'll pull the plug on the respirator."

"You can do that?"

"Somebody has to. It's legal in this state. We're getting no brain waves. Her EEG is flat, has been for three days now. [I didn't yet know what an EEG was.] It's putting her family through useless agony. She's dead now."

"But who pulls the plug?"

"I would; but others would, too. We have to agree. It's done at times. It's just not broadcast. It's the only humane thing to do."

I didn't really disagree. But I didn't understand it all either. I was still digesting the fact—now fact—that Marilee *was* going to die, period, no more questions.

Dr. McMahan went down in the elevator. I walked toward Intensive Care. As I reached the door, Dr. McMahan was being paged on the speaker and Mrs. Johnson was coming out . . . sobbing . . . but without tears. A nurse was with her. The nurse looked like she could have kissed me.

"She's gone. My Marilee. She died. Right now. I was watching, and she died." She walked aimlessly. It was only a few feet to the waiting room door, but she walked there in circles. She couldn't seem to stop and just cry. She kept walking and walking and zigzagging across the hall toward the door.

"She's gone. She's gone."

Mrs. Harris and the glittering lady minister were in the waiting room. They came out, heard the news, and began to wail, literally.

But Mrs. Johnson still was not crying. She still seemed to be in a strange trance. Dr. McMahan came out and took her into a little conference room to explain what happened medically. (No plug was pulled.)

He left and called me in. We sat there. In semi-darkness in the windowless room. She talked about Marilee, the things she did, the things she said. What she looked like when she was born.

I'm not sure she knew I was there. It didn't matter.

Then we prayed. In the middle, she wept . . . finally. It was beginning to make me nervous, her not crying.

A nurse came in and said she could see Marilee now, if she wished.

"Come with me, please." Mrs. Johnson took my hand and pulled more than really said anything.

I didn't want to go. But I did.

All the machinery had been unhooked. A sheet covered the little girl to her neck.

We stood there by the side of the crib. The sun was blazing in. The room was very white.

Tears were streaming down Mrs. Johnson's face. But she wasn't making a sound. The room was quiet.

She pulled down the sheet and touched her little naked daughter all over. She rubbed her chubby little legs, her little tummy and chest, her arms, her cheeks. She lifted her shoulders gently and looked at the wound in the back of her head. Then she covered her again up to the neck.

Would I pray?

It was short. I don't remember the words.

She didn't seem to be able to leave. I didn't either. Suddenly my mouth opened and words came out. "You know, right now she's seeing something we can only dream of. She's seeing God's face."

I don't know where the words came from. I hadn't planned to say them. I hadn't even had the thought, the mental picture, before. But it broke the spell. Her mother kissed her on the cheek.

"Would you like to kiss her?"

"Yes." I did. She was warm, still.

"She's all right now," said Marilee's mother. "I know she's all right now. We can leave. God has her now. She's all right. My little girl's all right."

We left.

The last thing I heard Mrs. Johnson do before I took them to "admitting" to sign the papers was call her husband. He was in California, I think.

He wasn't in. For the last five days she had been trying to get him to come home to see Marilee. "You tell him his daughter . . . you tell him Marilee . . . she died. *She is dead.* You tell him that. You tell him to call me if he wants to know when the services are. If he gives a damn."

I realized I couldn't unwind yet when I walked back to three-north and saw Katharine Hanley. Someone had to tell the pretty little twelve-year-old about her former roommate . . . about Marilee, her friend. And someone had to deal with her reactions. It was only fair.

Her mother, that was the first place to start.

"How's Marilee?" asked Katharine's mother as I stopped her in the hall outside Katharine's room. Katharine was watching television.

"That's what I want to talk to you about."

"She died?"

"Yes."

"I was afraid of that when she didn't come back to her room for so long . . . but I don't think Katharine suspects."

"Do you want to tell her or would you like me to?"

"No, I'll tell her. But I know Katharine. She won't break down in front of me. She'll try to be brave. So, if you could sort of go back and talk with her after I leave, about eight tonight, I know it would help. I think she'll get it out with you, where I know she won't with me."

"All right. I'll talk with her later. I won't forget." What could I say? That I had a date at eight o'clock and I really wanted to go because I wanted to think about something else and be with somebody else, somebody who would yell at me enough to remind me I'm alive, like David. Oh well, he'd yell anyway when I asked him to pick me up here, at nine. Good old David.

Katharine's mother was right. I found Katharine, the curtains half-drawn around her bed, her eyes pointed at the television, with big tears half in and half out . . . with no safe place to cry.

"Wanna take a walk?"

She understood. "Yeah."

She put on her furry blue slippers and her striped housecoat. We found an unused private room, closed the door, put on only the night light, and she cried—it had been pent up for hours— all over my shoulder and the daybed. Just went limp and cried. It almost scared me how hard.

She didn't talk for a long while. Neither did I. There aren't any rules for times like that, no pat set of answers, no pat set of actions. You just wait, and hope you can avoid saying the wrong thing, whatever that is.

"Did she have any pain? I mean a lot of pain?"

"No. None at all. She just fell asleep."

"Good. I'm glad. I'm glad she didn't have any pain."

Pause.

"I used to carry her around, and give her potato chips, and push her in the wheelchair, and talk to her when she cried. She was so cute. She was so happy. She'd say, 'walk, walk . . .' I kissed her good-bye before she went to surgery. She said, 'bye, bye.' Oh, I loved her so much."

She cried again, all over again, the same way, just as long.

"I loved her so much. Why? Why did she have to die? Why?"

Pause. She wanted an answer.

"No one knows why people we love have to die. Only God knows that. And he loves us. So he must always let happen what's best for us in the long run. Marilee was a sick little girl. Maybe God knew if she lived she'd have a lot of pain, that she'd never be well and happy. So maybe he let her die and come to him in heaven so she wouldn't have to suffer, to have unbearable pain. You and I wouldn't have wanted her to have lots of pain all her life, would we?"

"No."

"Well, maybe that's what would have happened. I don't know. But I do believe God knows best and, in the end, always lets only those things happen to us that are best for us, even if we don't always understand at the time."

She thought. "Yeah. I wouldn't have wanted her to have lots of pain. And I remember she did say, 'head hurt, head hurt' lots of times."

Pause.

"Is she in heaven now?"

"Yes."

"Will I get to see her when I go there?"

"Yes."

"Will she recognize me? I'll probably be old."

"Do you believe that in heaven God can do anything?"

"Sure."

"Then don't you think he'll make it possible for two people who loved each other to know each other again in heaven?"

"Yeah, sure! I guess he can."

Pause.

"I won't forget her. I'll never forget her. I loved her. I wish she wouldn't have died. But if she's happier in heaven and doesn't have any pain, I guess that's better. Is her mom OK?"

"Yes, I think so."

"Did you tell her about heaven and no pain?"

"In a way. But I think she understood. Mommies have a way of understanding. They always want what's best for their children, just like God."

"Yeah, my mom says that to me, sort of. I mean about wanting what's best for me. Can we sit here a little longer?"

"Sure. Do you want to say a prayer for Marilee?"

"OK, that would be nice." She took the "you" to be a personal you. I was glad.

"Dear God . . . Please take care of Marilee. I loved her so much. I really miss her. But I'm glad she's not having any more pain. I'm glad she's with you if she couldn't be happy here. But I miss her. I'll never forget her. I hope her mom's OK. Amen."

She sat very quietly. She got up and looked out the window. Beyond the street lamp. "See the star up there. Maybe that's Marilee."

"Maybe."

'My grandpa's in heaven. Now I know two people in heaven . . . and God . . . and Jesus . . ."

9

THE SUNDAY AFTER Marilee died I had the chapel services at both Adult and Children's. At Adult I decided to preach about God's love. I was going to steal a bit of Dr. Davies' theology about God's "unconditional love." It's a sound theology. I believe it, and maybe I needed to hear it that Sunday.

It was my first sermon.

(Here I must point out something, in retrospect. I wasn't wrestling with deep theological questions those first few weeks as a hospital chaplain, especially the theological questions related to pain and suffering and death and dying. I was simply flying by the seat of my faith, lots of times not sure where the next words or the next portions of gut strength were going to come from. When I went home at night I didn't always sleep. And when I did lie awake, the only things that went through my mind were the picture slides of memory. The people—the children—would flash over and over again in front of my eyes. *What* had happened to the people—the children—would flash over and over again in front of my eyes. But that was all. My head was full. There was no room for the "why?" Just no room.)

But back to God's "unconditional love" and my first sermon.

The services at Adult were held in an all-purpose chapel-conference room. Leftover styrofoam cups sat with dead cigarettes in musty ashtrays, and chairs had to be put aside to make room for the fifteen or so wheelchairs. Somehow I felt like I was preaching at a drive-in movie. The patients probably felt the same way.

"Most of you likely have heard God defined as 'love.' It's on bumper-stickers and buttons—and that alone should prove its validity! And it's also in the Bible: 'He that loveth not knoweth not God; for God is love.' [I John 4:8, KJV] And, as the verse says in the beginning, by loving we can know God—know his personality: 'He that loveth not knoweth not God.' Or, conversely, using preacher's license: He that loveth knoweth God; 'for God is love.'

"Now, let's test that, let's see what comparisons we can draw between God and love as we know it. And I'm not talking about people who use the word 'love' to get what they want. I'm talking about the most genuine forms of love that you and I have ever felt. And even these cannot come close to God's love."

"Amen!" stated an older black lady near the front.

A bit surprised, I smiled with her and went on. But my mind flashed back for a second to the black student in my preaching class at divinity school. "You whites miss all the *fun* of preaching," he had said. "We have help, support, from our congregations. It's real community!" I kind of knew now what he had meant. At least I knew someone was listening, was following.

"I assume most of us have experienced love in our lives: love for parents, brothers, sisters, friends, man, woman, wife, husband, grandparents, grandchildren . . . There are many kinds of love.

"But let's ask some questions about love. Can we see love? Can we touch love, literally? Can we buy love? Can we earn love by racking up points? Can we bargain for love? Can we turn love on and off like a light switch? Can we have control over love? Does love know the boundaries of race, creed, age, sex, nationality, wealth, social position?"

The lady had been shaking her head "no" with each question. So had—with less vigor—one or two others in the group.

" 'No' to all so far?" I asked.

"That's right!" said the lady.

"Can we reject love? Yes. Yes, we can reject love. But by rejecting love does that always stop the other person from loving us?

"Is love better when it is given with no demands, no strings attached? Is love better when it is there on our bad days as well as our good days? Is love better when it supports us, when it affirms us as persons, when it makes us feel totally safe and totally free at the same time? Some 'yeses' now?"

"That's right!"

"And, finally, is this love best of all when it is *all of these things*—all of these 'yeses'—and when we *respond* to it? When we feel the same way? When we try to love the other person the same way back? Another yes?"

"Amen!"

"Have you figured out my ploy yet?"

The lady nodded and smiled a huge smile. I smiled a huge smile back. Good for her! I sensed the others were with me, too. It felt good.

"Let's look at God now, as we see him—or as I see him, anyway—and ask the same questions.

"Can we see God? Can we touch God? Can we manufacture God? Can we buy God? Can we earn God by racking up points? Can we bargain for God? Can we turn God on and off like a light switch? Can we exert control over God? Does God know the boundaries of race, creed, age, sex, nationality, wealth, or social position?

" 'No' so far? Are you seeing the parallels between love and God as we know them?"

"Amen!"

"Can we reject God? Yes. But by our rejecting God does he cease to exist? And does his love for us stop?"

"No sister, no!"

"Does God come to us with no demands, no strings? Maybe we're not too sure about that one, even if we've answered 'yes.' *Does* God come to us with no demands, no strings?

"Is he there on our bad days as well as on our good days? Does God support us, affirm us, as persons? Does he make us feel totally safe and totally free at the same time? 'Yes' so far now?"

"Yes!"

"And finally, is God 'best of all'—do we feel him closest of all—when we *respond* to his love? When we try to love him back? 'He that loveth not knoweth not God; for God is love.' "

"Amen!"

"Now, if you think there are some variables in some of these last questions . . . then your *pride* is getting in the way. Yes, your pride . . . and my pride!

"What do I mean? Well, *were* you wondering whether God really makes no demands on us? Whether he really puts no performance strings on his love for us? Whether he really makes us feel totally free?

"Yes. The answer still is 'yes.' God loves us—each one of us—no matter what we have done, what we are doing, or what we will do. He may not approve of some of the things we do, but God loves each one of us equally, and totally without condition. Nothing, *nothing* you or I can do will make God stop loving us. Nothing."

"Tell it!"

"That is 'unconditional love.' And that is what makes God's love for us perfect and our love for each other, and for God, imperfect.

"For we, you and I can't love without condition. We can *try* to love without condition. But sooner or later, from time to time, our pride gets in the way.

"Someone we love will hurt us and we'll say, 'You can't do that to me!' Someone we love will ignore us, will do something of which we don't approve, not live up to our expectations, whatever. And sooner or later, we'll be too proud—whether it's hurt pride or snobbish pride—we'll be too proud to go on loving them. Our love will have been based on a condition."

"That's right!"

"And we do it to God, too. When all goes well, that's fine. But let us ask for something we don't receive, ask fervently and for a long, long time . . . And finally, when we don't get whatever it is we're asking for, our pride is hurt. 'I've lost my faith,' we sigh."

Softly, "That's right."

"So, strange as it may sound, if you—and I—think God doesn't love us because we've done too many things wrong, or because we've ignored him too long, or because we've simply rejected him, or because our prayers haven't been answered the way we want—it's just our pride getting in the way.

"Just because you and I can't love without condition doesn't

mean God can't love without condition. And that's *our* problem—yours and mine, not God's.

"For God is totally *prideless*. That means he's totally humble.
He'll love us always, without condition. He'll love us when we
love him back and he'll love us when we ignore him—whether
we ignore him because we think we've done too many wrong
things, or because we don't have time, or because we are afraid
we don't believe any more, or because we've 'lost' our faith . . .
or because we've *never* believed. It doesn't make any difference.
God will love us. Period."

"Amen!"

I smiled and lowered my voice just a bit. "But, in our lives
when we have had rare moments of loving and being loved by
someone who seems to love us without condition, someone who
loves us in the midst of our stumblings, in the midst of our
sufferings, how does that make us feel? Free? Not worried about
always doing the right thing or saying the right thing? Safe?
Secure that the love will not fly away on a whim?"

"That's right."

"And when we feel both free in love and safe in love, what
does that do to our lives?

"It makes them other people directed, doesn't it? Suddenly
we're not so worried about me, me, me: 'Nobody loves *me*,
nobody cares about *me*, nobody listens to *me*.' Suddenly, the
'me' is loved and cared about and listened to, so the 'me' is
safe, and free—free to see the world around him, free to see the
world around her, and the people in it. Free to care for and love
and listen to . . . somebody else."

"You said it! Amen!"

"And it's the same with God's love. When we *respond* to
God's love—something that has been, is, and will be ours, freely,
for all time no matter what—when we respond to God's love,
suddenly we are safe, and we are free. We are safe in the knowledge that God loves us, God cares about us and God listens to
us—unendingly; and therefore, we are free, free to see the world
around us and the people in it. Free to care for and love and
listen to . . . somebody else.

"Simple, isn't it? Almost too simple, too good to be true.
And that's why we continue to try to build a self-righteous for-
tress around God, to make him someone *we* have to 'find'

through good deeds and righteous feelings, rather than someone who *has already found us, where we are, today*; someone who loves us without condition and asks only that we accept that love and respond to that love.

"God *is* love, unconditional love. And knowing that and responding to that can make all the difference . . ."

"Praise the Lord and Amen!"

I was glad for the lady in the congregation. Not only did I know that at least one person was following, but I sensed that she helped others follow, too—or at least stay awake!

But I was also glad the sermon was over. I believe in God's unconditional love. It has made a major difference in my life. And it certainly has set me free. But that was the first time I had tried to put Dr. Davies' theology into a sermon, into my words. I was glad he wasn't there!

The people did seem to like it, though, afterwards. But I guess ministers never can tell for sure. I mean, very few people would go up to a minister and say, "That was a crummy sermon and it took too long and you speak in a monotone." They just say that to their spouses over brunch.

Anyway, I packed up my Bible and headed the one block west to Children's for the service there. This one would be easier, maybe. But what if a child got sick or a parent got really upset? It was going to be difficult to strike a happy medium of speaking both to parents and children.

There were fifteen children and ten adults at the service. I hadn't expected that many. My knees got weak, very weak. I had written a few notes, but I just put them aside and decided to wing it.

Gary Larson was there. Remember Gary, who knew everybody's name? And Lindsay Grice, the little girl I rocked so often that first week. Gary and Lindsay were side by side in their wheelchairs. And they were the only people in the whole chapel I knew!

First of all we sang a hymn and then we went around the circle of parents and children introducing ourselves. At least half the children were in wheelchairs or "banana" carts and had I.V. fluid bottles attached to their arms. There were bandages on heads, chests, arms, legs, backs . . . everywhere.

But the smiling and the chattering and the bashful glances, they were the same. Children are children are children, I guess.

We talked about praying, about talking to God, and that there are many reasons to talk with God, and that it doesn't have to be a particular time or a particular place or a particular way.

Sometimes we talk with God when we sing, like the hymn. Sometimes we talk with God about happy things. Sometimes we talk with God about sad things. Sometimes we ask God to help us. Sometimes we thank God for helping us.

"And sometimes we think God isn't listening to us . . . don't we?

"But does God stop listening to us? Or does he sometimes know what's best for us even when we might not agree or understand?

"For example: do your parents really want you to be in the hospital? Of course not. But is being here the best way to help you feel better?

"Do the nurses really want to hurt you when they give you a shot?" Laughter. "No, believe it or not, they don't. But is the shot to help you feel better?

"It's the same way with God. He doesn't like to see us unhappy, to see us hurt, but he knows many more things than we do . . . even many more things than our mommies and daddies and all the big doctors and all the nurses . . . and the chaplain! He knows, when all is said and done, what is best for us.

"And most important of all, God loves us. So in the long run, he'll only let what's best for us happen, even if we or our mommies and daddies can't seem to understand that right now, and even if we or our mommies and daddies get angry.

"We all do, sometimes, get angry because we don't understand what's happening to us and to those we love.

"But that's where faith comes in. God told us he loves us, and we have to believe he does—or go it alone. The choice is ours. Just like we really know our parents love us even when we don't always understand what's happening to us or why they tell us 'no' sometimes. Right?

"But it makes it better, doesn't it, when we talk with our parents about how we feel?

"And that's the same way with God. It's better when we tell him what we feel—when we're happy, when we're sad, when we're angry, when we don't understand. Because God is *always* listening. He always cares. And he'll always do what's best for us in the long run, because he loves us.

"And we'll also feel better about it if we talk with God. It will make us feel safer and stronger and braver. Because he'll be *sharing* our feelings with us!

"So that's what we're going to do this morning. We're going to talk with God. Each one of us will have a chance to say exactly what he or she feels . . . and we know God will be listening."

A little girl with her arm in a cast, suspended from a pole, went first: "Thank you God that I had a good operation and my arm will soon be better."

The others followed, happily without much prodding.

"Thank you God for my puppy. His name is Sam. I love him very much. He's a beagle."

"Please let me go home soon, God. And please help Mommy not to cry so much."

"Thank you for my grandpa. I wish I could see him. Please help him get well."

"Please let them let my sister come to visit me. I miss her."

Then we came to Gary Larson.

"Hi, Nina!"

"Hi, Gary!"

"Hi, Nina!"

"Gary, what do you want to say to God today?"

"What do I want to say to God today." It was a statement.

"Can you think of anything? God's right here with us. Don't you want to say something to him?"

"What do I want to say to God today." Statement.

"Can you say, 'Thank you, God'?"

"Yep."

Pause.

At the top of his lungs. "Thank you God!"

"Good, Gary! And this is Lindsay next to Gary . . ."

"That's Lindsay Grice!" clarified Gary.

"That's right, Gary. Lindsay, can you say, 'I love you God'?"

"Lindsay . . . say 'I love you God,' " Gary nudged her.

Lindsay mouthed the words, sort of. And smiled a huge smile.

"Good, Lindsay!"

And we went on . . . to some parents.

"I guess we don't understand all the time, God. Please give us courage. And help us turn to you more often. We've found comfort today. Thank you, God."

"Dear God, help us accept . . ." The rest was cut off by a choke.

"Dear God, thank you that we're taking Tommy home with us next week. Help us remember what we have learned in this hospital. It has been a priceless lesson."

Back to the children.

"Thank you God for my turtle. His name is Harvey."

All this time Gary Larson had been looking all around the chapel, at the ceiling, the floor, the altar, the walls, the doorway.

"Hey, Nina!" Right in the middle of the prayers.

"Excuse me. Yes, Gary?" He was too little to understand.

"Hey, Nina!"

"Yes, Gary, what is it?"

"Where *is* God?"

It broke the growing tension. The little boy had been looking high and low for God in the chapel!

"That's a good question, Gary." And a hard one! "God is here, but he's inside us. He helps us feel happy. Do you feel happy now, Gary?"

"Yes!"

"Well, God helps us feel happy. OK?"

"OK. Hi, God!" He looked at his tummy.

Whew! I thought, and looked up as one of the fathers was smiling and making a gesture of wiping his brow. At least I got some sympathy!

We finished prayers. We sang a hymn.

"May the road rise to meet you. May the wind be always at your back. May the sun shine warm upon your face, and the rains fall soft upon your fields. And, until we meet again, may God hold you in the palm of his hand."

It was over. But the service and that Gaelic blessing—later requested by parents whose dying child I never saw, never was on my floor—had so affected those parents that I received two letters and a Christmas card from them long after I left Children's. Here is part of one letter. You never know, I guess.

We will long remember the Sunday worship service you conducted in the hospital chapel the day we first heard the words of the "Irish Blessing." That was a most memorable half hour for us. It was perfectly done and so reassuring to us.

Every weekend Bill was in the hospital we attended those services, and for us, the Sunday you were in charge proved to be the most meaningful. You gave us a great deal of strength, and we want you to know that your ministry at Children's is much appreciated.

Having Bill gone leaves a huge void in our lives and a deep hurt in the pit of our stomachs. But we do have peace knowing that he is God's child and that he is with Him, suffering no more.

God bless you in your work.

You're right it made me feel good . . . and lots of other things.

10

THE FIRST TIME I saw Riann (pronounced: Ryan) Miles she was in room 383 sitting up in bed reading. It was early afternoon. Her hair was thick and dark, and about three-fourths of an inch long all over her head. If she hadn't been so pretty, she would have looked like a rosy-cheeked eight-year-old choir boy.

"Hi."

"Hi."

"What's your name?"

"Riann Miles—R-I-A-N-N, I'm a girl."

I smiled. "I can tell! I'm Nina Herrmann. I'm the chaplain on this floor. Did you just come in?"

"About an hour ago. My mother went downstairs for a cup of coffee. I didn't know they had lady ministers?"

"There aren't too many of us. I hope you don't mind?"

"Oh, no! I think it's a nice idea."

"What grade are you in?"

"Second."

"Where do you live?"

"Rock Shores."

"I like that town. It's pretty."

"Thank you, I like it too."

She was very polite, and very sweet, and very pretty. "Have you been here before?"

"Yes, three times: last August, then in October, and then at Christmas."

"Oh, Christmas; that's too bad."

"Oh, no, I was lucky. I got to go home just before!"

"That's good. I have to go to a meeting now. But may I come back to see you again?"

"Yes. I'd like that. I want my mommy to meet you."

"Thank you, I'd like to meet her, too."

I met Riann's mother and her father that evening on rounds. Dr. Verdi introduced us, mentioning that they, like him, were Roman Catholic . . . teasingly implying that that was obviously a step above Presbyterian. Dr. Verdi clearly liked the Mileses and Riann. It was more like a social visit between them than a medical one, or at least those were the overtones.

Dr. Verdi pushed on Riann's stomach a few times. One place hurt. Did her head hurt?

"Just a little, not much."

"A headache?"

"Yes."

"When?"

"In the mornings, mostly."

Dr. Verdi told Riann's parents he hoped it was her shunt rather than anything else. He wanted to get her through her adolescent developmental stages before he had to do anything more major . . .

They nodded in agreement.

I wondered if she had something wrong with her stomach . . . But a shunt? She didn't look like she had hydrocephalus.

About an hour later I saw Dr. McMahan in the room behind the nursing station. "Do you know Riann Miles?"

"Yeah, cute kid. Did you meet her?"

"Yes, this afternoon and again near the end of rounds."

"Didn't make rounds. What did Verdi say about her?"

"He pushed on her stomach and asked her about headaches and said he hoped it was her shunt."

"Yeah, me too. I'd be afraid to go in there again, afraid of what I'd find."

"Does she have hydrocephalus?"

"Oh—you mean because of the shunt. Yeah, in a way. She's got two shunts."

"Two? Why?"

" 'Cause she has a big, nasty, ugly tumor in her head."

Pause.

He continued. "She's a beautiful little kid with a very ugly tumor." He looked at my face. "I'm sorry. Didn't you know?"

"No. What does it mean?" I felt sick.

"We don't know for sure."

"Is it malignant?"

"No, not by itself. But it acts malignant because we can't get it all out and because it may grow. Sometimes tumors like Riann has grow slowly, very slowly. That's what we're hoping. Verdi thinks she can have fifteen to twenty years. But I'm never as optimistic as he is."

"What do you think?"

"I don't know. But I just don't think it will be fifteen to twenty years . . ."

"Why does she have two shunts if she has a tumor?"

"Because the tumor puts pressure on the intraventricular system and can obstruct the flow of CSF. And by putting in shunts, we can relieve the pressure. They—the shunts—keep the person from getting bad headaches and having lots of pain. That's why we think that one of her shunts is either loose or obstructed now, because she has headaches."

"Obstructed by the tumor?"

"No, not likely. Just by some foreign matter caught in the end, maybe the tummy end. That's why Verdi pushed on her tummy."

"And if isn't the shunts . . . if they aren't clogged, obstructed?"

"It may be her tumor . . . growing. That's why Verdi wants it to be the shunts. Not very pleasant is it, Rev?"

"No."

"But don't worry too much. I really do think it's one of the shunts this time. We'll know Monday after we do some tests. We're just going to observe her over the weekend."

Pause. "Did Pat Allen have a tumor?"

"Yeah, but a different kind. Other than shunts, we couldn't even operate on hers . . . it grew too fast."

"But it was a tumor?"

"Yeah, it was a tumor."

Saturday rounds are brief, around noon. Paul was going to pick me up at one o'clock for lunch and some shopping. Paul was just the opposite of David—sympathetic, easily moved, upset by suffering and illness. Visiting three-north, David would have calculated the amount of money spent on the surgical gauze used to cover wounds. Paul would have calculated the amount of suffering spent on the wounds that were covered by the gauze. But maybe I'm being a little hard on David.

Knowing Paul, I told him to go to the Information Desk when he arrived and ask them to telephone me on three-north and I would meet him in the lobby. Paul wasn't ready for three-north. But all Paul got out of his mouth was "three-north" and he was told to "go right up," and given detailed instructions on how to get there. (Paul was a public official whose face was well known.)

I was on rounds with the neurosurgeons, at the very farthest end of the L-shaped three-north wing. To get to me, Paul had to walk through about one-third of the orthopedic section, past all the private rooms on three-north, past the Constant Care room on three-north, and past all the four-bed wards on three-north. He had to walk past children with bandages and tubes and no hair and scars and casts and open backs and all those ailments I saw on my first day on three-north. He had to walk by all that. And he had to remember to smile pleasantly . . .

I was standing at the doorway of room 388, the last room in the hall. I felt a tug at my sleeve. I looked down; a child tugs at your sleeve. I saw a pair of highly polished boots and custom-tailored trousers: Paul. I looked up. His face was so white it was almost translucent. Poor dear. He looked so pathetic that I almost wanted to laugh.

"Oh, hi. We're just finishing rounds. Want to come along?"

His head shook no.

"Want to wait on that chair? I'll only be a few minutes. I promised to see one little girl for a minute before I leave."

His head shook no.

"Want to wait in the lobby?"

His head shook yes.

"Can you find your way back to the elevators?"

His head shook no.

"Ok, I'll show you."

His head shook yes.

I walked with him back to the elevator. He never said a word. He had that stupid, plastic-politician smile on his face. But behind it was silent panic. When we reached the elevator he kissed me, got in, and went to the lobby . . . or so I thought.

But when I got to the lobby, Paul was gone. I looked downstairs, and in the emergency waiting room; even in the chapel. Nowhere. So I decided to wait. After all, I couldn't look in the men's room.

Five minutes later he came in the front door.

"Sorry. You been waiting long?"

"No. Where did you go?"

"Come on, I'll show you."

We got to his green Continental and the right front seat was littered with scraps of paper. The door to his glove compartment was open and everything inside was arranged in neat piles.

"I was so frustrated by what I saw that I couldn't sit still. I cleaned out my whole glove compartment, found things I never knew I had, tried to forget. I couldn't."

And all through lunch he couldn't forget.

He still hasn't.

He never went back.

I knew he wouldn't.

They operated on Riann Miles Monday afternoon. It was her left shunt, blocked, at the top end—in her ventricle.

Dr. Verdi was optimistic. Just her shunt he told her parents. She can go home in about ten days.

But Dr. Praeder had done the surgery. "I think the tumor, it is growing. I do not know for sure. But I think it is bigger than before. I think we must watch very carefully." He was saying that to Dr. McMahan after rounds Monday evening. I overheard.

I remembered Pat Allen.

One evening Riann and I were playing the card game "war." I could see that she was getting tired. I was glad in a way. I hate "war."

"Wanna just talk?"

"Yes, I think so. Thank you."

That was another unusual thing about Riann, beyond her unswerving politeness. Winning was of no importance. Neither was finishing a game. What eight-year-old do you know who would have stopped in the middle of a card game—tired or not—without saying, "OK, but I win"; or, "OK, but we have to draw to see who wins." I don't know any, except Riann Miles.

"We say prayers at home in my room."

"You mean the whole family?"

"Yes. Or, at least Eric and Kevin and Allison and Mommy and me, if Daddy isn't home. We have relics, crosses and things my grandmother gave us. We use those in our prayers."

She started to giggle. "You know what my brother Kevin did?—he's so funny. The last time I was here I asked him to bring some of the relics so Mommy and I could say prayers here. And he brought them in—you'll never believe this—in a Seagram's bag!" Giggle. Giggle.

"In a what?"

"A Seagram's bag. You know, like liquor comes in. It was really funny."

"Oh," I laughed with her. "That is funny." I still wasn't quite sure what she meant, but I guessed she meant her brother had put the crosses in a blue velvet Seagram's Crown Royal bag. (I was right.)

"When did you say you were here before?"

"Three times! First in August; that's when they operated on my tumor . . ."

Grief, she said the word! For a moment I didn't realize that to her it was just a word.

". . . the second time in October for my shunts. And then at Christmas when my shunt got clogged, like this time. Both times it's been my left shunt. You know what my brothers call me?"

"What?"

"Rube tube! Rube because I was bald—though some of my hair is coming back now, thank goodness! And Tube because of the tubes in my head. They're so funny. Rube Tube! Can you imagine?"

We laughed. She was unreal. Totally unreal.

"Riann, if you want to say prayers at bedtime here in the

hospital and your mother has to leave early or something, I'd enjoy saying prayers with you."

"Really? Oh, good! Mommy does have to leave early sometimes, because of Allison and Kevin and Eric. I usually just say prayers by myself then. But I'd much rather say them with you. I'll ask Mommy to bring the Seagram's bag." Giggle.

"OK."

"She's gone already tonight. And I think I'm ready to go to sleep. Can we say prayers now?"

"Sure."

"You go first."

She folded her hands and bowed her head. I went first.

Then she thanked God for a good day and for helping her feel better. And she prayed that a long list of people would have a "good night's sleep."

"Wanna say the 'Our Father'?" she asked.

Fortunately I remembered that Catholics stop after "deliver us from evil," and say "trespasses" rather than "debts."

(I have heard Riann say the "Our Father" maybe fifty times now. But from that very first time on, I haven't been able to say it once—not once—without thinking of her, without hearing her voice. I wonder how long that will last. It's like a crystal bell ringing.)

I gave her a kiss good-night, turned out the light.

"Leave the door open, please."

"OK."

"Nina . . ."

"Yes?"

"Thank you."

Riann and I said prayers together a few times more, took a few walks together, talked about her brothers and sister, about school. She never asked questions. What eight-year-old do you know who never asks questions? Most of her sentences began "I remember one time when . . ." Or, "Do you know what Kevin did one time?" Giggle. Or, "I like to . . ."

She never asked questions. Never.

In the middle of the week after her operation she went home.

At the end of the week after she went home, she came back.

11

I WAS AFRAID of Dr. Jenssen—Dr. Ingrid Jenssen. She was the head of Neurology at Children's. Neurology and Neurosurgery patients shared three-north, I finally discovered.

Neurology is "the branch of medicine dealing with the nervous system and its diseases," according to Webster.

Dr. Jenssen was somewhere in her thirties, blond, attractive, married, mother of two. She always looked at me disapprovingly. I wondered if my skirt was too short or my hair too long or if she just didn't take me seriously.

I had heard good things about her from the nurses: "Kind, sympathetic, exacting doctor, sweet, friendly . . ." So it bothered me even more. I would smile, but the best she seemed to manage was a half-smile back.

The neurologists made rounds, too. I really wanted to go along. I was learning about neurosurgery, learning to read charts and be somewhat forewarned about what to expect with each patient's diagnosis. I was learning the terms. (I was the hit of the party circuit just explaining a shunt!) I wanted to know about neurology. But in no way could I get up the courage to ask Dr. Jenssen if I could go on rounds with the neurologists.

Then something happened that changed her attitude, or at least changed my reading of her attitude, I guess. It was a brave attempt on my part to give her a compliment, one she deserved . . . and her reaction to something I wrote for the parents of one of her patients.

Mark Heller was a handsome little boy, about three, with black hair and blue eyes. His mother was pretty, young, with dark hair and deep-set brown-black eyes. Mark had a private room across from the small waiting room. Mark's mother spent nights at the hospital, sleeping on the daybed in Mark's room. She would bring Mark out into the small waiting room and hold him in her lap in the evenings and talk with me.

We talked about casual things a lot, Mark's mother and I. Mark was Dr. Jenssen's patient, so I really didn't know what was wrong with him. I never got to see him on rounds or hear the doctors discussing his symptoms or his tests.

His mother said he had seizures. The doctors didn't know what caused them or how to keep them under control for sure.

But I had never seen Mark have a seizure and I really wasn't quite sure what a seizure was . . .

Other than that, Mark's mother didn't talk much about Mark's condition, just held him and cuddled him and loved him. I held him one time when his mother went to answer a telephone call. He seemed sort of stiff. And he didn't react very much. But he was an adorable little boy.

Each day Mark had a test. Then one day his mother said the results of one test had been sent somewhere in the West. Doctors there would look at them and maybe they'd be able to try some very new medication on Mark that might help. It would take a few days to find out.

I was sitting in the small waiting room talking with several mothers and fathers when Dr. Jenssen and Mark Heller's mother walked by. They went down the hall toward the other wing, then stopped and sat in a window ledge and talked. They talked for quite some time.

I watched out of the corner of my eye. Mark's mother looked sad. Dr. Jenssen put her hand on the girl's shoulder, shook her head, and left. Mark's mother sat a few minutes on the window ledge, then walked back to her room. She looked at me for a moment when she walked by, but she didn't stop. She left the door to her room open. I wasn't sure whether or not to go in. But I did. The open door . . .

"Are you OK?"

She shook her head no.

"Would you rather be alone?"

No again. "Could you please close the door." Choked.

I did.

She was like a little girl, like me the night Ethel Stone died, needing to cry but needing someone to cry on.

I sat down on the daybed beside her and she simply buried her head in my arms and wept . . . and tried to talk at the same time.

"They can't do it . . . it won't help . . . no use . . . they said there's no use . . . won't help. I wanted it to work . . . to try . . . just try . . . it was the last hope . . . last hope. Now there's nothing. They've tried everything . . . nothing more . . . they can't do anything more . . .

"How can I tell Barry . . . my husband . . . how can I tell him?"

She sat back, blew her nose, wiped her eyes. The worst was over. And just beginning.

"Is that what Dr. Jenssen was telling you now?"

"Yes. She tried to be nice. But she said the doctors in the West said the new medication won't help Mark . . . He's incurable."

It took everything inside her to form the word *incurable*.

"All we can do now is take him home."

I looked at Mark. He was asleep in his crib, eyes closed, hair tousled, light perspiration on his forehead, light blue sleepers with firemen on them. No wonder it hurt. He *looked* so normal, so healthy, so cute when he was asleep.

"He wasn't like this from the beginning. He was so normal . . . for a whole year. Nothing wrong . . ."

Then the entire story—the story which she had been afraid that verbalizing would somehow negate the last hope—came out, now when there was no "last hope" to tease the superstition.

"One day he had a seizure—just like that, out of the blue. It scared me, but the doctor said just to watch him. Then he had another one six weeks later, and another one two weeks later. That one lasted six hours. Six hours. I felt so helpless. My own little baby. And I couldn't do anything. Nothing.

"He hasn't stopped seizing, really, since. He's on lots of medication now, but even that may lose effect sooner or later.

"I don't think he even knows us any more. I hold him and talk to him and kiss him and love him . . . And he doesn't even know I'm his mommy. He'll never know. Never."

She got up and put her forehead down hard on the railing of the crib . . . as if she wanted to bang her head against something in utter desolation. I watched as one of her tears fell from her cheek onto the crib railing and trickled slowly down the metal bar.

I heard how Mark Heller's mother felt. I saw how Mark Heller's mother felt. Never, never could I, in those moments, *know* how Mark Heller's mother felt.

But seeing and hearing were enough.

"How do you think your husband will take it?"

"He'll try to be brave because of me. He always is. I love him for that. But I know how it hurts him inside.

"But there's something more. Something I'm even more afraid to tell him." She measured out the words as if talking in rhythm with a metronome. "Dr. Jenssen said since she and the other doctors can't determine what caused Mark's seizures, they can't be sure the cause isn't genetic. Which means we can't be sure if we had another baby it wouldn't develop the same thing. So she suggested we not have any more babies maybe . . .

"And Barry and I wanted five children." The tears came again. "We both wanted five children. We decided that the day we got engaged. We've built our lives around that. Even moved to a suburb we didn't especially want to live in just because we could afford a down payment on a bigger house . . . with more bedrooms . . .

"And Barry's father. He can't even admit there's anything wrong with Mark. He talks to him and plays with him and brings him toys . . . even though he never responds. He says it's a 'phase' he's going through. He's sixty-two years old. He has to know better. But he won't admit it. Mark is his first grandchild.

"And the neighbors. They look at Mark funny when I take him out. I hate that. I guess you can't blame them. We haven't lived there long. They don't know. But they're so obvious. All I want to do is take him for a walk, for some air. Just leave us alone.

"Now it won't change. Sooner or later I'll have to tell them. They'll build it up, too. I hate that. If they just wouldn't look, would just leave us alone. 'Can't he walk yet?' 'Can't he talk yet?' 'How old *is* he?' 'Well, some children are just slower than others. He'll come along soon.'

"Just leave us alone!

"My mother said we'd have to put him in a home if they

couldn't give him the medication. I can't think about that yet. Just an hour ago I still had hope. I can't put him away, not in an hour. I want him at home. I don't care. Barry understands. He says I don't have to put him anywhere I don't want to. Do you think I should put him in a home?''

Pause. ''I think that's something you may consider at some future time. But I don't think now is the time.''

''But do you think he'll have to be placed someday?''

''I'm not a doctor, so I don't know. But I can see you love Mark very much, which means you want the best for him, that you want him to be as happy and comfortable as possible under the circumstances. As long as that is with you and your husband in your home, then that's the place he should be. But if the time should come that you couldn't care for him properly, for one reason or another, you might want to consider placing him. But I don't think you have to rush into anything. Look at some homes after a while. Talk with staff. See the children. See if they look happy and cared for and loved. Take your time.''

''If I were *sure* he didn't know us, absolutely sure, it wouldn't be quite as hard . . . someday. But I wouldn't want him to think we'd abandoned him.''

''Yes, I can understand that. But sometimes children are happy, too, with other children in a place equipped to their needs. I'll tell you a story one of the parents here told me one time.

''He had a cousin who was retarded. The parents of the cousin had kept the boy home until he was sixteen, and they just couldn't handle him any more. Finally they placed him—with great fear. All the while they worried they hadn't done the right thing.

''But then the child came home for Christmas vacation. One day the parents saw him sitting unhappily by the Christmas tree. They asked him what was wrong. 'Mommy, Daddy, I love you but when can I go home? I want to see Billy and Freddie . . .'

''The boy was so happy where he had been placed that he called it 'home.' And rather than being hurt, the parents were happy because it made them sure they had done the right thing for the boy they loved.

''It's hard to know what's best all the time. But you love Mark. You'll know if the time comes to place him. I'm not worried about that.''

''I guess so. I just have to keep telling myself this is it. We go home. This is it. I guess I still really don't believe it. I guess I still expect Dr. Jenssen to come through the door and say, 'I made a mistake. We *can* treat Mark.' But I guess, too, I know she won't. I think I knew that all along. I guess I want to pray now.''

We did.

Mark Heller went home the next day.

That evening I wrote something for his mother . . . I guess for his mother . . .

"My name is Mark.

When you look at me,
You will measure me
    . . . by my awareness
    . . . by my response
    . . . by my age
    . . . by my development
And you will shake your head
And find me lacking.

But, for me, you are measuring
With the wrong cup.
For I have one possession
Which brims and overflows
Beyond all others.

I have my parents' love.

This cup they give me holds also their
    . . . agony and helplessness
    . . . waiting and hoping
    . . . tears and pain
    . . . aloneness and fear.

But in the end, all these are swallowed up
In the deepness of their love
Which now, in each same moment,
Both lets me go
And will never let me go.

So measure me, if you must . . .
But measure me, too, with my cup
And you will find me
Full.''

I saw Dr. Jenssen in the hall a few days later. I got up my courage. ''Dr. Jenssen, I just wanted to tell you how much it helped the way you talked with Mark Heller's mother, the way you took the time to explain things. It made my job so much easier. She obviously understood what you were telling her and all the implications.''

What I wanted to say didn't come out very well. But Dr. Jenssen still frightened me.

''Yes. She told me on the telephone that you wrote something for her. She liked it very much. What was it?''

''Just something I felt Mark might have said some day if he could. I'll show you a copy if you like.''

''Yes. I would.''

I got the feeling she thought I had given a medical diagnosis.

''His mother was worried about placing him,'' I ventured.

''I know. That is a hard decision.'' And she disappeared into the elevator.

''That was very good. What you wrote for Mark Heller's mother.''

It was two days later. I had left a copy of the poem for Dr. Jenssen at the nursing station. She returned it as we passed in the hall. And that did it, I guess. Something did it. The next thing I knew, Dr. Jenssen was showing me photographs of her children and I was asking her if I could go on rounds with the neurologists.

''Yes, of course. But I thought you only made rounds with the neurosurgeons . . .''

How funny. She apparently thought I didn't want to make rounds with the neurologists. And I thought she didn't want me to . . .

Mark Heller died that fall. At home. Pneumonia.

12

ONE OF THE first things I began to suspect was that "why?" cannot be answered, and that deep down inside, most people know that already. "Why?" theologically, that is.

It can be said what "why?" is not. Mary Smith does not have a tumor because the sins of the first generation are being visited on the third generation. At least not "sins" when they equal immoral or evil acts, as they do in the minds of most people. If that were the case, then Mary Smith would be merely a puppet in the hands of an evil "god."

Mary Smith does not have a tumor because her mother didn't go to Sunday school or her father had an extramarital affair. Not an eye for an eye, a tooth for a tooth. Some people might believe that. But I don't believe that. I don't believe in a puppeteer God.

Most theological conversations—the unscheduled type held while sitting in the little waiting room area with two or three parents dropping in and out—began with, "The first thing I asked myself was 'why? Why did this happen to my child? What did *I* do wrong?' I still think about it every now and then, but I know there's no answer. And intellectually I know God doesn't really work that way. But still you've gotta think every now and then, 'Was it me?' "

I point out that that's a normal reaction. And I reaffirm that "no, the God I believe in really doesn't work that way, either." And I reaffirm that "no, it wasn't your sins."

79

It works, of course. And it's comforting. After all, I wear the reversed collar, don't I?

But it still doesn't answer the question, "Why?"

But then, I still wouldn't admit to asking it . . . admit to myself. And I wouldn't admit, either, to a streaking wonder if it wasn't all a cheap game.

I don't remember the first time I saw Joey Collins, or my first conversation with his mother. But I know I saw them both a lot.

They were in and out of the hospital nine times between January and May. I say "they" because though Joey wasn't in a private room, his mother came at ten every morning and stayed until eight-thirty every evening. Joey's father didn't like hospitals, so he didn't come as often. But he loved his kid. Joey and his mother were lucky that way, I guess. A lot of fathers don't . . . love their kids like Joey, I mean.

Joey had myelomeningocele and hydrocephalus. Myelomeningocele is a birth defect, cause unknown. It's the worst form of spinabifida. But you almost never hear "spinabifida" around University Children's. It's "myelomeningocele"—which is what most children we got had. Helping a child with myelomeningocele takes the most intricate neurosurgical procedures.

When a child is born with myelomeningocele (hereafter referred to as "m-m," as it is at Children's) it means a severe malformation of nervous tissue and that a portion of the spinal column is open and protruding, usually covered only by a thin membrane which may rupture and provide an entry for an infection. (Thus the need for immediate surgery.) The lower this opening is on the child's back, usually the better it is for the child. For years, the mortality rate for m-m children was very high. Doctors simply didn't know how to treat it. But finally a surgical procedure for m-m was developed and perfected.

The surgery performed immediately on the child with m-m is surgery to close the opening in the child's back. Nerve endings, muscle tissue, and spinal cord tissue are involved, so it's a very delicate, very tedious operation. Every nerve that can be saved is important, because it may make a difference in whether or not the child will ever walk . . . whether with crutches, braces, or if lucky, by himself. Very few m-m children walk unaided.

And not that many more can walk at all. But it's a hope their parents cling to.

Once the m-m wound is closed, the child is placed stomach down on a wooden board called a "gingerbread board"— because it looks like a gingerbread man without a head, I guess. The child is cared for on that board until the back wound is healed.

(Does the word *wound* sound strange? It did to me for a long time. But it's standard hospital terminology for any skin opening, whether inflicted by nature, a gunshot, or a surgeon's knife.)

Once the child's m-m wound is healed, all problems are over, other than walking? No.

Usually m-m children don't have bladder or bowel control. In an infant, that doesn't hit home right away. After all, it's normal. But the day comes . . .

Often m-m children have trouble with their hips—they come out of their sockets. So they may have to spend months in a cast.

At times m-m children are born with club feet—more time in casts, more surgery.

And at least eighty percent of the time m-m children develop hydrocephalus.

Surprised? Remember CSF—cerebrospinal fluid? I mentioned that it is a fluid that circulates within the ventricular system (the four cavities) and over the surface of the brain, continuously? And that hydrocephalus was caused by an increase in CSF, in intraventricular pressure, and in intraventricular size?

Well, when the m-m is repaired and the skin closed, very often this brings on an increase in pressure, an increase in CSF, and an increase in intraventricular size—all leading to hydrocephalus.

And sometimes the hydrocephalus is present even before the wound is closed, even before birth. Cause, again unknown.

So the m-m child has another surgery, to insert a shunt to drain off the excess CSF and keep the head from growing.

All of which means that though children born with myelomeningocele will probably never have to have another surgery on their spines, they can spend weeks and months in the hospital for orthopedic work, urology work, and shunt revisions . . . year after year after year . . .

* * *

Joey Collins was three when I met him. Most of his hospitalizations during the time I was at Children's were for shunt revisions. The neurosurgeons just couldn't seem to get a shunt that would work right for him. Finally they inserted a V-A shunt—that means ventricle to aorta, or head to heart. Usually shunts are V-P—ventricular to peritoneal, or head to stomach. But the V-A shunt worked.

One time when we were talking about ministers and chaplains Mrs. Collins told me what it was like when Joey was born.

"Who expects that! I mean, you plan and pick out clothes and blankets and set up a nursery and all that stuff. Your first kid; you don't expect no trouble. You expect a baby, to bring him home.

"Oh, I'm not saying I never had fears. That's normal as you go along. But myelomeningocele! I'd never heard of it, so how could I worry about it. You know what I mean?

"But they sedated me real good. I didn't know from nothing for days. I almost lost my mind when they told me. Started screaming and yelling.

"I saw Joey. Lots of mothers don't. But he was bad. A lot of m-m kids don't look that bad. But Joey did. He got this hydrocephalus before he was born even. They didn't know if he'd live.

"Anyway, they were afraid of me. I just started to scream. So they kept giving me stuff and giving me stuff to keep me quiet. I was real out of it.

"And when I did come around I didn't want to see nobody, even Joe [her husband]. I mean nobody could do nothing. Nobody could change nothing. I'd have talked with anybody if it would have helped Joey. But I didn't want a lot of people shaking their heads and muttering how sorry they were. It wouldn't do him no good.

"That's how I think I scared the priest out of his collar. God, when I think of it! I really didn't mean to, but I just didn't want to talk to nobody.

"He knocked on the door . . . all in black with his black Bible and his stiff white collar. And he asked me if there was anything he could do. Like he was scared.

"I told him, yeah, there was something he could do. He could get out and leave me alone and never come back.

"And boy did he! He ran like a rabbit. He never came back, neither.

"I didn't mean to do that. If he'd have come back I'd have apologized. But I was really out of it. And well, he couldn't have done anything.

"It's been that way up here, too. You're the first chaplain I've ever really talked to. And that's because you don't push in. Before you came, every time we'd see a chaplain coming—those of us who 'live' up here—we'd run into our rooms and close the door. They never stayed. All they'd want to do was come in and say a prayer and leave. On their time, at their convenience. We didn't all feel like praying when they did, that's all.

"But you stay, and you seem to know when somebody wants to just joke and kid around and when somebody wants to be serious. Maybe it's because you're a woman. I don't know."

Maybe that's one reason why I liked Mary Collins. *She* always made *me* feel good! It helps to get a booster shot now and again.

There isn't any end to Joey Collins' story. It will go on and on. He'll be back for shunt revisions. He'll be back for ortho work. He'll be back for urology work . . .

He has learned to maneuver a wheelchair. Maybe he'll be able to maneuver leg braces. That's his mother and father's hope . . .

He's a cute kid. And I love him.

He just turned four.

Why the "hell," God? Why the four years of hell? Why the ten or twenty or thirty more to come?

Why?

13

Even when I wasn't on call I had begun going to Children's at least one weekend day. I told myself this was because there were a number of admissions over the weekend and I would get behind if I didn't take that opportunity to meet some of the patients and their families. It was true. But I really just *wanted* to go. That was the greater truth.

Doctors and nurses usually were more relaxed on the weekends. There was time to talk and learn to know each other. I was learning a lot about neurosurgery, and neurology now, too. And the more I knew, the better able I was to keep at least a half-jump ahead in trying to be in the right place at the right time as far as my work with parents was concerned. It really did make a difference, knowing what possible medical situations to expect.

But that Saturday in February I didn't expect to see Riann Miles.

Riann's shunt had stopped working. The same one that had stopped before. Dr. Verdi was out of town. Dr. Praeder had taken Riann to surgery. It was Dr. Praeder who had said he thought her tumor was growing the last time she was in.

I went to the surgery waiting room. Riann's parents were there. It was the first time I had a chance to talk with her father. He talked about business, about brokerage firms and the stock market.

In about an hour, Dr. Praeder came out in his surgical greens.

Riann was all right, in the recovery room. But he did think the tumor was growing. He said it out loud, to her parents, kindly. But that was only his "suspicion." He would talk with Dr. Verdi when he returned on Monday. But for now, Riann was all right.

That's what her father heard: "All right." It was as if Dr. Praeder hadn't said another word; had never mentioned "tumor" or "growing." He didn't hear it. He simply didn't hear it. He couldn't hear it.

It was late. Riann's father wanted to go home. Riann was all right, he repeated. And she would be "out of it" for the rest of the evening, he rationalized. He wanted to go home.

Mrs. Miles didn't. But she didn't say so. She understood. No, not understood—accepted. It would take months for her to understand.

They went home.

But I couldn't go home. Riann didn't need me. But I needed to see her, needed to see her back in her room and tucked in for the night, needed some completion to the day, to tie up the ends.

I went into the recovery room—Intensive Care on Saturdays— and sat on a small stool by the head of her bed. Actually, she was still on the surgical cart because in about an hour, when they were sure she was all right, she would be moved back to her room on the neurosurgical floor.

I remember sitting there and looking at her. Intensive Care is one large room with about nine beds and two isolation areas. It is very, very bright, all the time. I've never seen the lights turned down in Intensive Care. And with the white sheets, the glare is almost blinding, especially at night.

Riann's head was shaved, again. And she had one of those multicolored blood pressure cuffs on her arm, like Marilee Johnson.

She was naked, covered loosely by a sheet. The doctors had inserted a urinary catheter with a plastic collection bag hooked to the side of her bed. There were reddish-brown sterile wash marks on her neck, left over from surgery. And spots of blood, too, here and there.

She was restless, kept kicking off the sheet and lying there naked. It's a very inhuman, depersonalizing thing—a little girl lying naked with her head shaved and bandaged, with a urinary catheter sticking out and a blood pressure cuff wrapped around and an I.V. tube sticking in. I wanted to yank out all the tubes and wrap her in the sheet and make her hair grow long and throw away the bandages and hold her in my arms and say "everything will be all right."

But I just sat there and watched.

The nurse came and took her temperature, rectally, and her blood pressure. She talked with her, trying to arouse her. There was a slight response. "Not yet," said the nurse, "but soon."

About twenty minutes later the nurse was satisfied. Riann was answering questions coherently. But she was still very drowsy. That's normal. She was all right.

"Do you want your mommy?" asked the nurse.

"Yes." Then Riann dropped off to sleep again.

"Her parents have gone," I whispered to the nurse. No further mention was made. Riann didn't remember.

I helped push her down to three-north on the surgical cart. I tucked her in . . . tied my loose ends . . . and went home.

But I had heard Dr. Praeder.
So had Riann's mother.

The following Thursday they performed another surgery on Riann—a craniotomy.

Tests proved the tumor had grown. Dr. Praeder's "suspicion" was right. Dr. Verdi would try to get as much of it as he could. Maybe he could get it all.

At Children's they had "play ladies." Jane was the play lady on three-north. She was in her mid-twenties, cute, enthusiastic. Play ladies wore bright-colored smocks and came around every afternoon to play with the children, all the children who were well enough to get up and gather at the end of the hall in a small play area. On three-north the play area was at the opposite end of the L-shaped wing from the parents' smoking/waiting area.

Jane was attached to Riann, too. The afternoon before Riann's surgery, Jane had an ice cream party for the children on three-north. She brought an electric freezer and all the ingredients. The children helped make the ice cream and then Jane played records while the mixture was churning. The children loved it. "But I did it for Riann," said Jane. I knew.

The one thing Riann hated above all else was "needles." Most children are that way. They can be picked at and probed at and X-rayed and bandaged, but needles are a no-no.

With Riann the fear was acute. She'd start to cry before the syringe was even filled. Just the sight of a needle set her off. It was the same when they wanted to draw blood.

I was in her room the day before the surgery when they drew blood. She held onto my arms and hands, and screamed. I remember trying to get her mind off what was going on by asking her questions about other things. It didn't work. She screamed and sobbed and trembled until the bed shook.

Needle pricks for blood samples really don't hurt that much. But if you're afraid of needles, the mere word hurts. Especially if you've been a human pincushion for the last eight months of your life.

A volunteer with a lot of fourteen-carat gold bracelets and diamond rings brought a puppet theater into Riann's room after the ice cream party. The puppets acted out what would happen prior to surgery. It was a good idea, so children wouldn't be totally uninformed or unprepared for what was to happen to them the following day.

Other children crowded around Riann's bed to watch. Riann had seen it all before, before her first operation last August. But she politely didn't interrupt. Her mother arrived in the middle of the skit. She watched politely, too. But she was terribly on edge, as if she wanted everyone to "clear out" and leave her alone with Riann.

But they didn't get a chance to be alone all afternoon. People paraded in and out: visitor people, nurse and doctor people, technician people, a priest to give communion. It was after dinner until Riann and her mother got to be alone.

It was important, to be alone together . . . because Mrs. Miles couldn't spend the night with Riann. Not because the child didn't have a private room; she did. But because Mr. Miles wanted his wife home that night.

Whether or not to spend the night with Riann despite her husband's wishes was my first real discussion with Mrs. Miles. It had agonized her for days before the operation. She wanted to stay. I know I would have wanted to stay if Riann had been my daughter. There are no guarantees in brain surgery. She could die. No guarantees.

What would I do if I were in her place, Mrs. Miles asked.

I was in the middle. I thought I knew well what I would do: stay. But I couldn't say that. So I just listened. "I don't know your husband or his reasons for wanting you home tonight well enough to answer," was my only response.

I think I did, though, know his reasons . . . remembering how he had discussed the stock market . . . and hadn't seemed to hear Dr. Praeder's "suspicion." He couldn't divorce himself from the norm. And the norm was having his wife at home at night. He was still in shock, still denying. As if by denying the seriousness of Riann's tumor it would go away.

Mrs. Miles knew his reasons, too. "They'll give Riann something to make her sleep early anyway," she rationalized aloud. "And we'll be here first thing in the morning. She'll be all right."

But it bothered her, gnawed at her.

Me too.

Mrs. Miles's sister spent that pre-surgery night with Riann. She flew in from California. (Did you think I would offer? The relationship wasn't that close yet. The mutual bond of trust was building, but it hadn't reached that height. My offering to stay would have created another problem, not a solution. It was too soon, on both sides.)

Mrs. Miles and her sister were very close. It was as if someone had released a pressure valve that had been about to burst when Brooke Flynn walked into Riann's room. Mrs. Miles nearly collapsed into her sister's arms.

Mrs. Miles's sister and Riann and I said prayers together that night. We used the "relics" from the Seagram's bag, plus a special one Riann's grandmother had sent from Florida. Riann was very, very tired. It had been a long day. Tomorrow would be short—for her.

Jane, the "play lady," came in early the next day . . . at seven A.M. So did I. Both of us knew why. Neither of us was needed, or could do anything. But we couldn't stay home.

I went with Mrs. Miles's sister to bring coffee to Riann's room for her parents. I stuck my head in the door just long enough to hand in the coffee and say hi. Only the small night light over Riann's bed was on. Her mother and father were standing close, talking with her. The room was eerie. Maybe the room wasn't eerie at all. Maybe it was what was happening that was eerie.

Riann showed me some little stuffed animals a friend had sent her. I said they were cute. But I didn't stay. It wasn't a party.

I went and sat in the little waiting room and smoked.

I wanted to be a full-fledged priest. The Mileses were Catholic; and I felt that if I had been a Catholic priest I could have done something more, been more helpful. Right then I felt like a rookie sitting on a log. Riann deserved more than a student chaplain.

But in my anger, I turned the coin over. So, I was on the outside and helpless to effect change. Big deal. In the long run, when the chips are down, a tumor is a tumor is a tumor. . . . and what good is a chaplain? Any chaplain?

A blond nurse came by with a surgical cart. It was time. I heard Riann cry a little bit. Then I remembered she had to have a pre-surgery shot. The nurse came out of the room for a few minutes; gave them a little bit longer. Then she went back in.

The sheet was pulled high around Riann's neck as the nurse pushed her by on the surgery cart. And she looked so tiny and afraid. But her right arm wiggled out from under the sheet and she waved and smiled as a tear dripped on her pillow. "Bye, Nina."

I watched them go down the hall. Her mother and father walking along beside her.

I watched her mother and father return alone. He got his hat and coat, "to take a walk." Mrs. Miles and her sister and I all sat and smoked. Mrs. Miles and her sister didn't normally smoke. But they needed something to do with their hands, some rote motion in which to engage, I guess. There was nothing else normal. We didn't say much.

I had breakfast later with Jane, the "play lady." She had stayed with Riann outside the surgery door until the little girl had to go in . . . alone.

How we all fight helplessness.

How helpless we are.

Creature, not creator.

But *we* would have done a better job of it, now, wouldn't we? Or is that the very reason for this world?

* * *

Riann had come out of surgery by two-thirty that afternoon. She was all right, in the recovery room. But Dr. Verdi had called her parents into his office to talk.

Earlier Dr. Praeder had told me Dr. Verdi couldn't get all the tumor . . . just a tiny piece. It had spread too far too fast. They had suspected that all along. After all, they hadn't been able to get it the first time, he said; why should this time be any different?

"But it was big," said Dr. Praeder. "Bigger than I thought."

Nobody told me about their faces, the faces of patients who have had craniotomies; what happens to them. So I didn't know.

I saw Riann in the neurosurgery Constant Care room that evening. She was actually awake and talking when the nurse brought her down from the recovery room. I couldn't believe it. She sat up for a bit, looking at flowers and cards she had received.

"She's fine," said her father. He stayed with her longer than usual. She really looked bright.

But the next morning I didn't recognize her. Her face looked like a basketball with black eyes. "Oh, that's normal," said Mary Cooke. "People's faces always swell like that after a craniotomy. I guess nobody warned you. It is a shock the first time. You see, they pull the skin the whole way down off the forehead and . . ."

"That's OK, Mary. I'd rather not hear 'why' right now. As long as it's normal."

She laughed. "Yeah, it's normal. It'll go down in a few days. Don't worry."

Riann was pretty well out of it for the next two or three days. The swelling was incredible. Her eyes were swollen shut and almost blocked from view by the swelling above and below.

Every now and then she'd forget where she was. She thought she was at school one time, at ballet class another time.

But mostly she slept. And managed to cry when the nurses had to give her shots. And oh how the nurses hated to do it.

For Jennifer Bradford it was hardest of all. Jennifer was the P.M. charge nurse, from three-thirty to eleven-thirty . . . or twelve-thirty . . . or one. I was around more and more in the evenings, so I got to know her better. She was a central casting nurse: tall, slender, fresh-faced, well-manicured hands, very clean, and very efficient. But she would just agonize when she'd have to give Riann a shot.

One evening there were two shots ordered for the same time. "I just don't want to do this. She's hurting so much anyway. I just don't want her to have to cry again. Why couldn't I be off tonight?" Jennifer Bradford wasn't profuse about it; very quiet. She kept busy. Gave other medications to other children. But the two syringes wouldn't go away. They stared back at her from the medicine cart when there were no more pills to give.

I saw her go sit in the little room behind the nursing station and hold her stomach, trying to be inconspicuous. But finally she did it. What else could she do? And Riann cried and cried.

Jennifer didn't say much the rest of the evening.

That was when I realized the difference in our jobs. Jennifer—the nurse—had the worst bargain. I could care about the children and talk with them and try to comfort them and try to help. The nurses could care about the children and talk with them and try to comfort them and try to help—but they also had to hurt. They had to give shots and medicines and enemas and wound scrubs. They couldn't just be nice. And that was worse. I could be nice all the time.

No wonder Jennifer got so angry one evening when a doctor told a complaining child, "Wait a minute, I'm not going to hurt you. I never give you shots or pills. The nurses do that. They hurt you; I don't. Don't get upset with me."

No, being a chaplain is easier.

Except for that one question. "Why?"

It was happening. I was beginning to ask those questions. The gnawing of "Why evil, why pain?" was getting greater. "God won't let her suffer more than she can stand . . . He may have foreseen a life of constant agony and pain . . . and because he loved her so much . . ." Those answers alone weren't sufficient—for my gut as well as my mind—any more.

Fortunately—and this has never happened yet—I didn't withdraw from God. I didn't renounce him. But I was beginning to question, beginning to need a "theology" that would get me through these questions, my own questions. Maybe it would be a theology too deep to be used outright in crisis conversations with parents; but I needed a theology that would get me through three A.M. in bed awake . . . wrestling with the "why?" that now came between the mental slide pictures.

That theology became increasingly necessary as I got to know Riann Miles and Alex Felini better.

14

ALEX FELINI GOT a brainstem cyst for his seventh birthday. It's called a posterior fossa cyst. Just like Marilee Johnson had. Oh, he had the cyst before his birthday; that's just the day it was diagnosed.

I hadn't paid much attention to Alex Felini when he first came in. In fact, he had had a shunt inserted to relieve the pressure from the cyst before I even met him.

That was my fault. Lindsay Grice was admitted on the day of Riann's surgery. I was actually glad. I needed her. Can you imagine? But I was glad, nonetheless. I held her for hours that evening. She was in for another shunt revision.

But between Riann and Lindsay and the others I already knew, I just couldn't handle one patient more right away. I knew Alex was there and I felt appropriately guilty; but I would make up excuse after excuse to myself not to get acquainted yet. Maybe subconsciously I suspected he would be there for a while.

He was: for over five months, with the exception of one week.

"A cyst is usually benign, isn't it?" I asked Mary Cooke one day after I had finally met Alex Felini and his parents. In fact, Alex was in surgery right then.

"Yes, but don't count on that meaning anything. I don't want to be cynical, but I've been here long enough. It seems we have much more trouble with kids with benign cysts than with brain tumors. I hope Alex will be all right; but I'm not banking on it."

What a pessimist, I thought.

Mary Cooke was right: Alex Felini had every complication in the book, and some not in the book.

Alex's mother and father, Carrie and Tony, lived in the same neighborhood where both had grown up. They had two other children, Chrissy, who was four, and Sandi, who was five, and tons of relatives. I got to know them all.

But it was several days after Alex's first surgery—for the cyst— that we talked together at length, his family and I. I had copped out until then.

Carrie Felini's father was a construction worker, a heavy equipment operator. He would sit there in the small waiting room and look at me. "You really a minister?"

"I'm a student chaplain, studying to be a minister."

"Not a priest?"

"No. The Catholic Church doesn't ordain women."

"Yeah, that's what I thought. How come you wanna do that?"

"I don't know for sure."

"Seems strange, I mean for a girl. Can you get married? Have kids?"

"Sure, both."

"Don't you wanna?"

"Sure."

"Then whatchya doin' here? I mean, it's nice and all, but what about having your own family?"

"I want to someday. But it just hasn't happened."

"You probably got too high standards. No man can live up to all them standards some women holds."

"Yes, you're probably right at that. My standards probably are too high." Though I was sure not in the way Carrie's father meant.

"Take my advice. You're a pretty girl, really OK. Get a guy while you're still pretty. It'll change, ya know. Everybody gets older. Get one while you can!"

I could feel myself shriveling up and bursting with wrinkles and arthritis while I sat there!

"You know, I'm gonna buy a St. Jude candle for Alex." It was one of Tony Felini's sisters. She sat down beside us.

"We have a St. Jude candle in the chapel, I think. Actually, it's just the glass candle holder, but I'm sure I could fix it with a candle if you'd like."

"You're the chaplain, aren't you? Carrie was telling me there was a woman chaplain up here."

"Yes." We introduced ourselves.

"Yeah, I'd really like a St. Jude candle, if you could put it in the chapel."

"Sure."

"You know, Alex isn't doing so good. They say they may have to take him back to surgery. His neck is all swollen and puffy where they operated."

"Do you mean tonight?"

"Maybe. The doctor—Dr. Praeder—is with him now."

They took Alex back to surgery at six-thirty that evening. The wound was infected. It burst pus. Then they took him back to surgery at ten that night. Opened his stomach, trying to find something. I guess his fever was still up. They didn't find anything.

I put the St. Jude candle in the chapel between surgeries. I met Carrie's sister in the hall and told her. "Oh good, thank you. Can we go there now and pray for Alex?"

We did.

Just after we finished and were sitting on the little chairs in the chapel watching the lighted St. Jude candle, Alex's parents and grandfather came in and sat down. They prayed silently, and then we talked for a few minutes.

"Well," said Alex's grandfather, "you said you were a chaplain, didn't you?"

"Yes."

"Well, let's pray for Alex. That's what we're here for."

Tony Felini's sister tried to apologize . . . to say I had just done that. But I said I'd like to again.

After the prayer Carrie Felini looked up at me. "Gee, thank you. You done that just as well as any priest I ever heard. I mean . . . not that you ain't as 'good' as a priest . . . just that we, being Catholic, never knew . . ."

I knew what she meant. It was the best compliment I had gotten since I had been at Children's.

* * *

Alex Felini turned out to be a funny kid. Even when he wasn't feeling very good, he could still be funny.

One night Dr. Praeder was particularly worried about Alex. The little boy hadn't really been physically right since surgery: infection, fever, chills, headache. He just wasn't progressing as well as he should.

Dr. Praeder: "Alex, I love you so much. Alex, you have to get better, Alex. Alex, I love you so much. Alex, you are such a sweet boy. You have to feel better, Alex. I love you so much."

Alex: "Yeah, you're OK, too, Maxmillian."

The nurse who was in Alex's room at the time almost dropped the I.V. bottle laughing. From then on, all Dr. Praeder got from the staff was, "You're OK, too, Maxmillian!"

Another evening I was walking toward the nursing station when I heard laughter coming from the Constant Care room. Several nurses and Dr. McMahan were standing around Alex's bed. The little boy had been having trouble urinating on his own, and that was one of the requirements for him to be discharged from the Constant Care room to his own room. This was after the fourth or fifth surgery for one complication or another.

Finally, a tiny bit of urine flowed. Alex was exhausted. "But that ain't all, Doc. I really gotta go a lot. Rub some more, nurse."

"Alex, I think I'm going to have to insert a catheter. This just isn't working," said Dr. McMahan.

"OK, Doc. Whatever you say, 'cause I really gotta go!"

Dr. McMahan attached a catheter to a urine bag and then inserted it. It worked.

"Ah," said a relieved Alex. "Now, Doc, that's the *real* thing! That's the real thing!"

We still laugh about that. That and "You're OK, too, Maxmillian," and so many many others . . .

15

SUDDENLY I DIDN'T want to go to Europe. If anyone had told me the previous November that that would be the case, I would have laughed him out of the room. I love Europe. I think part of me always will see the Swiss Alps across the meadow from Interlaken's Grand Hotel Victoria-Jungfrau, or live by a tiny lake in Welsh Snowdonia.

But by March, with enough money and enough time to chew and digest Europe in a long, leisurely, comfortable meal . . . I didn't want to go. I wanted to stay on three-north at University Children's Hospital, and to be there completely . . . not have to make a pretense of liking to go to my general medical floor at Adult Hospital.

Under normal circumstances, that would have been impossible, staying at Children's. Normally, another group of students would have been arriving. But this March that wasn't the case. There was no spring quarter of CPE. No new students would arrive until June.

So I asked Craig Hatfield if I could stay. After making me sweat it out, he said yes.

And that "yes" of Craig Hatfield's, and those two and one half months made all the difference. They confirmed for me that I wanted to be a hospital chaplain. They added depth and dimension to my theological probings. And they confirmed, for me, the crying need for chaplains with concern and training—

and time—to work on a long-term basis with critically and terminally ill children and their families.

I wouldn't have traded those two and one half months for one hundred trips to Europe.

The St. Jude candle placed for Alex Felini was the patriarch of generations of daily St. Jude candles. Then one day Alex's aunt said she had found weekly St. Jude candles at a religious goods store and had bought several. Thus began the second succession . . . these changed each week.

If people always got what they wanted by praying profusely, Alex Felini would have had one surgery and gone home to play. Rarely in those weeks between the end of February, when Alex was admitted, and June 6, the day I left Children's, did I ever go into the chapel without seeing a member of the Felini clan praying for Alex.

But it was hardest for Tony, Alex's father. At first he wouldn't come to the chapel often. But as time went on, he began to try to pray Alex well. It seemed to become a test of his ability to convince God of his sincerity through prayer. At times the prayer tension was so great that I felt if God didn't come through and "let Alex get well," Tony Felini would punch Him in the teeth.

But nothing changed. It was like a merry-go-round. One week Alex was up and about, six-guns tugging his pajama bottoms. The next week he made another trip to surgery: drain the wound, exploratory laparotomy, one shunt, two shunts, fix a shunt, no shunts, burr holes to relieve pressure, on and on and on.

And each time, *telling* Alex he had to make yet another trip to the fifth floor operating room got more and more difficult. "Don't-get-emotionally-involved" Maxmillian Praeder was getting just that. For he was Alex's principal neurosurgeon. And he began to see it as a personal war, too. After all, Alex had a benign, posterior fossa cyst. He shouldn't be having all these complications. But the Felinis, rightly, never lost faith in Dr. Praeder.

Each time Alex had surgery he snapped back. After the initial surgery it had been a long, long pull. But from there on in, he just snapped back. It was like diving off a diving board and bobbing back up again. Except in this case Alex had to be dragged back to the board each round. And it began doing something to his morale, not surprisingly.

After the eighth surgery it looked like things had worked. Alex seemed all right. But the angiogram showed pressure. They had to put in a shunt. Just *one more* surgery. Better to do it now than send Alex home and have to bring him back in a week. That's what they decided. But Dr. Praeder was agonizing over telling Alex.

"How can I tell him that again? I am afraid he can't take it. The ninth time! He is old enough to know what is going on. And I love him so much. It really hurts me."

That was on a Thursday. They were to operate on Friday. On Saturday Alex went to a baseball game with his family. Dr. Praeder just couldn't do it. He had to give Alex that weekend to breathe. Even if it was his last surgery before going home, a few days more wouldn't make much difference. Alex took an eight-hour hospital pass Saturday. They would operate Monday.

I remember the Sunday evening when Dr. Praeder told Alex about that ninth surgery. I was sitting in the waiting area next to Alex's room. I thought the wall between us would crumble.

Dr. Praeder finally emerged from the room, ashen-faced, and hurried off down the corridor. My urge was to follow him. But he wouldn't want me to see the results of his doing what he told me he couldn't allow himself to do. So I stayed.

About an hour later, he found me sitting at the nursing station and asked if I'd like a lift home. As we walked past the little waiting room, there sat Alex and his mother and father. Alex had on his flannel cowboy pajamas and his heavy black wing-tipped shoes. He always wore those heavy shoes. His hair had begun to grow out and was in a soft brown crew cut brushed forward. His eyes were sad, like big chocolate drops ready to melt.

"Dr. Maxmillian . . ."

"Yes, Alex?"

"Dr. Praeder, Alex has something to say to you," said his mother.

"Dr. Maxmillian, I'm sorry I got mad and yelled earlier. My mother and dad explained how you don't really want me to have to have all these operations, but how it has to be if I want to be really well. But I hope you can understand," he added, looking down, "that it still makes me mad."

He said it like a man, the whole thing. But his hands shook quietly on his lap.

"Of course I understand, Alex. Thank you very much. I know that took a lot of courage. You are a very brave young man."

But Alex couldn't say any more. He tried not to cry, but it was beginning. He started scuffing the dangling toes of his shoes back and forth against the floor.

Dr. Praeder could tell. "Thank you," he said again, to all three, then turned back down the hall.

I didn't say a word. He was close to tears. "I don't believe it," he repeated and repeated, shaking his head. "I just don't believe it. Oh, God, why?"

I looked back over my shoulder. Alex and his mother and father still sat in the dimly lighted waiting room.

Too much happened to remember it all, that Monday of Alex's surgery. I don't remember how it began, because so many others had begun the same way: another dive from the high dive, another bob up.

Except it wasn't.

Surgery went all right. I happened to be sitting with the Felinis when Dr. Praeder came out of the O.R. "But we'll have to watch him closely. There was a lot of pressure."

On rounds that evening Alex responded to verbal communication. But he didn't wake up again all evening. I left at about eleven.

When I returned Tuesday morning, Alex was in Intensive Care—on the sixth floor. He had started to become decerebrate. That means, basically, he became rigid. You can't imagine, maybe, just how rigid someone can get.

They had made burr holes—that's four incisions, one in each "corner" of the skull—to relieve the pressure on the brain. Early that Tuesday morning they had made the burr holes—ten surgeries.

When I saw Alex lying there in Intensive Care I just remember getting very cold.

The Felinis were in the chapel. A St. Jude candle was burning. We prayed. We all were in shock. How dare the routine be broken! How dare God "not let" Alex bob back up!

"But Dr. Praeder said this happens sometimes," said Tony

Felini. "It's a form of brain swelling. A person with that can be unconscious for a long time . . . But it doesn't mean he will die . . . If the brain swelling reverses he can be fine."

Dr. Praeder repeated the same thing to me later. There was hope. It was bad, but there was hope.

As the day dragged on that Tuesday Alex got worse. They took him to surgery to insert a second shunt: eleven surgeries. He still got worse.

"We'll do an angiogram," said Dr. Praeder. "Maybe the shunts aren't working. Maybe we'll find something else." They took Alex to angio. It was about three-thirty in the afternoon.

"Go along?" Alex's father asked me. "If you want to," Alex's mother said. Her voice had changed. I sensed something had snapped. But it wasn't the time to talk . . .

I went to angio. It was a big room with a huge overhead X-ray machine that took a quick, running series of X-ray photos. The whole thing only took a few seconds. It was getting ready that could take hours.

Hollow needles had to be inserted into two arteries in the neck. As each artery was hit, the hollow needles were quickly plugged. *Finding* the two arteries could be tedious and tricky. When all was ready, the needles were unplugged and dye was squirted in through the needles. It circulated through the arterial system in the head. As the dye moved along the arterial path, X-ray photos were taken in quick sequence. The patient was heavily sedated for an angiogram, but general anesthetic usually was not used with children.

In the middle of Alex's angio, as he had one tube-needle in an artery of his neck, Dr. McMahan yelled, "He's going sour! We can't go on. Call the O.R.!"

They raced Alex to the operating room. "Find his parents and tell them I want to talk with them in the six-center waiting room," Dr. Praeder said to me on the run.

I did. And he did. "We have to take out the shunts and put one shunt on the outside," Dr. Praeder explained, "so we can be sure it is working, sure there isn't an infection."

The procedure is called "inserting an EVD"—external ventricular drainage. Instead of the excess CSF draining off into the tummy, it now would drain into a tube sticking out of Alex's head and attached to a clear glass container. That way doctors could measure the amount of CSF draining off into the container and then regulate the pressure. They also could tell by the clearness or opaqueness of the fluid whether or not the CSF was infected.

"OK, OK," said Mrs. Felini. "Anything."

"Will you go with Alex?" asked Mr. Felini.

I nodded. Mrs. Felini said nothing.

I couldn't believe it. When the incisions over the burr holes were opened, there was the brain—almost pushing out, grayish-white. I could see it.

To make a burr hole, the scalp is opened, than a round hole is drilled in the skull. Thus the brain can expand and pressure can be eased. It is through this hole in the skull that I saw the swollen brain.

But when I began to realize that it was *Alex's* swollen brain—I had to leave.

(*And that is all the difference.* That, I was to put together much later, is why a neurosurgeon must guard against getting too "close" to his patient while he [the neurosurgeon] still must operate. In the operating room, for the neurosurgeon, it must be "a" brain, not Alex's brain or Riann's brain.)

I threw my green surgical clothes—gown, mask, hat, and shoes—into their proper "used" bins, and went to the chapel. That was the third surgery I had watched. But it was the first one on a child I knew well. I was sick: exhausted, ineffective, powerless . . . sick. I wanted to be alone.

I was in the chapel five minutes when the Felinis came in. I whispered that surgery was nearly over. But we all prayed our own prayers.

"Will you pray for Alex?" It was Tony Felini.

"Yes! If you really want to pray for him, pray that he dies!" It was Carrie Felini. She was exploding.

I wasn't ready. I wasn't up for it. Her words hit me like a hammer. I didn't say anything at first. Was she right? I couldn't blame her. It seemed so endless, so predetermined, so stacked—the deck against Alex. But die? Pray for that? That Alex would die? Now?

"I'm sorry, but I can't do that," I said. "Not yet. I can't play God yet . . ." It was not the time to argue. But I had to be true to God, to the God I believed in, anyway.

"Oh no!" the voice pierced back, breaking in midsentence, angry, cold, sarcastic. "We can't play God. We have to have hope! Hope! Hope! Hope!"

Tony Felini started to cry.

"The time may come when I can pray that he dies. But not now. Not while he's up there fighting. Not while Dr. Praeder says there *is* hope, that the brain swelling could go away." (But as those words came out, the picture of Alex's swollen brain flashed through my mind.) "I'm sorry, Carrie, but I can't. Not now. Not yet."

She didn't say anything.

I started to pray. "Dear God, it's almost unbearable. The agony. We want to flail our arms and scream. At you, at the world, at the unfairness. 'Why?' we ask. *Would* it be better if Alex dies?

"Oh, God, we don't know. Only you know that. But in our unspeakable anger and utter helplessness, give us the faith to trust you.

"Give strength to the doctors. Help them draw on all the skills they know as they work to save Alex.

"And God, above all, please be with Alex. Let him know you love him and are holding on to him. Let him know that his parents love him, that they agonize to see him suffer so. Give Alex strength and love, oh God. And, please, hold onto us . . . to all of us . . . now."

The dam broke . . . about two sentences earlier . . . for Carrie Felini. It all fell out on the needlepoint chapel kneeling cushions with blue butterflies and suns and moons and winds and flowers on them.

And the dam broke for me, too. I've never known whether that was the "right thing" or the "wrong thing" for a chaplain to do. But I do know it was unavoidable. I sobbed, too. I just couldn't take it any more. The day had been beyond human comprehension, beyond human assimilation—at least my comprehension, my assimilation.

Unexpectedly, Carrie, still crying, came and sat next to me and put her arms around me. Tony followed. And so we sat there, three helpless individuals now a helpless group.

What difference did it make . . . ?

16

IF IT EVER entered my mind, which it didn't, whether or not I was happier as a chaplain at Children's than I had been in broadcasting, Manuelito Cerci gave me the perfect test.

Manuelito and his parents were from Italy. Dr. Verdi had seen Manuelito on one of his frequent European trips and had told his parents that if they brought the child to Children's there was a chance he could operate successfully on him.

Manuelito had an aneurysm. Basically, that's a mix-up of veins and arteries to the brain. To straighten it out is a very difficult and very delicate operation. Not only does it involve correctly redirecting the blood flow; but there's the danger that while the surgeon is doing that, he'll burst a malformed, ballooning vein or artery.

Correcting an aneurysm can require two surgeries. And usually it is only successful on adults or older children. Manuelito was not yet two. No one that young had ever before lived through aneurysm surgery.

When I met Manuelito and his mother and father the boy had already lived through the first half of this surgery, performed the preceding fall. If he, and Dr. Verdi, made it this time, the procedure would be complete and Manuelito would become the youngest child in medical history to have survived aneurysm surgery. And Dr. Verdi would be a medical hero.

Manuelito's parents didn't speak English. His father, who was a university professor in Italy, was learning. When his mother (who hadn't come to the U.S. for the first surgery) arrived, she spoke only one or two words. But she was determined to learn.

For the first few days, everyone just smiled at her. I wanted to talk with her—as I'm sure everyone else did—but I didn't know any Italian and didn't know for sure if she wanted to try.

But one day she solved the problem. I had on my clerical collar and was sitting in the small waiting room with Mrs. Cerci and some other mothers. During a brief lull in the conversation, Mrs. Cerci looked up a word in her Italian-to-English dictionary, then pointed to my collar and asked, "church?"

I nodded yes.

"Catholic?"—with a tone of disbelief.

"No," I answered. "Presbyterian."

A puzzled look.

I took her dictionary, but the word *Presbyterian* wasn't in it. So I looked up *Protestant*.

"Protestante," I answered.

"Ah, si! Protestante."

I realized the obvious lacking of my Italian pronunciation.

She looked up another word.

"Minister?"

"Si," I answered, very proud that I'd picked up Italian for "yes" so quickly.

She looked up another word or two . . . "Protestante . . . minister . . . female?"

"Si."

"No!" Surprise.

"Si."

"Non Catholic?"

"No."

"Si?" She pointed to my ring finger.

"No."

"Oh?"

Then I realized she probably was misinterpreting, thinking I couldn't marry because I was a minister. But how on earth did one say, "I can marry if I wish, but I haven't yet," in Italian? But by that time she had looked up the words.

"Church . . . rule . . . Protestante?"

"No."

She looked up another word. "Personal?"

"Si."

Another word. "Boy friend?" and she pointed to me.

"Si," I laughed, and held up three fingers.

"Bravo!" She seemed happier.

That was the beginning. I bought an English-to-Italian dictionary and began learning Italian for the duration. But she was much better.

It was fun. But it was also tense. The day for Manuelito's surgery grew closer. And Mrs. Cerci—Lana—and her husband got more tense. He would pace the floor for hours and take long walks. She would find me to talk with, just to relieve the tension.

The day before surgery I asked her if she wanted to go to the chapel. Yes, she said; but she wanted to wait to go while Manuelito was in surgery.

It was difficult in the chapel that Thursday. At least I felt so. There was so much I wanted to say, but couldn't. I guess that was selfish in a way. But I soon appreciated the reason for "Our Father" rather than "My Father."

I suppose we did communicate with our eyes, though. She seemed to want to stay a long time. And she kept holding onto my hand as if for me not to go. But how difficult it must have been for her—for both of them—to be in such an isolated situation at such a critical time.

Manuelito had gone into surgery at eight A.M. We went to the chapel at about ten. And all day long after that, whenever Mrs. Cerci saw me she would ask if I had heard anything about Manuelito.

"No," I answered, "I'm sorry. They're still in surgery."

"True? True?" she would always follow.

"True," I assured her.

Then she would tell me she trusted me to always tell her the truth, no matter what.

I said I would. But my knees would go weak.

At six-thirty I saw Dr. Verdi, in his surgical greens with white, blood-spattered shoes, race into the Cercis' room on three-north. Behind him was Dr. Praeder, who simply looked at me and said, "He's all right. So far, he's all right, Nina, honey."

Knowing the great amount of tension that fell off my shoulders at that moment, I can't even begin to imagine how much greater the relief must have been for his parents.

Dr. Verdi left and dashed into a stairwell as I was walking back down the hall. I hadn't seen his face at all, but I could imagine he was happy.

"Nina!" Mrs. Cerci was running down the hall toward me. "He is alive! He is alive! He is all right! Manuelito, he is alive!" She grabbed me and hugged the breath out of me . . . and started to cry.

They were still closing Manuelito's wound. It would be nearly another two hours until his parents could see him in Intensive Care. They decided to make some telephone calls and then get a sandwich.

I went to dinner with some nurses from three-north. Just as I was going in the cafeteria door, Dr. Verdi came around the corner, still in his scrub suit.

"Nina, honey, ["honey" always seemed to be my last name for both Dr. Verdi and Dr. Praeder], come to my office for a minute, can you? I have something for you."

I followed him into his office. He reached into his desk drawer and pulled out a bottle of French perfume. He had been to Paris a few weeks earlier and had promised to bring me some. I never dreamed he would remember.

But I was more fascinated by his face. I had never seen anything like it. Ever. He had just stood for a good part of twelve hours performing an operation that would make medical history. And his face reflected every moment of the agony, fear, exhilaration, and joy that had gone into it. I could barely carry on the amenities. I wanted to remember his face. I still do.

The next day that mental picture of Dr. Verdi's face was so vivid I had to tell him. So I wrote something.

I guarantee you, it is not nearly adequate:

. . . But in the vacuum of moments just after that surgery,
I saw what the journals could not see;
What the textbooks will not record;
What the surgeon himself cannot understand.
For I glimpsed the mystery of what *life* costs another human
    being.

I saw in his eyes,
In his face,

In his body,
The terrible price he pays.

And suddenly, for a moment,
   I touched the reason for the transcendent mystery of God
Because, for a moment,
   I touched the transcendent mystery of a man's soul—
And it was more beautiful than I could bear.

In all the careers of humanity there must be no moment greater
than that of knowing you were able to re-give life. And there
must be no moment worse than that of knowing you tried, so
hard, and lost. It is a rare person who is humble enough in the
first . . . and brave enough in the second . . . to realize in both
moments that he is not God.

With Manuelito, I saw Dr. Verdi's humility in the first moment. But with Riann Miles, I sensed Dr. Verdi's uncertainty in
the second moment.

I was in the middle of a parent-staff meeting on three-north
when I felt a hand on my shoulder. I looked up, and Mrs. Cerci
was motioning for me to come with her and her husband.

"We see Manuelito. First time. You come with. You pray."

All the blood in my body lumped in my stomach. It was
another of those totally unexpected, beyond belief happenings
that makes a job like chaplain worthwhile. I had thought that
moment between Manuelito and his parents would have been
the most private of private moments. I knew it was God and not
"me" that they wanted in Intensive Care. But I knew, too, that
they had understood my purpose.

The little boy was in the first bed to the left inside the door of
Intensive Care. His head was wrapped in a gauze turban, and a
large cake-carrier-shaped clear steam hood was over his face
and head.

He was asleep, but every now and then he made tiny whining,
half-crying sounds. Vaseline was on his eyelids and eyelashes
and the little multicolored blood pressure cuff was wrapped
around his arm. He had several I.V. bottles and a urine catheter.
There wasn't much swelling around his eyes, yet.

At first I stood back, dressed in the white sterile gown everyone entering Intensive Care must wear. Then they motioned for me to come closer. There really wasn't much we could do but stand there and be glad he was alive—and pray. And that's what we did.

How inadequate it is to try to write about something like that.

17

It WAS DECIDED that Riann Miles would be given X-ray therapy. That's cobalt. The tumor—the one that could take fifteen years or so to grow big—was huge. Huge. Perhaps cobalt would stunt its growth, would stop it. Perhaps not.

Six weeks of treatments, five days a week. Sometimes cobalt makes you sick, nauseated. Your hair falls out. Six weeks. She'd stay in the hospital the whole time.

Riann was out of the three-north Constant Care room and back in a private room about five days after her craniotomy. She stayed in the hospital recuperating for about ten more days. Then she got to go home for a week. And then she came back for cobalt . . . six weeks.

It's difficult to describe Riann. Not only have I never met another child like her, I've never met another person like her. She is too good to be true.

Granted, it's easier to see only the good points in someone very ill. But that isn't the case with Riann. Anyone on three-north would agree; anyone who ever knew her.

She is slender, like her mother, and has huge blue—clear blue—eyes and beautiful milk-white skin. She was eight when I first met her. And in the year I have known her, her face has matured, in moments here and there, to that of a wise woman. She is no longer a little girl. Yet her love is as innocent and trusting and complete as a little girl's.

During those six weeks of cobalt Riann enjoyed taking walks, often by herself, quietly, up and down the hospital corridors, looking. She would put on her pink quilted robe and dainty slippers and look much like the "lady of the house." But always quiet, always polite, never impatient.

The nurses would have parties in the small room behind the nursing station and they'd invite Riann. She was always so pleased, and somewhat awestruck, to be included in their fun. "Weren't they so nice to ask me?" she would say several times before being tucked into bed.

Saying prayers and tucking in became somewhat customary between Riann and me when her mother couldn't stay. She never counted on it, never asked to make me feel it was a duty. But if I was staying late, I could never feel the ends were tied until Riann had said her prayers and was tucked in.

It was during the time she was having cobalt treatments that I got to know her and her mother best. Six weeks is a long time.

Dr. Verdi had told the Mileses he thought they should get away for a week if they could, just the two of them. Mr. Miles still was having difficulty accepting the *fact* of Riann's tumor. And Mrs. Miles was exhausted and under mounting pressure. So it was decided that they would see how Riann got along during her first two weeks of cobalt; and then, if that went well, they would go away the third week.

Cobalt wasn't something one could just do on another floor of Children's. To get to cobalt treatment Riann had to go by shuttle to Adult Hospital. Riann and her mother took me along one day during those first two weeks so I would know the procedure if I ever had to take Riann, which I had offered to do.

It was mid-March when the daily treks to Adult started. Riann would dress in the mornings, go to school for an hour—there was a school at Children's—then go to Adult for cobalt. And sometimes, if she felt all right, she and her mother would go out for lunch.

Riann would wear tights and shiny black patent shoes with straps and buckles, and little plaid skirts with matching solid-color sweaters and a furry-lined peacock blue parka with a hood. She always looked so cute dressed. I had seen her so much in night clothes.

Her mother taught her how to tie a scarf over her head and

behind in a knot—right with the height of fashion, fortunately. She looked beautiful. You couldn't believe it.

Riann accepted everything—except shots and needles, and there were none with cobalt—and seemed to make a tiny adventure out of it.

The day I went with her and her mother "to cobalt" for the first time, she kept telling me about the slow elevator and the pictures on the wall and the small wooden playhouse in the therapy waiting room.

When I got there and saw the huge, ugly cobalt machine, I wondered how she remembered anything else. But she didn't even seem to notice. Or, if she did, she didn't say anything.

But that was the first time it went through me—the full impact—of how really sick Riann was . . . that one day she would be dead . . . one day, very likely, before her hair grew long.

The cobalt room was steely and barren. There was a huge metal table, above which hung the huge cobalt machine. Other than a small television monitor, there was virtually nothing else in the room.

Riann undressed almost completely and crawled up on the steel table. It dwarfed her. Then the technician lined up the cobalt machine with the red marks precisely painted on Riann's back and neck—red marks she wasn't allowed to wash off until all the cobalt treatments were over. Six weeks without a good bath.

Once that was done, we had to leave, all of us, even the technicians. Riann lay on her tummy, quiet and still . . . wearing only her white tights and her shiny black patent leather shoes. She looked so tiny and naked . . . and alone.

And she was.

In a few seconds it was over, she was dressed, and the three of us were on our way to lunch. Riann was doing better. The first week she had gotten nauseous four times. But so far this week she was fine. Her parents would be able to go away for a rest.

As Manuelito got better and better and returned from Intensive Care to his room on three-north, his mother felt more comfortable about leaving him for a few hours. One day she decided she wanted to see a "shop center."

I borrowed David's trusty Mercedes and took her to one. It

was a riot. She had two other children, she said—Mary, who was five, and Anthony, who was four—and she was trying to buy clothing for them and for Manuelito.

The girl was bigger than most children her age, she explained, and the boy was smaller . . . and of course, *I* would know exactly what size Manuelito should have since I had seen him! (I have never bought clothing for a boy between the ages of one and sixteen years in my life!)

She also went wild at the costume jewelry counter and in the yard goods section. The salesladies were helpful and amused as we wandered about with our pocket dictionaries.

When we started the day I wasn't sure we'd be able to get through without lapsing into periods of great silence. But I don't think we stopped talking all day. It was fun!

But the Cercis were ready to leave when the time came. It had been a long haul.

The publicity department decided they would have a news conference to publicize the successful operation. Manuelito and his mother and father were to appear and Dr. Verdi would explain the surgical procedure and its effect.

And that news conference gave me an unplanned test of the validity of my decision to leave broadcasting.

I had told no one on three-north at University Children's about my broadcasting background. It wasn't that big a deal, but I didn't want it to influence anyone's thinking about me one way or the other. So consequently, only one or two people knew—by recognizing me—and they agreed not to say anything.

But I knew if I went to Manuelito's news conference, the jig would be up. I would know every one of the television reporters and cameramen . . . and they would know me.

I was anxious to see how I would react, what decision I would make when the time for the news conference came.

Mrs. Cerci had asked me to come to their room to help her dress Manuelito for the news conference and to say good-bye. They were going to leave right after, and I had to take Riann to cobalt, so that would be our only time for farewells.

Mrs. Cerci kept the door closed. The lady from P.R. fluttered in and out. At one time the conversation was so confusing that Mrs. Cerci thought for sure the P.R. lady wanted her to paste false hair on Manuelito's head for the television cameras!

Finally we had Manuelito dressed and their suitcases ready. I had noticed a large button that read "Kiss Me, I'm Italian" in one suitcase. I laughed. Mrs. Cerci said Dr. Verdi had given that to Manuelito last week. I laughed again, but inside I flinched: Riann Miles had been so tickled when she had given that very same button to Dr. Verdi . . . I wondered why he gave it away. It bothered me.

The efficient P.R. lady knocked on the door. The press was waiting . . .

Mrs. Cerci scooped up Manuelito and thrust him into my arms for a good-bye hug. Then Mr. Cerci took him and they were ready.

"Come," Mrs. Cerci motioned to me.

"No, you go. It's for Manuelito and you, not me."

We hugged good-bye.

It was the last time I saw them.

The cameramen were all waiting at the corner of the hall. My ears were trained. When I heard the clicking and grinding stop and didn't see any more lights, I knew they had all disappeared down the hall to the conference room.

And not a bone in my body wanted to be on the other end of that story. They would write about a cute kid and a history-making operation. True.

But I saw the agony. I saw the real value of the reward.

No, I wouldn't have traded. The decision had been right. But then, I had never really doubted it in the first place.

The news conference for Manuelito was still going on when I left with Riann to go to cobalt. The little girl was all dressed and ready to go when I came to get her in her room. She had seen all the television people as they passed by the schoolroom door and had said good-bye to Manuelito that morning.

"He was so cute. Gee, I'll miss him. Mommy and I got him a little wooden toy at the gift shop last week. I gave it to him this morning. I hope he likes it. It was from all of us—Mommy and Daddy and Allison and Kevin and Eric and me."

"What about Silver Bullet and Gwennie and Marshmallow?" (one dog, two cats) I asked.

She giggled. "Oh yes, I forgot. Them too."

She was feeling good that day, thank goodness. The shuttle

car was full, so she sat on my lap on the way. Strange emotions went through me, realizing I was holding a child so ill—terminally ill; a child I was beginning to love. Maybe that was the difference—the love. I still remember that ride vividly.

After cobalt we went to lunch at a restaurant near Children's. The food was good and they had old-time silent movies with music background. Riann loved it. She ordered shrimp—her favorite—and sat absolutely engrossed in the Laurel and Hardy film, giggling softly when something funny happened. She sat long after she had finished her shrimp. I figured she'd know when she was tired and wanted to go. She did; but not before she had eaten both our pickles—she is a pickle freak—and taken the Miller Beer coasters under our Cokes "for souvenirs."

If I were with a healthy child would I have remembered all those details? I doubt it. But now I had begun to grab at moments. I think we all did, all of us on three-north. Not each with the same child, but each with any child we began to love.

Except possibly for Dr. Verdi. Dying children, and loving them, still were two things he was wrestling with, or wrestling with admitting, even to himself. At least so it seemed to me.

He and Dr. Jenssen and I had lunch together a few days later. He still said he would give Riann fifteen years to live . . . Fifteen years . . . after seeing that massive tumor.

I think he suspected differently . . . knew differently . . . knew it couldn't be fifteen years. It just wouldn't come out of his mouth. His heart kept getting in the way.

Not only was Christian Verdi one of the best—if not *the* best—pediatric neurosurgeons in the world, he was ruggedly handsome, sensual and virile. He was in his mid-forties, looked a bit younger, drove a Maserati, wore Italian boots and custom-tailored cords, and Gucci—almost everything Gucci.

His hair was graying brown, long and full and wavy. He swaggered down the halls with authority and racy dignity. And he knew just what to say to a woman in a two-second passing to make her not quite sure he hadn't seduced her on the run.

Of course he was married.

One day he and I were discussing what it is like to be a chaplain; and what, on his part, it is like to work so hard for children such as Riann only to discover, in the end, that you can't get anywhere, that despite all the knowledge of medical science and all your surgical skill, the child ultimately will die.

During the conversation I sensed a despair in his voice, his difficulty as a surgeon to "let go," to accept that the child would die. And once he did let go, the difficulty of still relating to the yet living child as a human being with potential. I sensed that once he admitted defeat medically, the child was dead in his mind.

Maybe I was wrong. But I don't think so.

Dr. Verdi is not the type of man who can accept discussion of his possible weaknesses. He doesn't seem to have many. But he doesn't want others to see any at all. So I hesitated to give him "The Gift of the Dying Child" a few days later. But I finally did. I guess if there was to be a real working friendship, it couldn't be a "yes, sir" "yes, ma'am" one. It had to be one of concern, of mutual growing and respect.

THE GIFT OF THE DYING CHILD

She's not the same.
She's not the same!
Her hair is shaved.
Her head is cut.
The tumor in her brain cannot come out.
She is dying.
Oh God! She's not the same.
She will never be the same again.
Look! She walks funny.
Look. She doesn't walk at all.
Listen! Her memory is slipping.
Listen. All is quiet.
There is no more to remember.
She cannot see.
She cannot hear.
She cannot smile any more, doctor.
She cannot even smile.

The tumor outran your cobalt.
The tumor outran your chemotherapy.
The tumor has outrun you, doctor.
Or did you stop looking weeks ago?

She is not the same, her parents weep.
We did all we could, you say and hurry on.
There is nothing left. But to wait . . .
  Hurry up and die.
  Hurry up and die.
  We cannot stand it.
Oh dammit, God!—Why?
  Forget it. There is nothing more.
    Someday we will find a way.
    Someday our sick children will not die.

Quietly now, slip into her room, doctor.
  The sheets are white and crisp.
  She is very pale.
  She does not know you.
  She will die before the next rounds.
Now take her hand that will not squeeze back,
And I will tell you what you missed.

You missed hearing good times remembered wistfully.
You missed easing the frustration of a thought
  Lost in midsentence, with a kiss.
You missed the time she gave her nurse
  A piece of rubber chocolate.
And the time she wore a big green button
  That read, "Bald is Beautiful!"
    And you couldn't cope with saving
    That simple moment of joy
    That came with the funny button she gave you . . .

You missed the waiting while she did things for herself.
  As long as she could.
You missed the time she prayed
  That the tubes in her head would "shape up!"
You missed the times she prayed
  That *you* would have a "good night's sleep."
You missed kissing her good-night.
You missed kissing her at all . . .
  When she was not the same.
And so, doctor, you missed the gift of the dying child.

For if you will but share time—
   If you will but enjoy the dying child,
   She will teach you something more.
She will teach you to measure her life, and yours,
   Not only by their accomplishments,
   But by their gifts—
      Both those given and those received.

For the dying child will show you, if you let her,
That the greatest gift
   Is not rewarded by acclaim,
   Does not hear the words "thank you,"
   Cannot see the smile of gratitude.
For the greatest gift is both given and received
WHEN YOU TRY TO LOVE WITHOUT CONDITION.
   When *you* can *do* no more,
   When you must set the dying child free—to die,
    Then it is hardest to love,
    For it is a love without condition.
    There is no reward to grasp.

But if it is here that you think you are farthest from God,
Then it is here that you are most mistaken.

For in learning to share this moment of time
   With the dying child,
You will learn to share in God's greatest gift to man:
   His unconditional love for us
   Despite his powerlessness
   In the face of our freedom to reject him.

If you can love the dying child, doctor,
   Despite your powerlessness
   In the face of her freedom to die—
    Then you cannot help but touch God.

   And your tears will fall on light,
   And you will have learned
   To share gifts with the dying child
   Beyond the diagnosis.

* * *

He said he liked it, understood its meaning. But I'm still not sure. He had told me he wanted to frame the writings I gave him about Manuelito. He never said the same about this.

It's walking a fine line to probe near a man's ego . . . especially a brilliant man at the top of his profession. They bruise more easily.

18

RIANN ALWAYS LOVED to talk about her family. It was obviously a close, happy one.

"Why don't we write about your family?" I suggested one evening while her parents were on their week's "vacation." "We can take one person each night while your parents are away, and then put it all together in a big card for them when they return."

"You mean like a welcome home card?"

"Sure."

"Oh, that's a good idea! But I'm not too good at writing; could you do that?"

"OK. You just tell me things you like about each person, one person a night, and I'll write them down. Then I'll put it all on big sheets of colored paper and you can write 'Love, Riann' and the date at the bottom of each sheet."

"That's really a good idea. They'll be surprised!"

I knew what I was doing. So would Mrs. Miles . . . and maybe even Mr. Miles? It would be a bit difficult to take right then. But someday it would mean a lot.

For Riann, it was just a nice idea for a welcome home gift. That's all it should have been.

We had fun doing it. Each night before prayers I'd bring my brown notebook and pen into her room and we'd think—or she'd think.

"Oh, gee, what can I say," she'd ponder. Then she'd sit in deep concentration for a while. And then, sort of embarrassed, as if it wasn't very earthshaking, she'd come up with something she liked, or some incident she'd remember, about whoever in her family we were writing that night. "That really isn't very exciting," she'd apologize.

"It's not supposed to be exciting," I'd reassure her. "It's just supposed to be the things you remember and like about each person. It's called 'stream of consciousness.' "

"What?"

"Well, that's sort of saying the first thing that comes into your mind about someone. Those things usually are the things that impress you the most about a person."

"Oh, I see." She did, too. Her vocabulary and usage were excellent.

"You mean I said all that!" She was absolutely elated when I showed her the "welcome back" book in its final form.

"Sure you did."

"Gee, that's really nice. And I love the pictures," she giggled.

I had drawn some cartoon illustrations around the edge. Primitive, very.

I liked "Daddy's" and "Kevin's" pages best:

DADDY

When Daddy walks you can always hear him . . .
   In the morning coming down the hall . . .
   Because his shoes always make this funny sound,
   —Kind of "clump! clump!"

In the summertime
   When we don't have to go to school
   But Daddy has to go to work
When we wake up in the morning
We usually hear his car go
   Because his car makes this funny sound.

Sometimes at the dinner table
   When the boys act kind of funny and stuff,
   Daddy goes, "Cool it, cool down!"

And Allison and me,
  Sometimes we say, "Cool it, cool down,"
  To be funny.
When we do that, we usually stand up,
  And when we say, "Cool it,"
  We kind of bend our knees as we go down.

Sometimes when Daddy says
  He has to get a haircut
  I think it looks just right,
And I don't think he needs a haircut.

I think he's a nice Daddy.

                    Love, Riann . . . March 17th

KEVIN

Kevin is my brother.
  He is twelve years old.
He has a bike and sometimes rides it.
  But now since it's winter he doesn't.

Kevin has a dog named Silver Bullet.
  That's a funny name!
Silver Bullet is a basset hound,
  And he always wanders.

There's a dog up our street
  That he always goes to.
My father and Kevin usually
  Have to go pick him up.
But he's a nice dog to have,
  Even though he wanders.

Whenever sometimes you pet Silver Bullet
  On his head . . .
It's like he has leftover fur on him.

Kevin has a girl friend,
　But we don't tease him about that.
He'll probably crush me for telling . . .

Sometimes Kevin is funny and tells jokes.
　He put my relics in the Seagram's bag.
Sometimes he calls me "Rube Tube"
　Most of the time, anyway.
And I think that's a funny name!

Love, Riann . . . March 17th

　Riann got out of bed three different times to arrange the card "just so" for when her mother and father would arrive . . . each time after someone had come in and looked through it. She was so tickled.

　"They'll bring a surprise for me, I'm sure," she said. "And now I'll have a surprise for them!"

　Saying prayers with Riann was difficult at times—for me. It was her frankness and her sense of humor, and her acceptance.

　Granted, the words "tumor" and "tubes" (shunts) likely didn't have the same connotation for her as they did for me. But hearing her use them so freely in open conversation with God made me cold.

　The ritual was always the same. First we'd get out the blue velveteen Seagram's bag that held several religious "relics." She would choose two, usually . . . or maybe three. Often she would comment, "This is my favorite," or, "Grandmother sent me this one; it has a real piece of the Cross in it."

　Then we would each choose a printed prayer to read. Her favorite was "Courage."

　And then we'd begin. She always wanted me to start. So I would read the prayer I had chosen, then say one extemporaneously.

　And then she would pray . . .

COURAGE

God make me brave,
　Let me strengthen after pain,

As a tree strengthens after the rain,
  Shining and lovely again.

As the blown grass lifts,
  Let me rise from sorrow
With quiet eyes,
  Knowing Thy way is wise.

God make me brave,
  Life brings such blinding things,
Help me to keep my sight,
  Help me to see aright,
That out of dark comes light.

And then she would continue on her own. "Dear God, I hope
Mommy has a good sleep and Daddy has a good sleep and
Allison and Kevin and Eric and Dr. Verdi and Dr. Jenssen and
Nina and all the other doctors and nurses have a good sleep . . .
and all the children in the hospital, too. And Bullet and Gwennie
and Marshmallow . . .

"Thank you for a nice day. Thank you that I didn't get sick
after cobalt. That's ten days in a row!

"Please don't let my tumor get bigger. Please don't let me
have any more headaches. And please tell the tubes in my head
to shape up!

"Please let tomorrow be as nice as today."

Then she would look up at me to let me know she had finished, so we could say the "Our Father" together. As I mentioned earlier, I still haven't been able to say the Lord's Prayer
once without thinking of Riann, without hearing her bell-like
voice praying along with me. Maybe if I tried hard not to remember, I could. Maybe I want to remember. Maybe sharing
the memory gives a deeper meaning to the prayer.

Soon the last day of cobalt treatments was drawing near. "I
can take a bath! I really can hardly wait. A real bath!" said
Riann anxiously.

Riann was growing tired of the cobalt treatments. And though
she didn't complain too much, we could tell that having all of

the little hair she had left fall out in clumps by its roots was getting to her.

Yet, still she was beautiful.

Her last cobalt treatment was to be on Friday and she was to go home Saturday morning. Everyone on three-north who knew Riann was happy for her. She had spent most of the winter in the hospital, and now, soon, she'd be free to go home. The beginning of the "grace period."

On three-north we all knew she'd be back, be a patient again, likely die here.

But when? How long? How much suffering? They're the horrible unanswered questions; the questions of each day, every day. The waiting for the other shoe to drop.

19

IN THE LITTLE hospital in a small town in the southern tip of the state that same Saturday that Riann went home to Rock Shores they were telling Ken Harrington that he had two choices. That his baby being born at that moment had such a large head that the doctors either could crush the head and let the baby be born naturally—but dead; or that they could do a Caesarean section and try to save the baby. But either way, they were sure the baby was severely deformed.

What could the poor man do? He said Caesarean section. It takes time to decide that "killing" your own baby may be best.

I took one look at Lisa Harrington as she was raced down the three-north hall in an incubator several hours later and I knew her diagnosis immediately: acute hydrocephalus.

Her head was immense; and when I looked closer, I saw that both her feet were bent inward—clubbed. But it was her head, so very very big.

"You'd better stay around, Rev." It was Patrick McMahan. "She may go soon. But come to think of it," he added, "the mother is still in the hospital and the father had to go back with the ambulance, so I guess you'd just be staying around for the kid, if you stay . . ."

"Oh, stay." It was Dr. Gary Suter. "I'm almost out of cigarettes!" He looked at my nearly full pack. (It's nice to be needed.) "We'll do an angiogram to see if there's much brain, and then we'll put in a shunt," said Dr. Suter.

I went along to angio. Dr. McMahan had a terrible time finding the arteries. Then, right in the middle of the procedure, the baby started not doing too well. "She may not get through this," said Dr. McMahan.

"I wonder if she's been baptized?" I asked. "If she's Catholic it may make a difference."

"You're right, Rev. Let's try to find out. That's important." Patrick McMahan is Catholic.

The word came back. The baby wasn't baptized, but there was no way, right then, to determine her religion.

"Go ahead, Rev. It can't hurt," said Dr. McMahan, who was still trying to find the second artery.

"OK." I was very nervous. I had never baptized a child before. I knew it was legal in an emergency, with the Catholic Church, I mean; but my knees still shook.

I didn't have much time to think, though. It had to be done quickly. We got a small paper lab cup. Patrick McMahan and I stood on either side of the baby . . . the baby whose head was held, tilted backwards, between two sponge rubber padded braces; the baby in whose neck was one needle piercing the artery; the baby who was lying bundled on a steel table under a massive X-ray machine . . . and I poured water on her forehead and said, "I baptize you in the name of the Father and of the Son and of the Holy Spirit, Amen. May the Lord bless you and keep you and make his face shine upon you, now and forevermore, Amen."

I kissed her. So did Dr. McMahan. Then Gary Suter lit a cigarette and "charted" the baptism and Dr. McMahan found the other artery and I watched. My knees still felt funny.

The dye didn't go anywhere. It just stopped. Lisa Harrington had virtually no brain.

In the complete, normal angiogram series, the dye looks like branches of a tree in the X-ray, with two main branches and lots of little continuous branches reaching and spreading from the front to the back of the head. But in Lisa Harrington's head, the dye just stopped. There were no spreading branches on the X-rays. Just two main branches. Then virtually nothing, virtually no brain system.

"I opt for no shunt," said Patrick McMahan. "It's useless.

It's cruel. Why make her suffer more? She's going to die. She has no brain system.''

"I agree, tonight at least,'' said Gary Suter, who was senior to Patrick McMahan. "C.B. [Dr. Verdi] will have the final say, though, you know.''

"Yeah, I know.''

It wasn't a matter of disagreement, really, between Dr. McMahan and Dr. Verdi. Because really there is no right or wrong. But the problem is a matter of growing concern: when to treat and when not to treat when you *know* the patient will die anyway.

The doctor in the small downstate hospital had left the decision at birth to the father. But in all fairness, did either of them have time to act beyond instinct in the crisis situation? And, in almost all cases, instinct tells us, as human beings, to preserve life.

Perhaps the child's hydrocephalus could have been controlled. Perhaps she would have had a healthy body and complete brain and intercranial system. That wasn't known for sure as she was pushing to get out of her mother's womb.

But now it was known. How much should the physician "treat" now? How many medical procedures should be performed now . . . when it was simply prolonging death rather than preserving life?

Dr. Verdi ordered a shunt for Lisa Harrington. So rather than a small basketball, the head soon began to look like a large prune. Orthopedic doctors put tiny casts on both of Lisa Harrington's legs and feet, and they put stiff moldings around her hands to try to straighten her bent fingers.

And the nurses moved her away from the window . . . so people walking by in the corridor wouldn't stare and point.

It may have hurt Lisa Harrington when each of these procedures happened to her. Under the circumstances, it could be asked, "Weren't these heroic means? Was it necessary? Couldn't she be allowed to die in peace, without surgery, without casts, without moldings . . . just be fed and held and let die in peace?''

What is life anyway? Does it end when the heart stops beating . . . when the brain doesn't function . . . or when a person is rendered incapable of both giving and receiving love?

I've never been sure why the doctors did all that to—or for—

Lisa Harrington. They seem to go in spurts. At times they use "heroic" means for a newborn who they know will die. But for an older child in the last stages of dying of a brain tumor, they will mercifully, quietly, "open the window and close the door," will not use heroic means.

But then, in each case, the doctors have had their day, their chance. They have *made the attempt to save life*, whether it be for the newborn or the older child. I guess when you're a surgeon, when saving life is what you breathe to do, you cannot do otherwise: Start out to save, despite the odds. End up quietly opening the window and letting the child go free . . . to die.

I dread the coming day when breast-beating moralists will engage in public uproar over the agonized life-death decisions made by concerned physicians in the quiet corridors of this nation's hospitals. The decisions are made every day—decisions to treat, decisions not to treat, decisions to use heroic means, decisions to pull the plug. But until I have to make one myself, I don't intend to write a rule book.

Lisa Harrington was ultimately taken to a nursing home where she died about a month later. She was Catholic. Her father cried in relief about the baptism.

20

ALEX FELINI WAS still unconscious. They took him to surgery three more times after the day we prayed and cried in the chapel. But it hadn't helped.

One Saturday—my last official Saturday at Children's—Alex stopped breathing. He was in room 383, a small, private room next to the Constant Care room on three-north. He had been there about a month. His head was bandaged and the CFS tube stuck out. He also had two I.V.s. He was still decerebrate. His eyes were open now, but they didn't react to light or movement.

We didn't know if he could hear us or not. But we would talk to him, all of us. We'd tell him hospital news and funny things that doctors and nurses did. His parents talked to him. About what was going on at home, about his sisters, Chrissy and Sandi, about horses and cars and baseball and horses and horses.

His father even made a cassette tape recording of each member of the family talking and asked the nurses to play it now and again when he and his wife couldn't be there.

Sometimes we'd believe Alex moved. Sometimes we'd believe we heard him make a sound. Maybe he did.

We would dream about him . . . waking up, sitting up, talking, running down the halls with his six-shooters saying "Quack, Quack, I'm a duck"—one of his favorite imitations.

But they were only dreams. And that Saturday he stopped breathing.

I was at the end of the hall in the small waiting room. I saw Tony Felini walk by to visit Alex. He was in a good mood. He stopped and chatted for a minute, then went toward 383.

About three minutes later, an agonizing scream came from the other end of the hall. No actor could duplicate it. It told a story without words.

Tony Felini came running out of room 383, screaming. "Oh God! Oh no! Alex, Alex! No! No! No! Oh God! Don't let him die. Alex, *don't* die! Alex don't die!"

"Code 1111—three-north, room 383. Code 1111—three-north, room 383. Code 1111—three-north, room 383. Code 1111—three-north, room 383."

Some hospitals are more subtle. They'll page Dr. Sam Smith, or Dr. Red, when they really mean "emergency." But it's all the same. People figure it out. You don't have to be around Children's long to realize that "Code 1111" is red alert—pull out all the stops, drop what you're doing, run—someone has stopped breathing.

Medical staff came out of the woodwork. The neurosurgeons, who had finished rounds only fifteen minutes earlier, came up the back stairway in a pack.

But no one could go near Tony Felini. He had run out of Alex's room and was standing in the middle of the nursing station flailing his arms and screaming. No one dared too near. If anyone had tried to talk with him, calm him down, he wouldn't have heard.

"Can you just stay with him," I was asked as the nurses ran back and forth.

"Sure," I said. But there was nothing to do but stand and watch. Even a strong man could have done nothing.

There's a large metal refrigerator on three-north by the nursing station. Tony Felini started beating his fists against it. His eyes were wild, his face damp and white.

He had nowhere to run.

He started beating his head against the wall.

"Neen"—Carrie Felini was the only person I had ever found who could shorten Nina—"Is he gone?"

Alex's petite, dark-haired mother stood by the nursing station divider wall . . . quiet, composed. Just one simple question.

She had been in the coffee shop when the "Code 1111" came. She recognized it.

"I don't know, Carrie."

"No." It was Mary Cooke. "He's OK, Mrs. Felini. He just stopped breathing for a few seconds. But he's OK now."

"Thanks, Mar."

"He's OK, Mr. Felini," Mary repeated to Alex's father. "He's OK. He's breathing fine again. Why don't you sit down? Go in the back room. He's fine. You can see him in a few minutes."

Somehow, Tony Felini dragged himself to the back room. He sat very still . . . unseeing, unhearing . . . just sitting, staring. "Alex, you can't die. Come on, Alex. Come on Alex. Don't die. God, please don't let him die. I've prayed so hard. Come on kid. I love you." The words came out in metered time, quietly, like an echo. "I love you . . ."

"You know, Neen, I guess I'm selfish, but I wanted it to be over. I wanted him to die, now. If he's not gonna get better, ever, I mean. *If he's gonna get better, I'll wait any of them out.* But if he's not, why let him lie there like that, day in and day out?"

Carrie Felini was still standing by the nursing station entrance. Tony Felini was still sitting in the back room. I was going back and forth. The doctors and nurses were still in with Alex.

"And all my friends and relatives," Carrie went on, "they mean well, don't get me wrong, but every day it's the same thing. They think they have to call. And then they ask the same questions, every day: "How's Alex? Any change? What about his temperature? What about his blood pressure? What about his brain swelling? Are his eyes still dilated? Does he seem to be more aware?

"If something has gotten worse, they don't seem to hear it. If something has gotten better, they try to latch onto it, to build me up—to build themselves up. I just wish they'd let me alone. If there's any dramatic change, I'll let them know. But nothing changes, day after day, week after week. I'd not answer the phone, but I'm always afraid it's the hospital.

"Tony can't take it, either. I think Alex is going to die. I really do. I think a lot of people around here are beginning to think so, too. But Tony doesn't. Tony still expects Alex to wake up and say, 'Hi, Dad! Hi, Mom!'

"Neen, I can't even hold Alex . . . with all those tubes and things. I just want to hold him. He's my little boy, my only boy. I'm his mother. I just want to hold him. But maybe it's best after all, that I can't hold him . . . with him this way, because he wouldn't respond, wouldn't hug back . . . and that would be worst of all."

I agreed with her then. I was beginning to think Alex would die, too. So, I think, was Dr. Praeder.

But even realistic Patrick McMahan wasn't one hundred percent sure. There still was that thread . . .

21

Rᴵᴀɴɴ MILES HAD a good summer, really good. Her father had wanted to take the family on a ranch/riding/camping-out vacation in the west. I can remember thinking it was a pipe dream as he talked about it the day of her surgery.

But they went, all of them. And Riann made it. She was so happy "just to have made it!" On their Christmas card of family pictures that year there was one of Riann standing in front of a tent holding a roll of bathroom tissue. It was a comment on her most difficult problem of the trip—how to crouch when what your brain tumor is doing to your body won't really let you crouch comfortably.

But it was a comment on the whole rotten deal, too.

The good summer turned into a relatively good fall. Riann went back to school—not whole days every day, but as much as possible.

Her classmates accepted her situation and, thanks to a perceptive, kind teacher, very likely learned a great deal from it.

I saw Riann in her home once before the camping trip and twice in the fall. It isn't difficult to visit Riann. She is always happy. She talks about her trip west and about school . . . and about University Children's. Her memories of the hospital and people there are quite vivid, and always positive . . . except for the needles.

Riann seems to have reached a plateau. Other than a slight limp, she can walk well. She can't run and play hard and she

133

tires easily, and her memory doesn't always work at one hundred percent in momentary things. But other than that, she seems not to be getting any worse.

"I have so many things going on inside me. I'm so *glad* she's doing well . . . but each morning I wake up and think—before I even get my eyes open—will *this* be the day? Will today be the one that she changes, that she starts going downhill? Will she suddenly be dead in her bed one morning? Each time she gets a headache I ask, 'Is this it, God? Is this one it?' If she has an upset stomach or throws up, I ask, 'Is it the tumor, or the shunt . . . or does she just have indigestion, or a flu-bug, like a normal eight-year-old?' " It was Mrs. Miles on the telephone one early fall evening.

"I try to tell myself to live each day at a time, but it's not always easy. And Eric [her husband] thinks she's fine. He'll hardly even talk about it. Ever since she made it through that trip west, he's sure she'll be fine for years.

"You know, when we had been on horseback for hours and finally got to the campground where we were going and Riann and I were alone unpacking some things, she started to cry. I was sure she was sick. I was so frightened.

" 'No, Mommy, I'm all right,' she told me. 'I'm just crying because I'm so happy. I'm so happy I made it . . . like everybody else.'

"I guess it was good for her. But that almost broke me in two. She was so brave . . . so brave. God! A brain tumor, two major surgeries—craniotomies—and riding horseback up some mountain. She could be dead next year at this time . . .

"Sometimes people say it's better if a child goes quickly. Others say we're lucky to have this time. I'm *glad* we have the time . . . but the uncertainty, the not knowing, the raw fear gets to me after a while. I worry about Eric, too. I don't want him to feel guilty about anything . . . when it's over. That's why I was *so* glad this trip went well. If something had gone wrong . . . with Riann . . . he may have felt guilty for years."

Guilt: That's the one major feeling parents have, I was finding out, that Elisabeth Kübler-Ross's patients didn't have. The sixth point. Yes, parents have the famous five: disbelief (shock), anger, bargaining, despair, and acceptance. They usually begin with disbelief—almost always; rarely end with acceptance simultaneous with or preceding death; and go through the other three in no particular order and often with one overlapping the other.

But guilt . . . With parents of critically and terminally ill children, it's a major point.

Guilt takes several shapes in this context. "I didn't get my child to a doctor fast enough." "I did something (took something, ate something, didn't do something) during pregnancy that caused my child to have a birth defect." "I haven't bought my child the things I should have." "I haven't loved my child enough." "I haven't really gotten to know my child." "Why didn't I take him to the fair?" "Why didn't I give him . . ." It goes on and on. And it's very, very real.

In my opinion, this guilt has to be affirmed—affirmed as normal. So often I'll hear a doctor or a nurse or a friend say, "Oh, you shouldn't feel guilty." If they're medical people answering a medical-genetic question, fine. But even then I think the answer should be preceded by, "Most parents ask the same questions, have the same guilty feelings; it's normal. But in your case, as in most cases, it is completely unfounded . . ." And then continue with their medical-genetic explanation.

But for other types of guilt, the more parents are told, "Don't talk that way; you have no reason to feel guilty; you shouldn't say that; you shouldn't feel that," the more they will suppress their true feelings and begin to imagine they're abnormal, or even losing their minds.

I have found it is much better to say, "I can see why you would say that . . . why you would feel that way. Johnny's situation was so unexpected . . . and your reaction is quite normal." Then make a transference to myself. "If my parents were to become very ill suddenly, or die—and they live in Maryland— I'm sure I would feel very guilty. I'd chastise myself for not going home more often, or writing or telephoning more often, or not being kinder . . . It's a normal reaction.

"But in your case, you have a choice. Are you going to let those natural guilt feelings overwhelm you and so engulf you that you neglect Johnny, who really needs you now . . . or neglect the rest of your family? Or, are you going to admit that the guilt feelings are normal—accept them—and let them subside naturally while you get on to more important things, like loving Johnny and sharing with him and appreciating him . . . or helping bring your whole family closer together in this important time? It's your choice. Nobody can make it for you.''

I talked with Mrs. Miles about guilt on the telephone that evening. And how they were lucky to have borrowed time . . . but how difficult it was not to know . . . to wait . . . for what?

Then I wrote again . . . about three in the morning . . . a prayer for Mrs. Miles to pray . . .

A PRAYER TO READ IN WINTER

One summer, I asked.
   You could have seen snow
On broad green maple leaves, and known
   That the warmth of April was best.

But no, my little one
   Wanted to pick daisies and catch fireflies.
So she melted waiting icicles with life's warm
   breath
   —she and You.
You work well together!

I live with hours; yet my heart dares to see
   Daisies in December.
But it *will* snow someday. And flakes
   Will blanket tiny petals and fool the sun.
For seasons live and die—and live again.
   Like God. Like man.

But, God, don't let me, shivering,
   Miss the gift of winter,
Whose frigid eyes now pierce me through
   With each morning's first breath.
For in stillness winter whispers,
   ''There is a secret. There is a secret.
Life will burst onto the face of the Earth,
   And leftover ice drip from daisies,

And you will call it spring.
But life is *made* while you wait on frozen soil.''

One summer, I asked. It is a gift glorious!
    But when winter comes, my little one will
    know its secret
    —of life, of love, of rebirth,
And winter will be *her* gift glorious.
    For she will see Your face; while I still wait
    and dream
And cry on naked branches.

Oh God! Don't let me be so frail at losing my
    gift,
That I fail to share the joy of hers.

That was for Mrs. Miles.
But I wrote some things for Riann, too. It started innocently with a short little story about ''Ferd S. Soap''—the bar of soap she used for her ''first bath'' after cobalt . . . Went on to a horse named ''Bruce''—supposedly the horse she would ride on her trip west . . . included a bluebird named Homer and a frustrated turkey named Thomas . . . And ended up with Clive Thurgood Bookworm, III, who was destined to become the subject of several stories, and Riann's favorite. Luckily, I found a red, orange, and yellow stuffed bookworm at a local department store and sent it to Riann. She carried him around with her for her remaining time.

He watched her die.
For in the interim of my writing, that has happened.

The first false alarm with Riann came at Thanksgiving. Like false labor pains in reverse. But she was all right, in and out of the hospital overnight. She had started to throw up, and had had a headache the Friday morning after Thanksgiving. But apparently one of her shunts had just clogged temporarily. Whatever it was, she went home again Saturday afternoon.
Home for Christmas.
It was a pretty winter day, the day I visited Riann just before

Christmas. I had borrowed David's Mercedes and I played Christmas tapes on the stereo all the way to Rock Shores.

When I arrived, Mrs. Miles was "at the grocery and would be right back." The day housekeeper was there with Riann.

One of my best memories of Riann is as she half-skipped, half-walked, half-limped out through the dining room to meet me. She had on blue slacks and a white turtleneck shirt, and it was the first time she wasn't wearing a scarf over her head.

"Riann! Look at your hair! All that hair! That's fantastic! I can't believe it."

She grinned from ear to ear, and giggled and giggled. She was so happy, so very, very happy. Her hair must have been one-quarter inch long all over.

She gave me a "big hug" (as her mother always called it) and a kiss on the lips.

Her right arm and hand were getting weaker each time I saw her. And the Christmas package I had for her was rather large. But when I held it up for her to see, that it was for her, she sort of reached for it.

I gritted my teeth and put it in her arms. And she managed! It was an immense effort, but she managed!

"I started to cry in the middle of the supermarket. All the people and the 'Merry Christmas' and the fruits and candies and goodies . . . all the smells . . . and playing Christmas carols over the loudspeaker.

"People must have thought I was crazy. I couldn't help it. I just started to cry, and I had to leave," Riann's mother whispered to me a few minutes after she came home.

The three of us had lunch and talked about Christmas and Santa, and about what Riann wanted, and about traditions and turkeys, and how her ninth birthday was too close to Christmas—"only two days after!"

Then Riann, grumbling as all children do who must take afternoon naps, went upstairs to rest.

"I just want it to be over—Christmas. I know that's awful. But I do. How can I be happy? I keep saying, 'It will be our last Christmas together.' And it will. Even Dr. Verdi admits that now. He says six months at best . . . probably less. Six months!"

"And Eric *still* doesn't seem to see. He still goes to meetings, meetings, meetings every evening."

Escape? Denial? I suggest.

"Yes, I guess it is his way of denying, his way of escaping the truth. But I don't want him to have regrets later . . .

"Last night I told him if he wants his family to be together after this—after all this—he'd better stay at home from now on. No more night committee meetings. He'll have years for that. I just can't carry all this by myself. I just can't. I need him.

"I can't be cheerful for Riann and answer the other children's questions—and they're beginning to figure this out; they'll have to be told the truth soon, just like Dr. Verdi said, we would know when they are ready—and keep house, and talk to relatives and friends, and be a wife, too. It's not fair."

(It wasn't. But it was normal, too. Men—at least the men I observed—seem to have greater difficulty accepting abnormalities of any kind in their children. Be it an assault on their maleness, or an unusually squeamish stomach by gender, or an inability to deal with interruptions in the normal order of things, or a prolonged state of shock, as it was for Mr. Miles. Any or all of them. These men couldn't accept the *fact* of sick or dying children as well as women . . . couldn't deal with their feelings about them as openly. And I think that's true of men—fathers— as a whole. Usually they just pack it away inside, layer on layer. And consequently, the statistics of broken marriages in this area are high.)*

We talked an hour more in the den as the sun slipped behind the trees.

"I read it. I read the whole book!" Riann walked hesitantly down the stairs in her heavy brown laced shoes. "It really was a nice book. Thank you."

As one of her Christmas gifts I had given her a copy of *Big Susan*, my absolute favorite child's Christmas book, about dollhouse dolls who come alive each Christmas eve.

We talked and laughed some more, and a light snow began

*See Chapter Five of *I Never Know What to Say* (my second book), Ballantine Books, 1987, for a more extensive discussion of this issue.

to fall. Oh, if only it had been a normal happy Christmas visit.
No hanging sword. No dangling shoe . . .

She stood shivering. "I'm glad when you come. I can always
get all that stuff out. It does me good."

I stuck the key in the frozen car-door lock. "Riann's so happy.
She's almost blissfully happy." And she was. "And that's the
most important thing right now," I said.

"You're right, you're really right. Thank God for that! I'll
just have to keep reminding myself of that, I guess. Over and
over. And you are right, she is happy. I can't believe it. And it
is the most important thing now. I have tons of tomorrows to
cry . . . Merry Christmas."

"Merry Christmas."

I drove down the driveway, waving.

Bah! Humbug!

22

ALEX FELINI DIDN'T have a good summer . . . from our human perspective. He died.

When I came back to three-north to visit that summer I always visited Alex, too. He had been moved from room 383, the small, private room, to a four-bed room. But it didn't make any difference. He lay there, getting thinner and thinner and looking less and less like six-gun Alex, and never regaining consciousness.

But his father kept talking to him.

His mother kept talking, too . . . about other things, to people other than Alex, laughing and joking and going on living. But she talked less and less *about* Alex. For there was less and less to talk about. There were no more questions. It was more than a coma; more than brain swelling. He was going to die.

He remained decerebrate; he developed an infection; and his pupils dilated—the worst sign. "Whether" one day turned quietly to "when," and I could have prayed Carrie's prayer.

A "no code" was ordered. No more "Code 1111" if Alex stopped breathing, no heroic means, no more torture. It wouldn't be preserving life, it would be prolonging death.

"Hi, Nina! Hey, Alex, Nina's here. Man, you should see the tan she has. You better get well fast so you can get a tan, too. The summer's almost over.

"Nina's working for a lawyer now, and she's also working part-time as a chaplain at North Side Hospital."

(When I had to leave Children's in June because the new stu-

141

dents were coming, Paul had given me a job, and I had volunteered to help the chaplain at North Side, near my home, in the evenings.)

"You remember North Side," Tony Felini went on, "where Mommy's doctor is. Yeah, Alex, Neen's got a real good tan."

Alex lay there, eyes open in a blank stare. Huge, huge eyes now, against this hollow gray-white face.

"Hi, Alex," I said. "If you think my tan's good, you should see Jennifer's! She loafs around all day in the sun." I went along. It would have been cruel not to. He knew; Tony Felini knew. But he had played the game so long now he didn't know how to change, didn't want to to "give up " in public. As if giving up in public would have "killed" Alex. But it was a superstition not teased by hope this time around.

"Hey, Neen, I was thinking," Tony Felini turned to me. "They've got a chapel at North Side, don't they?"

"Yes."

"Well, we've been bringing all these St. Jude candles for Alex, as you know . . ." High-strung laughter. "Well, we've still got all the empty glass jars—you know, after the candles have been burned up. Well, I kind of hate to just throw them away. I figure somebody somewhere could use them. For a while I just put them on the chapel desk downstairs, but then I seen them in the wastebasket. If I'd wanted them there, I could've done that myself . . .

"So, anyway, I was wondering if you'd like them to use at North Side?"

"Sure. I'm sure there are people there who would appreciate them." At the moment, I wasn't certain what I'd do with empty St. Jude candle jars. But of course, that wasn't the point. Those jars were wrapped up in the mystery of Alex's life and death. Tony Felini didn't want to see them in a wastebasket, not yet.

I guess I didn't either. Sometimes it's hard for gut reaction to travel to intellectual realism and acceptance.

"Well, I tell you what—now, these are all empty, you know—"

"Sure."

"Well, I'll drop them off at North Side some day next week on the way out here to see Alex. Do you have an office there?"

I explained how to get to the chaplain's office at North Side and told him to leave them on the desk if I wasn't there.

That was Thursday.

* * *

Alex died Saturday morning . . . two days later.

Three nurses from three-north and I went to the funeral Monday morning. It was an open casket. Alex was wearing a red plaid sports jacket and beside him was a plastic horse. That was the most real thing of all . . . the plastic horse.

I remember seeing Tony Felini sitting not more than three feet away from Alex's head, staring. He didn't see anything or anybody but Alex. The rims of his eyes—like the eyes of Ethel Stone's father so many months earlier—were like blood. His skin was translucent green. And when the lid of the casket was closed and snapped into place, his one solitary moan was beyond my experience to comprehend.

Another thing affected me, too, that August morning. It was the nurses, the fact that they came. One was Jennifer Bradford. The other two, Mary Katharine Soloman and Karen Greer, worked the overnight shift. I barely knew them. They all loved Alex a lot.

A few days later I put my feelings into words, but then I just put the pages away. It was too soon to show it to them. Maybe I would some day.

THREE-NORTH

The sun was blazing in the east window of the nursing station and the shifts were changing from night to day when Alex died.

The shifts kept changing and the sun crawled up over the roof and down the other side and around and up again, as its mission.

On its third trip, Alex was buried.

In a room that always wears soft orange lamps that look like vases, always wears the smell of flowers, always wears the silence of sick tension, stood three girls. Not everyone recognized them as they walked by the open casket. They were not "in place" without their nursing uniforms of white or pales of yellow, pink, or blue.

Alex was not "in place" either. He wasn't running up and down the hospital corridors going, "Quack, quack, I'm a duck!" or "Bang, bang, you're dead!" He wasn't playing "General Custard" with his everpresent plastic horses.

He wasn't trying to postpone the moment of medicine by saying, "Wait a minute, nurse; let's discuss this whole thing!" or "Wait a minute, nurse; I've just gotta go to the john! Things like that can't wait, you know."

Neither Alex nor the three nurses were "in place." No one had told Alex he would die without waking to see summer.

No one had told the nurses their jobs would make their hearts take them to the funerals of seven-year-old children.

I have watched these nurses, and all the neurosurgical nurses on three-north at University Children's, give greater human meaning to their profession than most people could imagine; than even they themselves would likely imagine.

I have watched their nursing care remain professional. But I have watched their faces tighten and their words get scarce as they see a child they have grown to love hooked onto a respirator, or diagnosed "malignant brain tumor," or lapse into uncontrollable seizures . . . or die.

I have watched them sit for a moment in the nursing station, trying to be unobtrusive as they hold their stomachs or clench their fists, knowing they have to go into the room of a child who has been through surgery and give him a shot that will hurt him *one more time* and make him cry. When all they want to do is love him and hold him and comfort him and make him happy.

I have watched them cry in a corner behind a curtain when a brave father whose baby suddenly died walked to a surgeon, shook his hand, and said, "Thank you, doctor, I know you did everything you could."

I have watched them grab any available moments to comfort a frightened child, or give cuddling and love to a newborn, or talk with worried parents.

And in the midst of the daily pain of three-north, I have watched these nurses make joy. I have watched them use their own money to buy clothes and toys for a sick and abandoned newborn, and have small parties whenever there is the most fragile excuse to celebrate. I have watched them grasp these moments of joy and hold fast . . .

In a few short months at Children's, I have watched all this. And I have developed a deep respect for these nurses for the *caring* in their care, and for the reflection of a Greater Love that shines through them on their patients, on each other, and on their profession.

For after all, no one told them their jobs would make their hearts take them to the funerals of seven-year-old children. They went, and will continue to go, because for them the word "nurse" means love, too.

Unlike Riann's parents, Alex's had no period of "borrowed time." By the time the "whether" turned to "when" there was no more breathing time, no responsive child. The other shoe had dropped, and the waiting was only for it to settle.

That same Monday evening after Alex's funeral I went to North Side Hospital. I usually arrived after the staff chaplain had gone, and this was the case that evening.

I got out my keys to the office, unlocked the door, and flicked on the light. On the chaplain's desk I saw a large brown paper bag. My name was written on the side.

I put down my purse and keys and opened the bag. Inside were seven St. Jude candles . . . four empty, and three still unburned. The accompanying note read: "To Nina, from Alex Felini."

I sat in that office a long time. It was the brown paper bag that got me immediately. The comparison between the brown paper bag of seven months earlier . . . the one that held Ethel Stone's furry pink coat . . . and this brown paper bag, which held said and unsaid prayers for Alex Felini's life.

But there was more. Was Tony Felini saying, in Alex's name, "Here, take your damned St. Jude candles . . . for all the good they did me! Look, three of them aren't even burned. Thanks, God. Thanks a lot. Thanks for nothing."

And if Tony Felini wasn't saying that on that Monday evening . . . was I?

About six weeks later, after all the autopsy results were in, it was determined that Alex Felini had an inoperable, undetectable brain tumor. That, and not the posterior fossa cyst, had caused his death.

At least there was a reason. People with posterior fossa cysts aren't expected to die. People with inoperable brain tumors oftentimes are expected to die.

That made it all all right, of course.

23

I WAS COMING out of my shell shock. Very slowly, very painfully, I was beginning to try to add one and one . . . add God and pain . . . and come up with a solution. I knew all along it was impossible. No one had to tell me there is no answer to the "problem" of pain and death. But now, in the winter of Riann Miles's life . . . in the winter after Alex Felini's death, I was beginning to want to think about it. I was beginning to want to wrestle with the "mystery"—aiming for an answer, but knowing that I would settle for a rationalization, a seeing "through a glass darkly."

I began to read, to see what others had thought on the mystery of suffering. Many theologians and philosophers chose to approach suffering and death as a "problem" rather than as a "mystery." Some wrestled with whether we were created good and went downhill from there, or whether we were created with holes—immature—and given the potential to lift ourselves up by our bootstraps. Many others compared pain with goodness as they compared hot water with cold: In other words, if there isn't pain with which to compare happiness (goodness, love, etc.), how can we know that we are happy?

Others spent a great amount of time discussing what happens when we die: the pan-cosmic nature of the separated soul; our total personhood achieved; our eternal "yes" or "no" to God. And still others wrote off the reason, the "origin" of pain, in deference to dealing with the cleansing "purpose," the trans-

146

forming power of pain. (Almost everyone I read had done this one.)

At the time the events of this chapter happened I hadn't read all these theories yet. I couldn't have coped with all of them then, not and had them make much sense. But I was beginning.

It was strange to be reading about pain and death as a theological-philosophical "problem" or "mystery." I would get angry and disagree. Or, I would stop at one sentence or paragraph that made some sense to me and then spend half an hour mentally applying it, reliving experiences, testing its validity in my own experience, and either building on it or discarding it as invalid for me. I didn't always get very far in reading numbers of pages that way, but I did get far in exercising my mind, in wrestling with *my* most relevant mystery about God—the mystery of pain and evil. There were still a lot of apples and oranges. But the potential for a jelly of sorts was there.

No great or small theologian I stumbled across told me why there is a world, answered the mystery of creation and history. An anthropologist and naturalist, Dr. Loren Eiseley, told me where I probably came from—a rather ugly Crossopterygian affectionately known as the Snout. But even Dr. Eiseley had to admit to "the eternal mystery, the careful finger of God," waving in the oozy pond of 300 million years ago. Still, no one told me "why creation?" Why we are here—humanity, or humanity up from Eden, or humanity up from Snout.

So I moved on to the next question: If there is a God and if that God loves us and if that God is all-powerful, why would what happened to Alex Felini, what was happening to Riann Miles, happen? And not just them, but the millions and millions like them in circumstances of suffering, pain, disaster, evil? I mean, if God is all-powerful and all-loving, isn't that a fair question?

Sure; and just as unanswerable . . . just as unanswerable as my question of "Why creation?" But that didn't stop me from asking, either. Not any more. I had been hooked by the mystery, first through experience and now through mind. And I anticipate I'll never be unhooked until I see "face to face."*

*See Chapter Nine of *I Never Know What to Say*, ibid., for a more extensive discussion of this issue.

I was reading one snow-filled February evening, reading about God and pain and evil, when the telephone rang. I'm not big on being disturbed when I'm nestled. The telephone has rarely been my third ear. I debated answering it.

I did. Riann Miles was in the hospital. She had been admitted that morning. She didn't look good. Could I come and talk with her mother? She had been pretty upset earlier.

It was a three-north nurse.

"Sure, I'll be right there."

Not now. I'm not in the mood. Not now. Make it go away. I don't want to. Besides, I had talked with Riann's mother just a few days earlier and she told me then that the family, including Riann, was going to Jamaica at the end of February. She can't die before that. They need that one last trip. I don't feel like doing this. Not now. No.

It's a natural rebellion. The mind doesn't want to accept. What will I find? Will it make any difference anyway, my being there?

I walked part of the way to Children's, in the snow, all bundled up. I wanted to . . . to kick clumps of snow and crunch through untrod plots of white and be cold and wet . . . to fight with nature . . . to feel, outside.

But I got there just the same.

Riann was all right. Another false alarm; another labor pain in reverse. She was sitting up in bed eating cherry jello, wearing her red nightshirt with a big "STOP" sign on the front.

Appropriate.

"Hi, Nina!"

"Hi. How *are* you?"

"Fine. I didn't feel too good earlier, but I feel fine now. Dr. Jenssen says I can go home Tuesday maybe. That's not too bad, two days. Want some jello?"

"No thanks."

"Mommy brought Clive, but then she left him in the car! She says he's sitting on the dashboard. He's gonna look awfully funny to people walking by," she giggled.

Mrs. Miles closed the door. "Want some wine?" Mrs. Miles was not all right. She opened the closet door and there was a half-gallon bottle of white wine. "Eric figured I'd need it. It beats jello."

Riann giggled.

We talked of pleasantries, the three of us, and drank wine, the two of us. Mrs. Miles was more tense than I had ever seen her.

"Dr. Verdi gave me some Valium. He said I have to be more accepting, more placid. But really I can't any more." She stopped. It was hard to remember Riann's presence sometimes. Mrs. Miles did pretty well. "Old nervous Mommy," she laughed and got up and put her arms around the little girl in the bed. "Good old Valium. They're better than my sleeping pills, Ri!"

"Yes!" Riann laughed. She began to tell the story again. How last summer after her first operation her mother was spending the night with her in the hospital. They were going to say prayers before bed. "But Mommy had taken a sleeping pill. They really work fast, I guess, because she kept falling asleep on the edge of my bed . . . in the middle of prayers! I would say, 'Mommy, it's your turn,' and she'd say, 'Let's pray silently tonight.' But I was sure she was falling asleep. And then she'd just keep saying how much she loves me, over and over again. I told her I love her, too; but she'd start all over again. I thought maybe she was sick or something. I almost called the nurse."

"But Mommy finally got to bed, didn't she, Ri? Dumb old Mommy," Mrs. Miles laughed again.

"Yes," laughed Riann, "she finally got to bed. But it really was a strange night." It was the third time, at least, that Riann had told me that story. I was to hear it several times again.

"Ri, is it OK if Nina and I get some coffee for a little? Will you rest? Then Mommy will come back and tuck you in."

"All right. See you later, Nina." We gave each other a big kiss.

Mrs. Miles told me how frightened she had been today. "I was sure this was it. Sure! She was *so* sick. She threw up the whole way here. I went through the whole thing in my mind, trying to accept, trying to resign myself that she was dying—now. I fell off the ledge . . . the whole way down. And I don't have the energy to pull myself up again. I just don't. Not knowing I'll have to go through it all over again. Someday. Soon . . . ?

"I'm glad she's alive, you know that," she went on, scrunching back on the three-north corridor window ledge; "you know what I mean. But to watch her be *so* sick, and know it still isn't the end. Will it be worse than this? Will she be in agony? Will she lie there like that little girl last winter—what was her name, in 378?''

"Pat Allen?''

"Pat Allen; that's it.''

"I was hoping you hadn't seen her.''

"I wish I hadn't. She was right across from Riann in December.''

"Her tumor wasn't the same kind.''

"I know. But I still see her lying there . . .''

So did I. But I didn't say that.

Mrs. Miles clenched her fingers. "I just want to ask 'Why, God? Why do this to her? Why do *this*? Why the agony?' It's not fair!'' She paused. I waited.

"You know,'' she went on, "it's an awful thing to say, but I guess I'm just mad at God right now. Really angry. That's an awful thing to admit, and I'm sorry . . . But I can't help it. That's the way I feel.''

That was it. On that window ledge that winter February Sunday, that was it. It all crashed together in my mind—Mrs. Felini: "Pray he'll die,'' bitterly; Alex: "But I hope you can understand . . . it still makes me mad''; Mrs. Miles: "Really angry.'' It was the missing link, the unacceptable, the negative feeling that no "moralizer'' had the right, or the ability when all was said and done, to strip away: Anger—at God—in the face of unbearable, unexplainable suffering.

Guilt, bargaining, disbelief, depression—they are all normal feelings as long as they don't last an abnormal length of time and overcome the emotional balance of their subject. But anger—anger at God: It is there when everything else is stripped away, in the basement of the human gut.

It is an anger that asks, "Why am I human?'' and "Why can't I stop what's happening?'' and "Why don't I understand?'' And it's an anger that says, "If I were God and I loved Riann the way everyone says You do, You can damn well bet I wouldn't let this happen to her!''

I wanted to shout, "Look! Revelation! I put some pieces together! I understand something! I see a truth—for me; something that makes sense!'' But the words that came out of my mouth sounded calm, as if I had said them a thousand times before.

But I hadn't.

"This may sound strange," I said, "but I'm glad you said that, about being angry at God. It's a normal, healthy reaction. It's focusing all your frustrations and mixed feelings where they really belong . . . saying, admitting, 'I'm helpless; I want to change things and I can't; but you can, God, so why don't you?!' There may be a part of you that never will be totally without anger at God. I don't know. But it's better than being angry at family or friends or doctors or other people. God can take it; he understands."

"Then I am normal? It isn't wrong, this feeling? I've felt it for a long time . . . but I didn't want to admit it. I mean, you're not supposed to get angry at God . . ."

"Jesus did." Where did that come from, I wondered? I hadn't been thinking it. Not at all.

Her eyes widened. Her mouth opened. She knew when. It had struck her, too. The Revelation. The truth that her feelings were justified. Her humanness, her personhood, was of value to God—her total personhood, including anger. Jesus Christ, in his death, among his dying words, had justified her in this moment.

For the first time in my life I *felt* Revelation. No, I can't explain it in words. And that, of course, gives validity to the reality of the "mystery." I had *read* about God in Jesus Christ participating in the human experience, participating in suffering, knowing rejection, knowing aloneness, knowing pain, knowing fear, knowing *anger*—anger at God? I had *read* it; but it had not been Revelation. Until now.

"Believe first, then you will understand." Dr. Davies had repeated it again and again. "Respond first, and then you will find . . . you will find that you already have been found."

I had believed. I had responded. I had read. But only now had I understood . . . just a fragment . . . a meteor—beautiful, bright, swift—blazing through the dark sky, then gone. But not gone.

A Revelation; a pinpoint of understanding never to be forgotten, nurtured and bundled in belief.

"I remember; you're right!" Mrs. Miles said. "It was just

before he said, 'Father, into thy hands I commit my spirit.' Jesus did get angry! He did ask God why he had forsaken him . . . And Jesus was our example, wasn't he . . . ?''

"Yes, he was." We didn't say any more, just sat on that window ledge. I'm not sure what she was thinking, but my mind was racing on . . . on . . . talking it out with myself. Yes, Christ was our example, a human being, participating in that which is human—pain, suffering, anger, and death . . . even death. Christ was God's own Son, and God didn't even save him from dying. Sure Jesus was angry—not with vindictive anger, but with an anger that claimed the very intensity of his being; which is what I realized Mrs. Miles was doing—claiming the very intensity of her being, her humanness. But she *wasn't* saying she felt *hopeless*. And Jesus wasn't either, when he asked "My God, my God, why hast thou forsaken me?" He didn't say, "God, I can't go on anymore." He didn't simply *stop talking*, as so many people do as they slip into the isolation of hopelessness. He cried out with a *"me"* . . . a "how could You do this to *me*?" Just as Mrs. Miles was doing, really.

But in the very object of the question, the very object of the anger—in God—came the *hope*, the knowledge of a love that "had been."

My mind wouldn't stop now. The fragment of Revelation was taking hold.

We don't get angry with someone for seeming to forsake us if we haven't been loved by that someone to begin with. And we don't get angry at all—and tell them so—if we don't have hope that that love still exists.

And the climax of this was on the cross. It is the mystery of grace, the mystery of faith, the mystery of God's unconditional love that will conquer all in the end that crept in in those moments on the cross between, "My God, my God, why hast thou forsaken *me*?" and "Father, into *thy* hands I commit my spirit."

It was Jesus' choice. God didn't dazzle him into it or manipulate him into it. And Jesus didn't say, "God, I'm sorry I got angry." It was *despite* his anger, *despite* his unanswered question, that Jesus chose not to go it alone.

Somehow, in those moments, Jesus realized the responsibility of his freedom. He realized in those moments that it wasn't up to God to choose him—God had already done that; but that it was now up to him to choose God, to claim in faith the love that stood beyond his anger, beyond his humanness, beyond his powerlessness, beyond his question that *remained unanswered*: "My God, my God, why hast thou forsaken me?"

Jesus Christ died on the cross, but his life, given to God, did not end. For in the final moments, in the darkest, deepest, cruelest, most painful moments—moments in which he had claimed, in anger, the very intensity of his being, and proved in fact that he was truly human—Jesus freely chose to return his spirit to God. And God, freely given back his power, snatched life from death eternally. The *"me"* became *"thy"* and death became life in God.

And, I thought, today that same choice is up to you, Mrs. Miles, and to me, and to each of us. That's what our freedom as human beings is all about. I believe God loves each of us without condition, no matter what we ever do or say or think or feel, no matter what. His grace is not "cheap grace," but it's *free* grace, given freely in love. And we are free to accept that love, respond to that love—"Father, into thy hands I commit my spirit"—or reject that love and try to go it alone. It's up to us.

I breathed. Something had made sense. I had caught it. I wouldn't forget.

The look of Revelation was still in Mrs. Miles's eyes. "My God, my God, why hast thou forsaken me?" and "Father, into thy hands I commit my spirit." That was all she had needed. And, after all, it is enough. That is it, those two feelings: "me" giving way to "thy." When we scrape away everything else—everything—that's what we as human beings, as Christian human beings, have left: anger and acceptance; anger and the free choice to respond . . . beyond our unanswered questions, to God's everlasting, unconditional love. "Me" becomes "thy" and we are safe and free and upheld in more than our finite dreams can imagine.

It was quiet in the hallway. The lights were dim and the courtyard beneath the window was dark and full of snow. Only the whir of a floor polisher in a distant corridor could be heard.

Reading words is vital. But alone, it's not enough. Meditation on written words is good. But alone, it's not enough. At least for me it was not enough.

Do when you don't want to do.
Go when you don't want to go.
Plod through the snow.
Kick fresh clumps of frozen white.
Wrestle with cold and wind.
Go when you don't want to go . . . and when you least expect
it, you may glimpse through the open door to Revelation. That
was my lesson that cold February night several years ago . . . a
winter night above other winter nights.

Sometimes, when you experience a certain feeling, do you
believe that everyone around you is feeling the same thing? I
had wondered that about Riann's mother late that same Sunday
night. Just because I had put pieces together in my mind that
evening did I just imagine that she had too?

"I had to thank you for last night." The phone had rung early
Monday morning. "All of what you said meant a lot. But the
part about Jesus being angry, and then putting himself into God's
hands anyway . . . That's what I remember most. I talked with
my sister in California last night after you left and told her. It
meant a lot to her, too."

Yes, I was embarrassed in a strange way. But yes, I was glad
Mrs. Miles had called. It was something I needed to know, an
affirmation of a feeling, an affirmation of a direction, an affirmation of meaning and interpretation. An affirmation.

Maybe Jesus was reciting the twenty-second Psalm. "My
God, my God, why . . . ?" But wasn't the psalmist angry, too?
And why *that* Psalm? Why else if it was not indicative of his
mood?

24

THERE'S AN ANECDOTE I forgot to tell earlier about Manuelito Cerci's mother.

One day after Manuelito's surgery we were sitting in the waiting room talking. Mrs. Cerci interjected suddenly, with a very puzzled look on her face, "What is an ascidulator?"

"A what?"

"An ascidulator?"

"I've never heard of it; I don't know," I shook my head and shrugged my shoulders. "Can you spell it?"

"No . . ."

"Can you use it in a sentence? Sentence . . . ?"

"Ah, si. Doctor, come in Manuelito's room. Smile. Examine Manuelito. Smile. Ask one, two question. Smile. Say 'ascidulator.' "

I paused for a moment to let the sentence sink in . . . then burst out laughing. So did two mothers sitting there. Mrs. Cerci looked puzzed. "I'm sorry," I apologized, still gasping for air. "It's an American saying. Four [I held up four fingers], four words. 'I'll—I will—[she nods] see you later.' In other words, the doctor will return again sometime soon."

"Oh! I see," said Mrs. Cerci, relieved. " 'I'll see you later!' " She laughed now too.

* * *

Sometimes it's a good thing our minds protect us enough that we can't think about what we're doing as we're doing it. Afterwards, yes; but not during.

It was that way for me the two weeks Riann died. If I had stopped to think about *what* was happening, about what I was doing . . . stopped to think about it for very long . . . I wonder if I could have done it. Even now, nearly a month later, my mind will let me *feel* only a little bit. I can recite what happened. But I still can't feel the total impact.

I'm glad for that.

It was Thursday, the Thursday before Easter. I had seen Riann, had spent the day with her, just one day earlier. Now she was in the hospital, dying. She would not go home again.

I had a sandwich, a Coke, and a television set—it was one of those evenings. My telephone rang at seven P.M. It was a nurse from three-north. Riann had been admitted.

She went on to describe her condition. But I stopped hearing with the word "admitted." It was as if I couldn't find a place in my brain to absorb the additional information. It just kept tumbling around with no home.

I finally asked the nurse to stop talking a minute.

"I just saw her yesterday, spent the day with her." I repeated it.

"Yes?" she said. "Well, she's here now and she doesn't look good at all. I just thought you'd want to know."

"Thank you."

I hung up. I went back to my sandwich, my Coke, and my television. The information was still tumbling about. No home.

The phone rang again, ten minutes later. I hadn't moved. It was another nurse from three-north, the same information.

"I just thought you'd want to know. I told Mrs. Miles I would call you."

"Thank you."

Back to the TV, the Coke, and the sandwich.

I decided not to go to the hospital that evening. The second nurse, Jennifer Bradford, had said she didn't think Riann would die that night. And with both her parents there, I didn't want to be the "minister of death," hovering. That was my rationalization. But I don't know if it was my reason. Maybe I just couldn't absorb it. Maybe I couldn't accept it. The *now*ness.

The other shoe had dropped.

It was just one day earlier, Wednesday, that we had had such a good time, Riann and her mother and I.

But I saw then that she had weakened, considerably, since I had seen her before their trip to Jamaica. Her right eye teared a lot and her right side drooped and she was terribly, terribly thin, wasted.

But nonetheless, she was happy—unbelievably happy. From the time I walked in that Wednesday she didn't stop talking. She had on a little blue and white jersey dress and a bow in her hair and heavy brown Buster Brown shoes and white socks. She was sitting propped up in the corner of the red and green sofa in the playroom. She had thrown up her lunch just before I arrived and she was afraid I would notice the smell on her breath when I kissed her.

"Nope, I can't smell a thing. [I couldn't.] And besides, you don't think a thing like that would keep me from kissing you, do you?!"

She giggled.

She had her program all set, things she wanted to say and do. First, she wanted to give me the gift she had brought from Jamaica.

"Do you like to munch on things . . . like when you're concentrating on your work and you're not really thinking?" she asked.

"No, not usually?"

"Well, I just wanted to warn you not to munch on these!" She handed me some seed and nut beads wrapped in tissue paper. " 'Cause they're poison!" she giggled.

"Oh! I'll remember! Riann, they're really pretty!" I put them on and gave her a big kiss.

Her mother had fixed us a drink and was sitting on the chair next to me at the other end of the sofa.

"Thank you again for the beanbag chair," Riann continued with the next thing on her agenda. "We tried to get me in it, but I guess I'll have to wait until I can bend a little better! But I really love it a lot. I can hardly wait to tell Dr. Verdi that I have *my own* beanbag chair and I don't have to sit in his any more!''

Giggle. Giggle.

Talk about the ironies of life . . . I had ordered the red bean-bag chair for Riann for Valentine's Day. Not that her parents couldn't afford it. Not that she'd get a lot of use out of it. But simply because it was *doing* something to make her happy, to add a little bit.

Twice at least she had mentioned how much she wanted a beanbag chair ''like Dr. Verdi's.'' She had said it to me in con-versation; not as a hint—she wasn't like that—just as a stream of consciousness. I happened by one in a department store in late January and decided to order it for Riann for Valentine's Day. *Then* she still could have sat in it, enjoyed it a little bit more . . .

But it didn't come. And it didn't come. The saleslady had casually promised delivery in ''five days.'' That would have been February 4. This was April, nearly mid-April. When weeks dragged on I asked the saleslady to telephone me when it came in. I didn't want it delivered ''after the fact.'' On April 5 some-one called. ''Your red beanbag chair is in! Shall we deliver it? By the way, the card reads, 'Happy Valentine's Day.' Should we change it to 'Happy Easter'?''

''Sure, 'Happy Easter!' ''

I almost didn't have it sent. I sensed it wasn't very long. But what the heck. It wasn't Riann's fault she was dying.

The tickled look on her face that Wednesday was enough. She had enjoyed it. It was all hers, her very own.

But I wanted to wring someone's neck at that department store.

You can't buy it, can you? . . . Time . . .

''How was your trip?''

''That's next! I want to tell you about that, and then show you the pictures, and then read you a funny book, and then we'll have lunch, and then we'll go to school . . . if you want to, that is?''

''Sure.''

''Good!''

She did . . . everything. She told me about her trip and showed me the beautiful pictures and told me how Kevin and Eric "drank so much beer they got sick . . . especially Eric—he threw up! And Mommy said she could hear him and Kevin in the bathroom . . . and then trying to clean things up . . . and she laughed."

And she told about the calypso singer who sang about someone with a brain tumor in his head and how the doctor had to take it out and how she laughed and pointed to her head when he sang it and how everybody probably thought she and her family were "crazy!"

And she told me about her aunt Meg who came with them on the trip and how funny she was. And about the live animals on the lawn outside her Jamaica hotel room. And she showed me a "funny" picture of her waking up in the morning "still half asleep."

Then she read me *The Elephant and Grape Book*—all of it! Giggling and laughing and having fun, nonstop. I forgot she was sick. I forgot she was dying. We just had fun.

We had lunch, then put her wheelchair in the back of the station wagon and drove off to school. It was a small private day school that looked like a rambling old army barracks with atmosphere. Four little boys, about nine years old, ran out and gallantly helped lift Riann in her wheelchair up the few stairs into the school.

We went into a "communications" room where the children were using various communication aids. Riann introduced me to her classmates as the "writer of the Clive stories." (She had taken one to school for the class to read.) She was still happy and cheerful.

Then we went into a room to watch a special television program on ballet. Riann was wheeled to the front and her mother and I sat in the back.

The television was terribly loud. It kept pounding and pounding in my ears. How could Riann stand it, I wondered, being so close?

But Riann was being bothered by something more than the television. Her tumor had changed, or moved, or done something . . . at least that's what must have happened . . .

A little boy came up to us. "Mrs. Miles, Riann wants you. She's upset."

The little girl was in tears. She wanted to go home. Her head hurt.

I was glad to get out of the loud room, but not when I saw Riann. It was unlike her. She was sobbing and sobbing and making sounds of pain. I got sick in my stomach.

We tried to get her parka on her. "My head hurts. Oh, my head hurts. It hurts." She sobbed and sobbed.

Finally we got her into the car. But the pain didn't stop. "It was probably the confusion," said her mother. "Too many people. She seems to get upset when she's around too many people all at once. Too much confusion. But I don't think I've seen it quite this bad," she added to me as she slipped into the front seat beside Riann.

I have never seen Riann upset by confusion, so I had to take her mother's word for it. But her cries certainly scared me. To me, she looked like she was in pain, in agony. I guess my face showed my fright to Mrs. Miles.

Riann sobbed all the way home. We tried to calm her, but we couldn't. I did notice some change in the sound, though. More from pain to a need to get settled, to be quiet. Maybe it had been that way all along, the confusion.

Whatever, she did stop crying, did calm down, when we got her home. Her mother carried her in to "Daddy's side of the bed" where she could "rest" a little. In a few minutes she seemed fairly comfortable.

"Could I please have my schoolbooks? My math?" she asked.

"Sure, darling." Her mother gave her her books. "Now you just rest. Mommy has to get the car pool. It'll only take a few minutes. But Nina will be here with you if you want anything."

She turned to me as we left the bedroom. "I know it sounds awful, but I have the car pool today and the kids are waiting right now. There's no way to get anyone else. I'm sure she'll be all right. She's calm now. I'll be back in ten minutes. Do you mind?"

"No! Go ahead; I understand. We'll be fine."

My knees went weak. I went back into the bedroom.

"How do you feel?"

"OK, thank you. My head feels much better."

"Can I get you something?"

"No, thank you. I'm just working on my math. I have more

trouble with math. I don't know why. Are these right?" She showed me some addition. Thank goodness it wasn't "new math"!

"Yes, all but this one. Three and three and three equals eight, doesn't it?"

She hesitated a minute, then broke into a wide grin. "You're funny! It's nine!"

"Oh, I'll be! Well, I never was good at math, either."

She giggled.

"I'll let you rest. If you want anything, I'll be in the den, just call." (The den was next to the master bedroom, where Riann was.)

I just made it to the sofa before my knees gave out. I sat for a few minutes, then found the liquor cabinet. There are times when liquor *is* medicine, and this was one of them. I drank a glass of white wine and sat with clenched muscles, listening.

But all went well, Mrs. Miles was back in ten minutes. She found Riann comfortable and resting. "No more headaches."

Neither of us could talk for a bit. She was as shaken—or more so—than I.

A few minutes later Riann wanted to get up. So her mother wheeled her to the den for a bit, then into the playroom to join her little sister, who had returned from school a few minutes earlier. (I can still see Riann sitting in that wheelchair by the den door, in her little blue dress with the matching bow in her hair. But her face was not the same. She was holding back pain. I'm not saying that because I know what happened the next day. I knew it then. The pain showed through.)

Finally Mrs. Miles and I had about ten minutes to relax, to unwind a bit. But we still were in shock, I think.

When Mr. Miles came home I realized for the first time how late it was. The three of us talked for a few minutes, then Riann was wheeled out to the front door to say good-bye. The look of pain was still there.

I thanked her for a nice day, said I hoped she felt better, and wished her a happy Easter.

But tears formed in her eyes. "She doesn't want you to go," said her mother. "Good-byes are getting harder and harder for her.

"Wish Nina a happy Easter, dear."

She did. But it didn't come out well. She kissed me and her eyes were heavy with tears. Then she looked away.

I felt empty, strange. I hadn't expected it. Maybe she knew about tomorrow. Maybe she knew the whole thing, and we were fooling ourselves. Maybe she really did know she was dying. Maybe she was just too kind to tell us, to drag us through it . . .

Or maybe it was just the pain. Or maybe just not wanting to see a good day end.

We'll never know.

25

I GOT UP at eight A.M. on Good Friday. I could have been at Children's, in Riann's room, by nine-thirty. But I moved like wet cement, holding back. An unrealness had set in. I was operating by radar.

Finally dressed and ready, I decided to stop by my church on the way—not to attend the noon Good Friday services—but just to sit, quietly.

But in my church there was nowhere to sit quietly, not after about five minutes. The ushers started arriving in the old gothic sanctuary and their echoes of greeting rolled down the empty rows and bounced off the concrete walls. They bustled about, being efficient.

Of course it was normal.

But my world wasn't normal any longer. It had changed . . . like never quite before. Someone I loved was dying.

I couldn't stand the "normal" noise. I went to a small chapel, one recently redecorated in polychrome and beauty. Here it would be quiet. I could think.

But someone was practicing the organ. It wasn't fair! It was my church! Why couldn't I find quiet in my own church?

There is no such thing, of course, as "my own church."

Riann was in room 381, the room she had been in when she had her second operation, the morning she waved "Bye, Nina," the morning the "play lady" and I had come early, the morning just over one year ago.

I knocked on the closed door. "Come in." It was a whisper, as the knock had been.

Inside it was dark, the shade pulled, the lights off. Riann's mother was there with two neighbors. All was hushed.

"Hi, come in. Riann just fell asleep. She had a bad night. Here, give me your coat. You remember Mary Alice Krider and Betty Armstrong?"

"Yes, hi," I whispered. Then I had a chance to look at Riann. I went numb. She was lying on her left side. Her spine and her neck were arched back so drastically that she formed a "C." Her knees were bent up. "She can't straighten them," her mother said. "She can't straighten anything. She can't get her head any farther forward than that. Dr. Verdi says it's the pressure from the tumor."

"Oh."

Riann was wearing a pink and blue checked flannel nightgown with a ruffled bodice and ruffled sleeves. She looked so frail, like a sleeping flower. The change in two days was overwhelming.

There was no doubt she was dying.

The only questions now were "How long?" and "How much worse?" and "How much pain?" and "How much agony?" The same old questions. Only now the answers were coming. The "when?" had become "now."

It was 12:45 P.M. Mrs. Miles asked me if I had had lunch. "Yes." (I hadn't, but I didn't want any.)

"Mary Alice has to go soon. She and I were going to go down and get some lunch and Betty was going to stay with Riann, but now that you're here, would you mind? That way Betty can come now and then she can get home too. She's been here— they both have, bless their hearts—all morning. Can you stay for a while? Or do you have somewhere to go, too?"

"No, I'm fine. I have no plans. I'll stay with Riann now. You go on to lunch."

"You're sure you don't mind?"

"No, not at all."

"I don't think she'll wake up. She needs some sleep. She was awake with me most of the night."

"OK."

"If anything happens, we'll be in the coffee shop, Dr. Verdi thinks it will be soon, but not likely for a day or two . . ."

They left to get lunch. I sat on the chair by the bed and looked at Riann. I wasn't feeling anything.

As I had opened the door I had wondered if it would be the same, our closeness—or what I felt was our closeness—now that the chips were down. Or would the family draw inward? It was possible. I was prepared to sense it, to leave gracefully, to not intrude.

But it wasn't that way. When I walked into that dark room that Good Friday afternoon, I became part of the process. And from that point on, I was unable to think about *what* was happening. I was just there. The mind is a fantastic protector at times . . . a friend.

I looked at Riann and didn't feel anything. Maybe it was shock. But I was numb. I just sat on the wooden chair looking at her face through the metal bed railing.

She opened her eyes. "Hi, Nina." She smiled.

"Hi, Riann. How do you feel?"

"OK, I guess. Where's Mommy?"

"Your mommy and Mrs. Krider and Mrs. Armstrong went to get a bite of lunch. Do you want me to call her? She should be back in a few minutes."

"No, that's OK. When did you come?"

"Oh, about a half hour ago. You were asleep. At least you weren't snoring!"

Giggle. "I bet you didn't expect to see me again so soon!"

"No, I sure didn't! I like to see you, mind you; but couldn't we pick a better spot than here?"

Giggle. "Yeah, you're right! Could I please have some water? Mommy had some in a cup with a syringe."

"Oh, I see it. It looks warm. Do you want me to get some fresh, with some ice?"

"That would be nice. Thank you."

I got some ice water in the ice room at the end of the hall.

"I had trouble with the straw last night, so Jennifer suggested Mommy use the syringe. It works much better, doesn't it?"

"Yes, that was a good idea."

(The "syringe" was just that, just like ones attached to shot needles, only without the needle and bigger than the average syringe. Instead of the needle, there was a small hole at the end. Liquids could be drawn into the syringe and then pushed back out through the hole and into the patient's mouth by depressing the sliding center stopper—just like a shot. It did work well. But what a weird thing to be doing . . . dropping water into Riann's mouth through a syringe. One more human dignity out the window. But she didn't seem to mind. She just accepted it as fact. No complaints. If she could accept it, I guess I could.)

"That's enough, thank you. That was good. Did you know that Jennifer went to Jamaica this morning?"

"Yes. She's really lucky!"

"I hope she has as nice a time as we did there."

"I do too. I'm glad you had such a nice time."

"So am I. I want to go back someday. It was so pretty. What time is it please?"

"Just about 1:30."

"Clive is here. Do you see him?"

"Yes. Who's his friend?" A stuffed doll in a pink plaid dress sat smiling beside Clive on the window ledge.

"Oh, that's Mrs. McPatches. I've had her for a while, too. A friend of mine has one just like her, only hers has brown hair."

"She's cute."

"Thank you."

I was amazed at her conversation. Granted, it was weaker and slower than I had heard before, but it was still Riann. The tumor hadn't gotten to her mind, to her disposition.

"I didn't sleep too well last night. My neck sort of hurt. Maybe I'll try to go back to sleep now."

"OK, that's a good idea. I'll be here if you want anything. And Mommy will be back soon."

She fell asleep. I sat on the wooden desk chair that Mrs. Miles had placed by the side of her bed.

All the private rooms at University Children's were much the same, reasonable in size and reasonably well furnished. As you walked into Riann's room, there was a bed to your left, its head-board in the middle of the left wall. Next to it on the same wall was a daybed which lined the wall lengthwise and flush. In the daytime it served as a sort of sofa, with a wooden built-in back-rest that opened to reveal a pillow. Opposite the door was a window. An orange vinyl chair with matching stool sat underneath. A radiator was behind the chair. Directly to the right of the doorway was a closet, then a natural wood desk and matching chair, and finally the bathroom door, all three along the same right wall. The bathroom was white tile and contained a sink and toilet.

The walls were yellow. A six-inch strip of flowered paper ran around the top edges of the walls, next to the ceiling. The spread on the daybed was green. Riann's junior bed was shiny chrome. Its top and bottom adjusted up and down by turning knobs underneath. Above the bed against the wall were several lights and a nurse-call button. Behind the orange vinyl chair was a floor lamp. And over the desk was a framed picture of children at a carnival.

I knew Riann would die here, in room 381. When? Today—Good Friday? Tomorrow? Easter Sunday? Somehow it seemed the ordeal wouldn't last beyond Easter. Symbolic. I guess I wasn't the only one thinking that.

"Wouldn't you know it would be Holy Thursday, Good Friday, Easter," said Mrs. Miles about an hour later when we were sitting in the room talking. Riann was still asleep.

"I thought about that," I said.

"I've thought about it a lot. It really brings home what you and I were talking about last February. It's almost like God planned it this way.

"She's much better now than she was last night, though," Mrs. Miles continued. "She really looked awful, and had a lot of pain in her neck. But they aren't going to let her have pain any more; not if they can help it. Dr. Verdi promised me that.

"But they aren't going to do anything extra, either. Just let the inevitable happen as quickly as possible. I can't stand to see her like this. I don't want to keep her any longer if this is the price she has to pay."

The acceptance was there. For the duration, there were no more questions. Not for either of us. We had worked it through. I knew I had. And now I knew she had, too.

Grief and emptiness and the real realization of the magnitude of what had happened—to Riann, to us—would come. It wasn't all cut and dried. But from now until she died we each knew we'd make it.

   . . . If it just didn't take too long.

   . . . Or bring uncontrollable pain.

   . . . If . . .

Mrs. Miles was exhausted. Dr. Verdi had told her to go home, to spend Friday night at home. He said he didn't think Riann would die that night.

She wanted to. But still she was afraid to leave, afraid to leave Riann alone.

This time it was different. This time we were close enough, had shared enough—Mrs. Miles and Riann and I—that I could offer.

"I'd like to stay."

"Oh, we couldn't ask you to do that. If she's like last night, you won't get any sleep at all."

"I'm prepared for that. Please. I want to."

"Well, Dr. Verdi doesn't want me to stay. He said if I start staying at night, soon—if there is a soon—I won't be any good at all, for Riann or the other children or Eric or me—or anybody. I hate to leave her . . . But I suppose he's right.

"But do you *really* want to? I'm sure the nurses will look in on her often. That's asking a lot, for you to stay. I know you won't get much sleep."

"Don't worry about me. I had today off from work so I was able to sleep later this morning, and I can go home tomorrow afternoon and go to sleep."

"OK, if you're sure. I would feel a lot better . . ."

"I'm sure."

I took a bus home, picked up a nightgown and toothbrush and a pair of slippers and returned to Children's. Mrs. Miles was going to leave with Mr. Miles soon after he arrived at the hospital from his office. If they had gone by the time I returned, she said, they would leave a note if there was any new information.

It was warmish out and sort of humid that April Good Friday evening. The world looks different when your eyes are not only yours, but surrogate for someone who is dying. I looked at the Lake. It was glassy blue dissolving into a pink sky. Boats weren't out yet, and the Lake lay undisturbed in the setting sun's reflection. Riann would never see it again; not see the boats this summer, not make her second trip to Jamaica, not see another squirrel, or bird . . . or grow up to love a man . . .

Well, most of the time I didn't think about *what* was happening . . .

The Mileses had gone when I returned to Children's. I opened the door to room 381. The bright light over Riann's bed was on. But I didn't see Riann.

A knife slashed through my stomach. Tiny needles pricked my whole body.

Finally I moved closer. She was there, sleeping! But the bed had been turned around so her head was now where her feet had been that afternoon. She was all covered up, a blanket was over the head railing, and since her knees were bent, all I had been able to see from the door was the empty bottom of the bed!

I sat down . . . on the edge of the orange vinyl stool . . . a long time.

Riann was asleep. The overhead fluorescent lamp was very bright. But perhaps she had wanted it on? I left it.

I put my night things and trench coat in the closet and sat on the orange vinyl chair. I realized it squeaked each time it was sat upon, and I was afraid the noise would awaken Riann. But it didn't.

I sat for a long time without thinking, barely breathing. Just looking at Riann in her little pink and blue checked flannel nightgown.

She slept peacefully. So much so that I began to listen for her breathing. I couldn't hear it! What if she had died in those few moments I had been sitting on the orange vinyl chair? What if she had just stopped breathing?

I was frightened. I got up to look. Her chest was moving, up and down.

I carefully sat back down.

What if she had died? What then? It wasn't that I wasn't prepared. I think I was, as much as possible. But I didn't want her to. Not while I was there, alone. Selfish? Perhaps. But I still didn't want her to. Not while I'm with you alone, Riann. Please don't die while I'm with you alone . . .

"With you alone." Taken apart from the rest of the sentence,

that didn't make sense. And then it just didn't make sense at all.
For we were not alone, either of us. My panic lessened.

I looked at the little milk-white face, the little neck bent back
so far, the thick black lashes, the pink lips, the soft brown
hair . . . a fuzzy blanket over a brain tumor that was winning.
I looked at the sleeping child . . . and realized how close,
how very close she was to the answer, to knowing for sure
about God, about transcendence, about life . . . knowing the
secret . . .

> But when winter comes, my little one will *know* its secret
>   —Of life, of love, of rebirth,
> And winter will be *her* gift glorious.
>   For she will see Your face; while I still wait and dream
>   And cry on naked branches.

As I realized this in that quiet, blue-bright room, I sensed that
the agony, somehow, was worth it. No, it wasn't *my* agony, *my*
brain tumor, *my* suffering . . . *my* death.

But for a fleeting moment, part of me wished it was . . .
wished for the secret.

My mind reached randomly beyond my experience . . . "Just
think," I wanted to say to Riann, "soon you'll *see* God, soon
you'll know more than your mommy and your daddy and your
brothers and sister and I can wildly imagine . . . soon . . ."

The reality of pain was put aside for a sense of awe in those
moments in that room. Part of the awe was fear—fear that Riann
really would die soon, like that evening, that night. Part of the
awe was the mystery—the mystery of death, and life, and hereafter, and God. Part of the awe was faith—faith in a love that is
unconditional despite our unanswered questions, a love that
keeps its promise, a love that will *never* let us go . . . a love
that is God.

And in the face of that awe, in those first moments with Riann
that Friday night, the anger was gone. It was pushed aside,
pushed out. I *knew* there was a God who was good, and a
heaven—a hereafter where "there shall be no more death, neither sorrow, nor crying, neither shall there by any more pain:
for the former things are passed away." (Rev. 21:4, KJV) "And
they shall see his face; and his name shall be in their foreheads.

And there shall be no night there; and they need no candle, neither light of the sun; for the Lord God giveth them light: and they shall reign for ever and ever.'' (Rev. 22:4-5, KJV)

But then, when someone you love is dying . . . heaven is a reality . . .

No! It was more than that, more powerful than a not wanting to let go into nothingness. For me, through Riann, it was the assurance, confirmed again.

Other times and other places, the anger would return in my humanness. But hopefully, ultimately, I will not forget the assurance.

For I am persuaded, that neither death, nor life, nor angels, nor principalities, nor powers, nor things present, nor things to come, Nor height, nor depth, nor any other creature, shall be able to separate us from the love of God, which is in Christ Jesus our Lord.

[Rom. 8:38-39, KJV]

I don't know how long I sat in that orange vinyl chair. I don't know to what reaches my mind roamed. I do know you must respect those moments if you respect me. For I was journeying on untried soil. And as I write this I discover that the mystery is aided in its preservation by the inadequacy of words. Fortunately, we can grasp more than words can describe.

More than one year now has passed since Riann died. Most of the preceding pages were written long ago. And they have remained unchanged, a testimony to edges of feeling and to the embryo chaplain, and as a reminder of the worth of discovery.

But despite the passage of time, I find that these last pages are to be written from a memory still almost too personal to commit to type. I have put off these pages until time has run out. They must be written. But I shall deny the task while doing it.

I had thought that with time writing about Riann's death would become less personal. But it hasn't. I do not yet want to share it with you. But I must trust you enough to trust that you will understand. Though, forgive me, I cannot yet believe you will . . .

* * *

Riann awoke. She said her mommy had told her I was going to spend the night and she was glad. Though she certainly hoped, for both our sakes, that she would be able to get more sleep tonight than she had last!

She decided she wanted the bright lights off. I was glad. And maybe she could eat some cherry jello. And then she would try to get some more sleep.

As I was feeding the jello to her she asked me why her leg hurt so. "It never did before; not like this . . ."

"I don't know for sure, Riann. Why don't you ask Dr. Verdi tomorrow? But I do know that while you've been sleeping you've kicked your knees against the metal bed railing a number of times. Maybe you just bruised yourself?"

"Maybe that's it . . ."

"Why don't I get some blankets and cover the railing where your knees are. Then maybe it won't hurt so much."

"That's a good idea . . . Kevin has a friend who has muscular dystrophy. He's in a wheelchair all the time . . . But he doesn't seem to mind. He's always happy . . ."

"That's good."

Later that night I wondered at her train of thought. Was she afraid *she* had muscular dystrophy? Was that why she went from her leg hurting to Kevin's friend? It hadn't struck me at all at the moment. Maybe I didn't want it to . . .

What if she did ask, I thought. *The Question:* "Nina, am I dying?" or "Nina, am I going to die?" God, help me. I tried to think of an answer. But I couldn't. I couldn't anticipate the setting, the circumstances. I would just have to grit my teeth and pray for the "right" words . . . if it happened.

Riann fell asleep. Slowly, I felt more free to move about quietly. I checked her breathing a bit less often. I wasn't quite as afraid the "baby would break if I picked it up," so to speak.

I telephoned Mr. and Mrs. Miles to tell them all was well— it's amazing what "relatively speaking" can come to mean— and went back to Riann's room. She was still asleep.

I changed into my night clothing and pulled down the covers on the daybed and got out the pillow. Only the night light was on in the room. A street lamp outside was pouring orange light through the window.

My interlude of mental floating was over. I was back to not

feeling, not thinking, just doing. I was beginning—though I didn't know it then—what was to become a routine.

Riann awakened as I was brushing my hair.

"Nina?"

"Yes, sweetheart?"

"Do you think there's any more cherry jello?"

"I don't know, but I'll check. Do you want anything else?"

"No, just that, thank you."

"OK, I'll be right back."

I put on my robe. The jello was there. I returned and began to feed her.

She was feeling better. It was obvious. "You know, when I was little one time Eric and Kevin and Allison and I went out and we were with my cousin and he ordered a hamburger and 'wrench-wries.' " She giggled. "He was too little to say 'french fries,' so he said 'wrench-wries.' So after that, when we were alone with just us, we always teased and said 'wrench-wries,' too. But we didn't tease him." She giggled again, remembering.

We talked and she ate her cherry jello and the street lamp watched.

"Nina, do you think I can get up tomorrow?"

I almost dropped the jello. "I hope so, Ri. We'll see how you feel. OK?"

"OK. I sure hope I can . . ."

"Me too."

A nurse came to turn Riann and straighten the sheets and wish her good-night. I slipped into the daybed.

She woke up several times afterwards, but all in all, she didn't seem to have too bad a night. When she did awaken it was from pain, in her neck. Usually, she would ask me to move her head or move her pillow or sometimes turn her. I felt OK about doing the first two, but I would call a nurse if she needed to be turned.

I slept, but lightly. I realized for the first time how a mother actually can sleep, yet hear her restless child in the next room. It's strange.

Riann would always say "thank you" and "please." Despite the pain, she would think to say "thank you" and "please"— to the nurses, to the doctors, to her family, to me, to everyone. She never forgot. Not once.

Saturday morning came "later" for Riann. The last time

she had awakened had been about 5:30 A.M. and now it was 8:30 A.M. and she was still asleep. Thank goodness! I got up about 7:30, sink-bathed, dressed, and went to the nursing station for some coffee.

I telephoned Riann's mother about eight o'clock and told her how the night had gone. She said she would come in about eleven and I said I would stay until then. We both agreed I didn't have to. But we both knew I would.

About an hour later, Riann took a turn for the worse. I was giving her some cherry jello for breakfast and she was in midsentence, saying that eating all this jello was like being on a diet. "But I love . . ." Her eyes slipped back in her head and her tongue shot out and back and her lips shook and her head and her right side jerked: a seizure. It scared the life out of me. I ran into the hall and called Mary Cooke, who was walking in my direction. She turned stark white and ran. She took one look at Riann. "She's seizing." She looked at her watch, and rubbed Riann's arm, and said, "It's all right, Riann, don't be frightened. It's OK."

She turned to me. "Scared you, huh?" I nodded. "They are scary. When did she start?"

"Just now."

"I think she's lost consciousness."

Riann kept on seizing. Five minutes. She seized nonstop for five minutes. Then she was fine.

"What happened?" Riann opened her eyes and asked a bit groggily.

"You had a little seizure," Mary explained. "But everything's OK. How do you feel?"

"A little funny, but OK. My tongue feels funny."

"That's from the seizure." Mary turned to me, quietly, aside, "I don't think in her position there's any danger of her swallowing her tongue. But I'll get you a wrapped depressor. If she does it again—and I have a feeling she will—just hold her tongue with it. It may help keep it from getting too sore. I'll get her medication in a syringe. You can give it to her with her breakfast."

It was scary. I hoped Riann wouldn't seize any more. She did. Five minutes later. For four minutes. But this time she didn't lose consciousness. And the tongue depressor annoyed her and scared her. "It's OK," said Mary. "I have a feeling her tongue will get sore regardless. She's not going to stop this."

(And she didn't. Soon, even it became routine. Sometimes Riann would even try to talk while seizing, try to finish a sentence. Her tongue did hurt, though. I would hold a cold wet rag on her lips while she seized. It seemed to help. Then we'd just pick up talking where we had left off. What else could we do?)

I didn't go home at all Saturday, to freshen up or anything. I don't remember details of the day, but I do remember that our tension mounted with the number of Riann's seizures. They had been a shock for Mrs. Miles, and a worse shock for Mr. Miles, who came in mid-afternoon. I left them alone with Riann.

About 5:30 P.M., as I was sitting reading in the small room behind the nursing station, Mrs. Miles came to the glass partition and motioned to me. "Eric is going across the street to bring back some martinis. Do you want one—or two?"

"Sure."

"Come sit with us while he's gone. You didn't have to leave, you know."

"I know. Thank you."

Ten minutes later, Mr. Miles returned with a dejected look on his face. "It's against the law. You can't take out drinks! I never knew that."

"Neither did I," Mrs. Miles and I said both at once.

They had brought Riann's dinner but she hadn't eaten much. Now she was asleep, had been for an hour or so, in between seizures.

"You know, let's all go out to dinner. Let's just go. We have to get away a bit." Mr. Miles was right.

"I'll ask Riann's nurse to keep a special eye on her," said Mrs. Miles. "She does seem to be sleeping well. And if she wakes up, the nurse can tell her Nina is coming back soon. Anyway, her nurse this evening is Cheri, and Riann really likes her. We *do* have to get out. All of us!"

I couldn't disagree. It was hard to go from quiet panic to unwinding to quiet panic to unwinding. Sooner or later you had to jump off the treadmill for a few minutes.

We went to a French restaurant and had our martinis—plural.

Definitely plural. And we talked. We went through a sort of eulogy and mourning and laundering of our nerves. We were on an island in the middle of land, unaware of our surroundings, yet using tools of those surroundings to help keep us in perspective. Life was still going on. At the backs of our minds somewhere, we remembered that.

When I returned to Children's, Riann still was asleep. Cheri said she had awakened several times, but seemed to be feeling better. Only three seizures. She had had some Coke and some cherry jello, too.

I got a book, crunched into the orange vinyl chair, and read.

"Nina, are you there?"

"Yes, Riann, I'm back. What is it sweetheart?" I got up.

"May I please get up?"

"Do you really feel like it, Ri?"

"Yes, please, in the wheelchair."

"OK, let me ask Cheri. We'll see what she says."

"You're kidding! She really wants to get up? I don't believe it!"

"Ask her yourself. I didn't believe it either."

It was a slow, painful process, but Riann finally was sitting up in her wheelchair—on top of two pillows and in front of two folded blankets for support. Her head tilted back far.

Cheri had put a pillow behind her neck for support. Riann's body would no longer bend to fit a chair.

But she was up! And it made her *so* happy . . . for about three minutes. Then the pain came—real, horrid pain, by the look of her face.

Cheri was just finishing changing the sheets on her bed.

"Nina, may I please get back in bed now?"

"Sure, Riann, right away. Does it hurt?"

"Yes . . ."

I could see how much in her eyes. Dammit! She was so happy, so proud that I could "tell Mommy and Daddy when you call that I was up in my chair!"

But what did I expect? *She was dying.* It wasn't false labor pains any more. But Riann just wouldn't give up her personhood without a fight—so much so that those around her could actually begin to forget the truth, could almost come to accept things like seizures as "routine." Good for her!

Do not go gentle into that good night.

. . . .

Rage, rage against the dying of the light.
[Dylan Thomas]

We got her back into bed. But it took a long time to get her comfortable. Finally, she was.

"Shall I call Mommy and Daddy now?"

"Yes, please. Tell them I was up . . ."

"I won't forget. That will be the first thing on the list. Do you want anything before I go?"

"No, thank you. I'll try to sleep."

"OK. Ri, that was fantastic, getting up that way. You really are brave." I kissed her.

"Thank you. I wanted to stay longer. But it kind of hurt. Maybe tomorrow . . ."

The Mileses were elated, and just as unbelieving as Cheri and I had been.

"I just can't believe it," said Mrs. Miles. "She's . . . dying . . . and she wanted to get up—got up!"

They asked for all the details. Eric and Kevin got on the extension to hear. A weird state of euphoria set in. Maybe Riann would live forever. That kind of feeling.

Eight thousand miles away, the Easter morning sun was rising in the Holy Land. And it was, for us, in that moment, as if Riann's spirit was taking over . . . as if she was showing us . . .

the ultimate meaning of that prodigious spiritual energy born of the Cross . . . A growth of spirit arising from a deficiency of matter. A possible Christification of suffering. This is indeed the miracle which has been constantly renewed for the last two thousand years.*

*From *L'Energie spirituelle de la souffrance* by Pierre Teilhard de Chardin, as quoted and translated by Christopher F. Mooney, *Teilhard de Chardin and the Mystery of Christ* (New York; Harper & Row, 1966), p. 114.

26

I DON'T REMEMBER much about that Easter other than that I didn't go to church. I have always looked forward to Easter for a conglomeration of reasons. But coming home in a cab that Easter Sunday just after noon, seeing all the people walking home from church, hearing the bells . . . It was like watching a movie.

I slept a long, long time—until about 11:00 P.M. Then I got up for an hour or so, and went right back to sleep.

Monday I packed fresh night clothes and went to the office. At some point I had talked with Paul, told him what was happening. He told me not to worry, to come to the office when I could and go to the hospital when I had to. He knew I would do my work sooner or later.

Mrs. Miles telephoned me at the office once or twice. Riann had had an all right night, but not great. I told her I would be at Children's about five-thirty. That's about when Mr. Miles would get there, too, she said, and they'd leave for Rock Shores soon after.

When I arrived, Riann was lying on the daybed. It was a change of "scene," and, I think, a bit softer than her own bed. Riann was very, very thin. I have no idea how much she weighed, but it couldn't have been much.

She was having her "dinner"—soup, Coke, ice cream and cherry jello. But a couple of bites of soup and the jello were the only things she had eaten.

Mrs. Miles explained that Riann had been so uncomfortable very early that morning that they had decided to try the daybed.

"And Mommy slept in my bed," Riann giggled.

"Yes," laughed Mrs. Miles. "And you'll never guess what my dear, sweet, little daughter said!"

Riann giggled again.

"What?" I asked.

"I asked Riann what would happen if Dr. Verdi came in and found me in her bed," said Mrs. Miles. "And my love over there said, 'Oh, that's all right, Mommy; he could just do brain surgery on you!' "

"Riann!" I exclaimed, playing along. "Your poor mother."

"Well," said Riann with a half-laugh, "all I know is he's not going to do it on me any more! Two times is enough!"

Yes, we agreed, two times is quite enough.

I could see that Mrs. Miles's nerves were scraped raw. The teasing and laughing, done for Riann's sake, had become higher pitched.

Mr. Miles arrived and I went to the cafeteria with some nurses for dinner. When I returned, the Mileses were ready to go.

"If there's any change, call," said Mrs. Miles as I walked with them down the hall. "And can you call around ten, regardless?"

"Sure, don't worry, I'll call."

"I didn't get much sleep last night . . . And I have a feeling you didn't either, on Friday and Saturday. Are you sure you still want to do this?"

"I'm sure."

"Well, we do feel better with you here. Dr. Verdi is amazed it has lasted this long . . ."

"Life has been happy for Riann," I said. "She's not eager to give it up. And that's a tribute to you two, to your family . . ."

Riann was in a good mood that Monday. She was still seizing, but not quite as often and not losing consciousness. Her tongue was raw, however, and giving her a lot of pain. We tried salves, but they didn't help much. (Of all the stupid things: dying of a brain tumor and having so much pain from your tongue, rubbed raw from seizing. Grief.)

There was a note for me on Riann's bulletin board. It was from Dr. Jenssen. She said Riann told her that when I had spent the night with her Saturday I had put some rollers in my hair, and that I "looked funny."

"Riann! This note from Dr. Jenssen says you told her I look funny with rollers in my hair! Shame on you!"

Giggle. Giggle. "Well, that's what you said, too."

"Well, I guess I did. But, gee, you didn't have to tell Dr. Jenssen!" I laughed.

"I wore curlers once . . . for my first communion."

"I saw that picture. Your hair was curled. You looked very pretty."

"Thank you. It was nice, my first communion . . . just before I got sick."

"Was that Natalie with you?" Natalie was Riann's cousin, next-door neighbor, and best friend next to her sister, Allison.

"Yes. She was in the picture you saw. We went together . . .

"You know, I don't know what to eat first when I get home. Mommy says we can go to the Japanese Village, too. I love it there!"

"Well, I'm sure you're not going to want any more cherry jello!"

"No, but I like it here. It tastes good."

"Do you want some now?"

"No, thank you, but maybe later."

"OK."

Riann was becoming less and less comfortable. She asked—always politely, but with great pain in her eyes and voice—to have her pillows "fixed" every fifteen or twenty minutes. After about three or four "pillow fixes" I knew, and she knew, that the only thing that would help would be to turn her. But it was *so* painful, so very, very painful.

By early Easter Sunday morning, with permission from the nurses, I had started turning her myself rather than call for help each time. Her mother had done the same. There was simply no medical trick to it. It was going to hurt, agonize, no matter what.

And Riann really couldn't help much in the turn. The only things she could move were her arms and hands, and even they were becoming stiff. Her neck and head were bent back farther and farther, nearer to the small of her back than to her chest.

Her knees were buckled up as far as they would go. Her mouth was chapped and sore and her body was covered with red marks from her thinly covered bones rubbing against the mattress.

But strange as this may sound, she was still beautiful. No, not just because I loved her. In all that pain, she was still beautiful, outside as well as inside. Her clear blue eyes had become huge—partly because her face was getting thinner and partly because her pupils were dilating (a sign of impending death). Her hair seemed thicker and her cheeks were pink.

But turning her, that was a problem. No, it didn't hurt her mother and me—literally hurt us—as it hurt Riann. But figuratively it did.

By late that Monday night, there was no way even to touch her, let alone turn her, without causing great pain. Yet, the pain from *not* being touched, not being turned, must have been greater still.

This particular time I had spent five minutes trying to "fix" her pillows, a large one and a small one. But it wasn't working. We knew . . .

"Ri, should I turn you?"

"Can we try the pillows just once more?"

"Sure, sweetheart, as many times as you want."

But it didn't work. Her face had that look of resigned fear, and I bit my lip. I was having trouble steeling my nerves for another turn, too.

"Ri, why don't I ask your nurse to turn you this time. Maybe she can do it better than me."

"OK."

I walked toward the door to call the nurse.

"Nina . . ."

"Yes, sweetheart?"

". . . not to be mean . . ."

I turned back and kissed her. "Riann, you couldn't be mean if you tried! When you hurt less, I hurt less. You haven't hurt my feelings!" I kissed her again. "I'll be right back with Cheri."

Once again, Riann had been unbelievable. In that much pain, and she had worried that she had hurt my feelings, had been "mean" by asking that her nurse try to turn her. Unbelievable.

Cheri turned Riann the next two or three times.

It was an hour or so later. ". . . Maybe you'd better turn me again."

"I'll get Cheri."

"Nina, you can do it. It doesn't make any difference."

"Are you sure? Cheri doesn't mind."

"I know, but it doesn't matter."

My stomach started to knot again. It's awful to try to help someone and know you're hurting them at the same time. I had been glad Cheri was turning her.

"It's going to hurt, you know . . ."

"Yes . . . I know . . ."

I had to laugh. "That was a kind of stupid thing for me to say, wasn't it, Ri?! I guess you do know."

Riann laughed a tiny, ironic laugh. "Yes . . ."

I turned her. It hurt. Naturally.

There really wasn't any medicine that would help Riann's pain beyond what she was already getting. The doctors tried, but nothing else helped much. Even her seizure medication didn't keep her from seizing. Other than simply drugging her out, there was nothing that could be done.

About midnight Riann decided she was "ready to go to sleep." Cheri came and put her back into bed from the daybed, again with much pain. We "fixed" her pillows and I turned out all but the night light.

"Do you want to try to say prayers, Riann?"

"Yes, that would be nice. Maybe I can make it . . ."

She had been seizing so much on Easter Sunday morning that all we had tried was the "Our Father," and even then she had had a seizure right in the middle of it. But she went on anyway, trying to finish the prayer. I told her God would understand. (A person ought to be able to get through the Lord's Prayer without seizing . . .)

"Do you want to go first?" I asked.

"OK. Dear God, thank you for a nice day. And it was a nice day, even if I was a little sick. God bless Allison and Kevin and Eric and Mommy and Daddy and Grandma and all my friends. Please make my tongue stop hurting. Please make me better so I can get out of here. I'm so happy that I got ten dollars from my cousin and an Easter basket. Even if I didn't get to the Easter egg roll or have Easter . . ."

She opened her eyes—the signal that it was my turn. I prayed. Then we said the "Our Father." Made it! No seizures!

Riann awakened more often Monday night than she had Friday or Saturday nights. But she did get some sleep. Once she awakened and wanted to play a game—"I spy." And another time, as the sun was coming up, she wanted me to read her the funny papers. I guess something reminded her of a Sunday morning at home.

At about 6:30 A.M. she and I both fell asleep, for over a whole hour! The neurosurgeons stuck their heads in on morning rounds at about 7:45, but I just pulled the sheet over my face.

Later, as I was drinking coffee at the nursing station and Riann was still asleep, Dr. Craig teased, "You certainly sleep late! What do you think this is, a hotel?" Dr. Craig came very close to having hot coffee all over his long, straggly brown hair and long, straggly brown moustache!

"You know what's happening, I think," he added. "Riann's getting her nights and days mixed. It happens a lot."

"Goody," I said. "Thanks for telling me. You're a delight first thing in the morning!"

"I know."

27

I THOUGHT RIANN was going to die Wednesday night. She was so sick. Not only was she seizing more often—at least every fifteen minutes—and not only was she in more pain, but now she could barely swallow and her lungs were full of mucus.

Her mother said that between seizures she had slept most of the day. And, true to Dr. Craig's prediction, she was awake most of the night. She could barely talk, and didn't much—just to ask about her pillow and turning.

They brought in a suction machine and suctioned her two or three times, but the pain must have been great each time. Once she was able to cough up a tremendous amount of thick, ugly, green-black mucus by herself. I was alone with her. I held Kleenex and held her head and encouraged her to keep coughing. It was awful—and my description is mild. But she really got a lot out.

If anyone had told me before the fact that I could have gone through this I never would have believed them. My stomach was sick for a long, long time. But Riann seemed to feel better.

It worried her that she couldn't swallow. She would try to eat cherry jello, but it would just stay in her mouth and squish around her teeth. Finally she gave up.

She didn't sleep all night. Neither did I. I was scared, really really scared.

But morning came. And Riann managed to swallow some soup.

184

I went to work, and counted the minutes until five o'clock, when I went home and slept.

Friday night she was better. She still had her days and nights mixed, still was awake all night. But this time she was more comfortable—relatively speaking. The seizures had lessened again, or maybe we were just accepting them more. Her tongue hurt less, or maybe it had just developed calluses?

She could swallow better, though her swallowing had a funny sound.

"It sounds like I'm swallowing bones . . . like a goat," she joked one time. It did, actually.

At three in the morning, just after a move from the bed to the daybed, we decided to read stories. Her neck was hurting. Maybe a story would take her mind off it.

We read—I read aloud—about "Flat Stanley," who somehow managed to become flat, which was nice because he didn't have to watch his weight and he could fit between the grating in the pavement to retrieve a ring his mother had dropped. But it wasn't so nice, either, because sometimes people laughed at him. However, true to all such stories, something wonderful happened and Flat Stanley became round again.

"Flat Stanley" was a funny story and Riann giggled a lot throughout. I hated for it to end. I read some others, but none was as funny as "Flat Stanley."

Later, back in bed, Riann looked over at the window ledge. Clive the Bookworm and Mrs. McPatches were sitting there, kind of facing each other. "Nina, look . . . Clive and Mrs. McPatches are getting to know each other." She giggled. It did look funny.

"You know, the other night, when you weren't here, I woke up and saw Clive in the middle of the night. I remembered that story you wrote about when Clive wanted to become a neurosurgeon. I pretended to picture him in the operating room saying, 'Give me a knife. Give me this . . .' That was a funny story." Giggle. Giggle.

Finally, at six A.M., she fell asleep. Me too. At eight o'clock Dr. Craig stuck his head around the door, saw me still in bed, and went, "Tsk, tsk." I stuck out my tongue, and pulled the sheets over my head.

It was Saturday morning, so I didn't have to go to the office.

I was up and dressed by nine. Riann awakened as I was straightening the daybed.

"Do you think you can sleep any more?" I asked, ready to get her breakfast if the answer was no.

"No, but I think I'll just loll in bed for a while."

"OK," I smiled. "You tell me when you want breakfast."

"I will."

She fell asleep again.

I went to the nursing station for coffee. I was really tired, and not quite as awake as I had thought. As I sat in the back room with my feet up and my second cup of coffee in hand, looking out toward the hallway, I saw a huge yellow bird walk by.

I put down the coffee cup with both hands and rubbed my eyes. It was still there. "I'm losing my mind," I figured. Then I realized that it was Big Bird from the "Sesame Street" television program. He and several other "Sesame Street" characters had come to visit children. I had to laugh at myself.

I went back to Riann's room. She opened her eyes as I went in. "Ri, do you ever watch 'Sesame Street'?"

"Sure."

"Well, I just saw Big Bird in the hallway. He's come to visit. Would you like to see him?"

"Yes! Please!"

"OK, I'll be right back."

I found Big Bird at the other end of the hall. I asked if he could come to room 381. I explained that Riann was "pretty sick," but that he could talk with her and ask her questions . . . just please not be too loud.

He was great. And Riann loved it. It really perked her up.

Then she asked me to pull down the window shade and she went back to sleep. After all, it was her night now.

I went to the cafeteria with one of the nurses for a cup of coffee.

When I returned, Riann's day nurse was giving her a thorough bed bath and changing her nightgown. That had to hurt. I couldn't watch. I was chicken. She couldn't have been that dirty. Why not let her alone? But I didn't know this nurse. I couldn't say anything.

When I saw the nurse leave, I went back in. Riann was lying on the daybed and she looked more beautiful than any time I saw her during those last days. She had on a very feminine little blue nightgown that matched her blue eyes perfectly. Her cheeks were pink and her lips were washed clean of the dried mucus. She did look much better . . . but she didn't feel better. I still don't know if it was worth it.

"Riann, you look so pretty!"

"I don't feel pretty . . ."

"I know sweetheart. It's miserable being back here again, isn't it?"

"It sure is. You know, Nina, I wish I could just snap my fingers and make it all go away . . ."

"I wish you could, too, Ri . . . I wish you could too . . ."

28

SATURDAY NIGHT I had an actual date! Nothing big, just dinner, a long, long dinner. But it was nice, so nice.

Sunday morning I went to church. Dr. Davies was preaching. It was like a shot in the arm.

"You look pale," he said after church. "And where were you last Sunday? I didn't see you."

"Riann Miles is dying. I've been spending some time with her."

"You watch it! You're too involved."

"Yes, but I love Riann. Why, how it happened, I don't know. But it's very hard not to love her, for anyone who meets her."

"Well, watch it!"

"Yes, sir."

We didn't talk farther about it. But I could tell in his eyes he understood.

He'll die, I realized once again, as I walked out into the blinding Sunday sunlight . . . long, long before I die, very likely. Will he ever know how much he's given me, in his sermons, in our long discussions? Will he ever realize how many sheep he's fed?

Are not all lifelong friendships born at the moment when at last you meet another human being who has some inkling . . . of that something which you were born desiring, and which, beneath the flux of other desires and in all the momentary silences between the louder passions, night and day, year by year, from childhood to old age, you are looking for, watching for, listening for?*

I went to brunch with David, who yelled at me, as usual. Good old David.

On Tuesday, a depression came over Riann. Her nights were still her days. The pains were still there. The seizures were still there. The fact that, for all practical purposes, she couldn't move had begun to set in . . .

"I don't know why she [the nurse] worried about putting the side of the bed up, I can't roll off . . . I can't move! Oh, I want to go home . . ."

It was said, that last sentence, with a hesitancy, a tone that said, "I know it will never be." Maybe that was my imagination. Maybe it was just that I had never heard Riann that depressed before, though I had often reminded her that she could feel free to tell me exactly how she felt, that she didn't have to "put on a happy front" if she didn't feel that way.

But nonetheless, the old fear came back that Tuesday. What if she asks *The Question*? What can I say?

Finally, I got up my courage. In all fairness, maybe she wants to talk, to get out how upset she is. Just don't let her ask The Question, please, God . . .

"You know, Riann, I've said before that I want you to complain whenever you want to with me. Anyone in the hospital has a perfect right to be in a bad mood now and then. I'm glad when you're in a good mood, mind you, but with Mommy and Daddy and me, we want you to tell us exactly how you feel, no matter what. OK?"

"OK."

"And Riann, today you sound awfully depressed, unhappy. Are you?"

". . . Yes. I just wish I didn't have this neck problem. It bothers me like crazy."

"I know it does, Ri. It doesn't seem fair, does it?"

"No . . . You know, when I was in the hospital before, I got

*From *The Problem of Pain* by C. S. Lewis. Copyright 1944 by The Macmillan Co. and used by permission.

so many stuffed animals . . . Mommy said someday we could give some to the poor . . . there are so many . . .''

At that moment the neurosurgeons came in on rounds. Riann's was their last room. I walked out with Dr. McMahan. ''You know, I'm afraid Riann knows she's dying.''

''Why?''

''Well, first of all, she's more depressed than I've ever seen her, which, of course, she has reason to be. And then, just as you guys were coming in, she commented on how, when she was here before, people sent her presents . . .''

''Sure, the old 'Dying Child Syndrome.' People are afraid to send cards and gifts . . . afraid they'll arrive 'after the fact.' A bright kid like Riann can figure that out fast . . . or at least begin to wonder.''

Later, on the telephone, I told Mrs. Miles about Riann's comment and Dr. McMahan's comment. She said the next day she would bring some things to brighten the room and hang some cards. It made sense. Or, it fed the denial. I'm not sure which. Maybe both.

But Riann still didn't ask The Question. Maybe we should have given her more chance. But I know I was too scared. Now, maybe I wouldn't be. I don't know. But then I was.

Tuesday night rivaled the previous Wednesday for Riann's lack of comfort. In desperation I probably asked Mary Katharine Soloman—who was a superkind, perceptive, and understanding nurse—at least five times for something to help Riann's pain. Anything! Usually, Mary Katharine just came and turned Riann or stood by her for a little while . . . or stood by me. Anyway, I was grateful for Mary Katharine that night.

All night long, every five or ten minutes, I would ''fix'' Riann's pillows, stand by her bedside to make sure it had worked, then tiptoe back to the daybed and slip under the sheets. At times I would pray that she would sleep—for just thirty minutes uninterrupted. Pray as much for my sake as hers. Now, it sounds selfish. Then, it was for sanity.

But the ''fixed'' pillows would last only five minutes . . .

''Nina . . .'' Very softly.

''Yes, sweetheart?''

''I'm sorry, but my neck . . . my pillows . . .''

''It's all right, Riann. You call any time, sweetheart. I mean that. I don't mind. The most important thing is for you to be comfortable."

"Thank you."

It was the most important thing. That's why I jumped up each time without hesitation. But it didn't keep me from dreading to hear the call, gripping my fingernails into my flesh, trying to race to see if my muscles and nerves could relax even the slightest before she would call again.

But she couldn't help it. I kept reminding myself. I would have months to rest, years to relax my muscles. Who would I rather be in those moments of pain, Riann or me? That was the question that kept me going. For her, now was the rest of her life. For me, it was a few nights of no sleep. The comparison—that's what did it.

"Nina . . ."

This time it took an hour. One hour. And I'm not exaggerating in the least. One hour of "fixing" the pillows, turning her, moving her to the daybed and then back to bed. Nothing was working. I wanted to scream. I'm sure Riann did, too.

Finally, we hit the right combination. Her relief was genuine. "That's it! That's it, that's perfect! Thank you."

"Good, fantastic!" I kissed her and stood there a moment. But she didn't say, "No, wait a minute . . . could you please try again . . ." All was quiet.

I crept back to the daybed. Slipped under the covers.

"Nina . . ."

Oh, no . . . no . . . Oh, no . . . "Yes, Riann?"

"Have a good night's sleep."

29

FRIDAY I HAD to go to New Jersey. I had known all along I would have to go.

An emeritus professor from my divinity school, Professor Beaver, was now director of a missionary study center near Atlantic City. He had asked me to speak at a seminar. The center would pay my way.

I had planned the mini-vacation well. First, from Friday evening until Monday morning, I was going to visit close friends, Nancy and John Miller, in Morristown, New Jersey, where John is pastor of the Presbyterian church. Then Dr. and Mrs. Beaver were going to pick me up in Morristown and drive me to their home. I was to speak there Tuesday, then go home to Maryland on Wednesday to visit my parents through the weekend.

I had been looking forward to it. It would be good to see my parents, and, I hoped, my Aunt Helen and Uncle "Doc"; and good to have a long talk with Nancy, my dearest friend, who had moved to Morristown just as I was beginning my chaplaincy. I was anxious to see their children, Amy and Andrew—how they'd grown!—and even their dog, Bambi. Something normal. A reminder of the rest of the world.

My involvement with Riann was deep. But I realized my limits. Staying in the Midwest, canceling my plans, wouldn't have given her life, wouldn't have made her well. I had done what I could when I could. If she was still alive when I returned, still aware, I likely would spend every other night with her again, just the same. I could do that. It wasn't killing me.

But going to New Jersey and Maryland, as planned, was the right thing to do. On one condition: if Riann died, I wanted to return for her funeral. Her parents understood that. They agreed without question to telephone me if Riann died while I was gone.

So Thursday was to be my last night with Riann, for a while at least. And, all things considered, it was a good one. Compared with Tuesday, it was fantastic.

Riann's depression seemed to have gone. Maybe it was decorating her room with cards and some flowers and balloons . . . Maybe the tumor had moved to a better spot . . . Maybe Riann had asked God *The Question* and together they had gotten it resolved . . . I don't know. But I do know she was in much better spirits. Still in pain, but in much better spirits.

A note from her mother said Riann had been awake a good bit that day. "Maybe you can get some sleep tonight!"

I had my suitcase with me. Mrs. Miles and her sister, Meg, who had come in from New England the past week, had insisted on driving me to the airport so I could have as much time as possible with Riann on Friday.

I went downstairs with some nurses for coffee. Riann had been asleep when I arrived and was still asleep when I returned from downstairs. I changed into my nightclothes and read.

"Nina . . ."

"Hi, sleepyhead! How do you feel?" It was about 10:15 P.M.

"OK. May I have some cherry jello, please?"

I laughed. "You know, they've had to hire a special cook just to make cherry jello . . . to keep up with you!"

She hadn't been eating much. A few bites at each meal. I anticipated the same this time.

But she didn't stop eating and she didn't stop talking for two solid hours. She went through nearly two tubs of cherry jello—which was monumental—and her whole life's history.

They say people relive their whole life in their mind before they die. I didn't think about it that night, but that may have been exactly what Riann was doing. Whatever it was, I heard about experiences in all of her nine years, from as far back as she could remember.

"I remember . . . there's this boy . . . his name is Henry
Alexander . . . when we were babies . . . there's this picture of
him kissing me . . . so everybody teases me and says he's my
boyfriend. He's not . . . but they tease me. I remember riding
in a car pool with Henry one time . . . and I hid so people
wouldn't see us together.

"And one time I went swimming and Henry was going to be
there . . . and I had these two bathing suits . . . one was a bikini
and the other just a regular halter . . . and I decided to wear the
regular one . . . so people wouldn't say I was wearing the bikini
for Henry.

"I have two boyfriends now—at least two! One is John
McArthur . . . he makes a funny sound with his mouth. I love
to see him do it. He makes me laugh. He makes everybody
laugh. He's so funny. I think he's handsome, too. I'll try to make
the sound, but I'm not as good as John . . ."

She tried, really tried. She could barely move her facial muscles and her arms and hands, which were also required for the
"funny sound." The procedure involved putting her index fingers into her mouth. Finally, she succeeded as best she could.

"That's kind of it," she said. "But I'm not as good as John.
You should hear him!"

I laughed. "As far as I'm concerned, you're pretty good! That
is a funny sound. No wonder John makes you laugh."

She giggled. "He really does. He's so funny."

"Allison has a boyfriend, too. Though I don't know if she
likes him as much as he likes her. He gave her a present at
Christmas. It was pretty . . . a ring.

"Her birthday is coming soon. I'm making her some needlepoint. Mommy has been helping me. Maybe we can work on it
tomorrow . . . I want to have it done by her birthday. I hope I
can . . .

"You know, I did something I shouldn't have once . . . I
guess. But I don't think Daddy would get mad. You see, I get
ten cents allowance and Daddy gives it to me every Friday. But
sometimes he's in a hurry and I'm afraid he's going to forget.
Well, this one time I kind of reminded him as he was going out
the door. He reached in his pocket and gave me a quarter. I
guess he didn't have a dime. I was going to say something, but
then I decided not to . . ."

When she stopped talking and said she had had enough cherry jello it was nearly 12:30 A.M. The nursing shifts had changed and we hadn't even known it.

I turned out the light, kissed her good-night, and she slept for three hours . . . slept right through her seizures. And even after that, she only got awake five or six times. I couldn't believe the change.

And, you know, we really had fun those two hours of talking. I forgot for moments that we weren't just at home having some dessert and relaxing. The mind can be a great protector . . .

If this had to be the last night I spent with her—and it was—at least it was a "good" one, a fun one . . . all things considered.

When I returned to Children's from the office that Friday it was about 12:45 P.M. My plane was to leave at 3:30; so we were going to leave the hospital about 2:30.

I ran into Mrs. Miles and her sister as I got off the bus in back of the hospital. They were on their way back from lunch. We went to Riann's room. Dr. Jenssen was with her. Riann was lying on the daybed. Dr. Jenssen was showing her some red clogs she had ordered for her from Sweden.

Dr. Jenssen had been upset earlier because the clogs had taken so long to get here—like the beanbag chair. She was afraid to give them to Riann this late.

"Go ahead," Mrs. Miles had said. "She'll love them! Really she will. She won't mind that she can't use them right away. Just having them, seeing them, will be enough. And red is her favorite color."

Riann did like the clogs. They made her happy. She showed them to me when I came in.

"They're great, Riann; and I love the color!"

"Yes, me too."

She was buried wearing them.

Mrs. Miles and her sister and I sat and talked with Riann for a while. Then Mrs. Miles and her sister went "to get a cup of coffee."

They were leaving us alone to say good-bye. It was thoughtful of them. But neither of us could. If we knew it would be our last time together we didn't let on. And I think we knew.

We kissed good-bye, and she whispered, "Have a good trip . . . I love you . . ."

There is so much I have told you—all of it true, none "made-up" to convey mood. But there is so much I haven't told you—not on purpose, but because exact memory fails me.

Mrs. Miles and I had many long conversations—survival conversations, detail conversations, emotional conversations, plain ordinary conversations. She was suffering far more than I have been able to relate. So was Mr. Miles; but somehow I always felt inadequate to "minister" to him. I guess part of me still figured I needed to be a priest. And part of him was still in shock.

If you have become a bit impatient in these last pages, that was my desire. Dying—*real life dying*—is not like the movies. It can take longer than expected. Riann lived eighteen days beyond Holy Thursday. It can become routine—frighteningly routine. And it is not pretty: Seizures, mucus, pain . . . they are not glossed over in real life dying, and they *purposely* were not glossed over here.

Yet for all my description of Riann's pain, her discomfort, I haven't begun to convey its magnitude. What I have conveyed, I hope, is her sense of humor, her outlook, her hope, her faith, her love, her "hanging in there" that remained constant to the end.

I wasn't soothing the Mileses when I said Riann loved life and wanted to hang onto it as long as possible . . . and that was a tribute to their family. I meant it. I sincerely believe that home and family was so wonderful for Riann, and that she felt so secure in her parents' love and her brothers' and sister's love, that she couldn't even imagine that anything could permanently separate her from "home." "Home" and "love" were synonymous for Riann.

Perhaps that is why she may not have been afraid to die.

Love bears all things, believes all things, hopes all things, endures all things. Love never ends.

[1 Corinthians 13:7-8]

30

IT WAS MONDAY night. I was in New Jersey. The professor and his wife and I had just returned from dinner. It was an enjoyable evening.

Mrs. Miles had said when they dropped me at the airport Friday that either she or her sister would telephone me on Monday evening to give me a "progress report."

So when the telephone rang and it was Mrs. Miles, that's what I expected.

"It happened. This morning at ten o'clock. She died."

I wasn't prepared. I didn't know what to say.

She went on. She told me the whole story. I know I didn't move. The professor and his wife could tell by my face. Kindly, they left me alone.

Dr. Praeder had looked in on Riann at about seven-thirty that morning. He checked her briefly and gave her a kiss. Riann had teased Dr. Praeder in the past because he didn't kiss hard enough.

"How is that?" he asked as he gave her a big kiss.

"That was hard enough!" Riann replied.

At nine that morning she went into a seizure. But this time she lost consciousness, went into a coma.

Her day nurse called Mary Cooke.

"Call her parents and call the doctors. It doesn't look good."

Mary stayed with Riann from then on . . . until she died, about an hour later.

It had been Mary Cooke who had said to me that Saturday

sixteen days before, when Riann got her first seizure, "I pray to God I won't be here when she dies. I don't want that. Anything but that." But at 10 A.M. that Monday, Mary Cooke was there. And she was the only one who knew Riann well who was there.

Riann's mother and father couldn't physically get there in time.

Dr. Verdi was giving a seminar at University Medical School.

Dr. Jenssen was taking some medical exams in a nearby suburb.

And I was in New Jersey . . . mailing Riann a postcard.

Ironic, wasn't it? Mrs. Miles was to say that time and again afterwards. "It must have been God's plan," she would say. "None of those who were closest to Riann were there when she died."

I don't know if it was God's plan or not. But I'm glad I didn't have to see Riann dead. I'm glad the last things I remember about Riann are "Have a good trip . . . I love you . . ." and how beautiful she looked that Saturday morning in her blue nightgown. They are better memories than seeing her dead, I think.

Mrs. Miles continued on the telephone late on that Monday night. The funeral was to be Wednesday afternoon at a Catholic church in Rock Shores. The church where the Mileses were members.

"But Nina, Riann had such a beautiful 'last day' on Sunday, with the whole family. The children came in—even Kevin, though it was awfully hard for him. Dr. Verdi talked with him a long time—man-to-man—and it helped a lot.

"And Riann was so good, so very good. It was a good 'last day.' I'll always be grateful for that."

I think I knew what she meant. I was grateful for the "good" last night I had had with Riann. Things like that are not to be taken lightly. They're important. They're part of the memory that lives on . . . after the bad memories, the mental picture slides, of pain and seizures fade away.

I gave my talk the next day before the assembled missionaries and flew home that same evening . . . home for Riann's funeral.

I could end these writings with details of Riann's funeral; or with what happened after the funeral; or with how Mr. Miles has grown to accept the fact of Riann's death and become able to talk openly about his feelings; or with how the Miles family has grown even closer; or with how I still can't say the Lord's Prayer, the "Our Father," without thinking of Riann; or with what a unique and priceless gift it was to have known Riann Miles in living and dying.

I could end these writings with a discussion of the theological mystery of pain and death.

All would have validity.

But I shall end it by telling you how I felt on the first anniversary of Riann's death.

I had been on edge for several days. I don't know if it was because of that or not. But I do know on the first anniversary of Riann's death I had to go to her gravesite. I didn't rationalize why or worry about whether or not it was healthy. I just knew I had to go.

I was back working at University Children's, as an advanced student chaplain. I told Craig Hatfield that I was thinking about leaving for a few hours, told him where I wanted to go.

He seemed to understand. "Sometimes we have to bury people again."

Maybe he was right. I don't know if that's what I had to do with Riann or not.

Maybe never having seen her dead, I hadn't buried her in the first place. Though I'm not sure that's it, either.

Regardless, I went. And I sat on Riann's tombstone for an hour and a half. And I had a wrestling match with God.

I was claiming "me," crying out, "My God, my God, why hast thou forsaken me?" Yes, I knew better. But yes, I was justified. Anger is a reality, a human reality, in real relationship with God. In those moments, sitting on Riann's tombstone, I was claiming the intensity of my being . . . and claiming God's love in the same breath.

That evening I wrote this:

Some theologian or another once described ministry as "one person's attempt to give God's answers to men's questions." Or, to put it another way, one person's attempt to answer the unanswerable.

Today I sat on a tombstone alone in a small cemetery and had a long talk with God. I told him I was figuring out that the child beneath the tombstone really was dead: Not first "in God's arms" or "seeing his face" or "alive in his heart" or "one with him." But first and foremost and above all, she was dead. Had been dead for 365 days and three hours. And I couldn't talk with her anymore. And I couldn't hold her. And it wasn't fair . . . or rational . . . or answerable . . . or reasonable . . . or very loving, when all was said and done, by a God I kept calling "love."

The only *real* thing I knew as I sat on that tombstone—knew firmly, gut-level, for the first time—was that that child was dead.

What sham we feed these people! I hurled at God. You're second-best . . . the crutch . . . the aspirin to ease the pain of nevermore. You're the lost future—better than no future. You're the hope unseen that beats no hope. Eschatology—fantastic word!

All these people who sit in small waiting rooms and shake on plexiglass chairs and wait for someone to tell them it's not true. Their child is alive. That's what they want to hear. "It was a mistake." Or, "There's been a miracle. He's alive!"

So what do I do . . . minister . . . reverend person? I tell them he's alive. Oh, he's dead all right. But he's "seeing God's face" or he's "in God's arms" or he "won't have to suffer any more pain." Check out Revelation: no pain, no sorrow, no darkness. Whee!

But sitting on that tombstone, I couldn't tell God where to go. I couldn't tell him to leave me alone. Was I too scared, worried about my insurance policy? I am a kind of chicken. Was I not hurt *enough*? Could I have renounced God if it had been my own child, my very own child beneath the tombstone with the recent rainwater oozing and bubbling over the naked rectangle? Was this the biggie test of faith? My freedom-to-reject being tested to make my freedom-to-accept more real?

Maybe. Maybe not. Maybe there is no God. Maybe he has sold out and left town. Or maybe the strict fundamentalists are right . . . or the Hindus . . . or the Buddhists . . . or the atheists. Maybe the Maharaj Ji is it?

When I got that far, I stopped.

* * *

Yes, it is unanswerable. Yes, I am going right on attempting to answer it. That's ministry to me.

The unanswerable has many faces: faith, hope, prayer, sacrament, revelation . . .

The attempt to answer has many faces; words, no words, caring, touching, worship, silence, strength, weakness, sharing . . .

All I *know* is I'm not alone. But I sure am curious about the nature of the Being who walks with me. And I guess I'll never really be happy being human . . . despite the lip service . . . until I get my unanswerables answered . . .

Of course, I won't . . . on this Earth . . . get my unanswerables answered. So, as I see it, this moment, it's my choice.

Today I choose God. I hope forever. I know anger will come back . . . and frustration . . . and fear . . .

But I know I'll never be alone.

And that is everything.

All through life's day we shall walk with the Christ, often as the Stranger, because He never obtrudes or overrides. Before the journey's end we shall ask many questions, experience many heartaches, be molded by many of life's disciplining disappointments.

And then, suddenly, whether we shall be young, middle-aged, or old we shall find that the day is far spent, that the shadows are gathering and at last the night descends. In that moment our eyes shall be opened and we shall know Him, but now no longer as One who will vanish from our sight, but as the living, traveling Companion along the unknown valley's way to the highroad of God's eternity. Then shall come to pass the saying, "Death is swallowed up in victory" (I Corinthians 15:54, RSV).*

Riann and I had given each other the same gift one time. Mine from her sits still on my office desk: a small, wooden, orange-and-black ladybug attached to a clothespin. Hers from me sits

*From *This Side of Eden* by Elam Davies, © 1964 by Fleming H. Revell Co. and used by permission.

still on her bed next to the window in Rock Shores: a large, stuffed, orange-and-black ladybug.

Out of the muddy ground that April afternoon . . . where spring's grass was being made . . . from the crevice next to the chilled marble tombstone, came a tiny ladybug marching toward me. I put my finger in its path and lifted it up.

It marched forward, undaunted.

Not the End

WHAT HAS HAPPENED

To
Riann Miles' Family
Alex Felini's Family
Joey Collins' Family

15 YEARS LATER

A TRUE STORY

A NOTE TO THE READER

PERHAPS HERE IT is only fair to tell you a bit about what has happened to me in the last fifteen years.

Well, I've certainly gotten older! I am forty-five as I write this—an age which in the last fifteen years has turned from "old" to "the young side of middle-aged."

After I left University Children's in 1975, I received my master's degree from The Divinity School of the University of Chicago, an institution I still hold in awe. In 1976 I became an ordained Christian minister in the now Presbyterian Church, USA, and the same year began a job as Director of Chaplaincy at The Rehabilitation Institute of Chicago.

I chose to leave that position in 1989. But I am still affiliated with the Rehab Institute, as well as, once again, with the Department of Neurosurgery at University Children's.

In 1980 I was married—not to David, but to a businessman who knows as much about hospital chaplaincy as I do about business! With the husband came two stepchildren whom I adore, and who seem to think I'm "okay too . . ."

In 1987 Ballantine/Epiphany published my second book. *I Never Know What to Say*. This book offers suggestions on how to help your friend who is in mourning or who is dying. It also was issued as a book on tape by Simon & Schuster in 1988.

I continue to rebel emotionally against writing or speaking about death and disability while at the same time working "hands on." But I continue to do so from time to time. It *does not* get easier, however. Perhaps that is a good thing. Perhaps it means that I have yet to develop calluses.

But never will I be as raw, as innocent of suffering, as I was when I ripped the words for *Go Out In Joy!* from my insides.

Nor would I wish to be. Even writing these epilogues has caused me a sharpness of pain I thought had been dulled by the years.

In the last fifteen years I have learned three things:

1. I have learned to say no.
2. I have learned that I can't please everyone.
3. I have learned to ask for help.

And in the last fifteen years I have known all along that I never, never will be abandoned by God. Nor will you.

. . . But, still, I have a lot of unanswered questions. . . .

As for others you may be curious to know about:

Dr. Verdi has left the chairmanship of the Department of Neurosurgery at University Children's. He is writing more and spending time living and teaching abroad. One of his children died tragically in an accident about ten years ago.

Dr. Praeder is in private practice as a neurosurgeon and continues his affiliation with University Children's.

Dr. McMahan is Professor of Surgery and has become Head of the Division of Pediatric Neurosurgery at University Children's. He continues to merge professionalism with understanding and compassion in a manner not easily rivaled.

Dr. Jenssen is in private practice as a neurologist and continues her affiliation with University Children's.

Neurosurgical nurses *Jennifer Bradford* and *Mary Katharine Soloman* have become my close friends. They both remain at University Children's. Jennifer was married in 1989 and is expecting their first child; Mary Katharine was married in June— or August (that's a joke I couldn't resist)—of 1974 and has two children.

David was married a few years after I was and has two children. (I still can't believe it!)

Paul never remarried and died of a heart attack a few years ago. (He is not the same person I discuss in the opening chapter of I NEVER KNOW WHAT TO SAY).

And now the epilogue . . .

The Collins Family

Mrs. Collins and Joey and I have maintained infrequent but regular contact since I left University Children's.

Mr. and Mrs. Collins amicably separated a number of years ago. Joey lives with his mother, but his father remains involved in his life and lives nearby.

I interviewed Mrs. Collins and Joey separately on a hot summer day in 1988.

Mrs. Collins: "I can't believe Joey's almost eighteen. He's coming along great! But, you know . . . we live day to day. . . ."

"I guess the hardest thing we've been through is the spinal fusion. They did it to keep his spine from curving. But it's curved anyway. . . . [This doesn't regularly happen to each m-m child who has spinal surgery.]

"Don't get me wrong. It's hard as a rock where the doctor did the fusion. So it may have been worse if he hadn't done it. I can't say. . . .

"But I'd never put Joey through it again. He hemorrhaged on the table. It was a long recovery for him. . . . He was only eight or nine. . . .

"I'd never put him through that again."

Joey Collins: "I'm not a complainer. Like . . . other people complain, but I'm not one of those types.

"Well . . . I do complain on one thing. . . . Like, if my ma puts some clothes out for me . . . I say, 'Ma, that don't go with that!' Like the other day she put out a red shirt with blue pants

. . . but they didn't go together right. I said, 'Ma, these don't go together!' She makes a lot of my clothes . . . you know, like these shorts I got on.

"I even tell her when she wears stuff. I say, 'Ma, that ain't going to look good together!'

"But I don't complain *all* the time. Something's got to be *right*, you know. I complain . . . like . . . ten percent of the time. . . ."

"One problem, though, is transportation. That's tough . . . trying to use public transportation. I haven't even used it in a long time. . . . My dad takes me. He takes me when I gotta go some place. He lives right next door . . . close to me. . . ."

Mrs. Collins: "I don't really want to talk about my marriage. You can say we're separated. It's friendly. . . ."

"Joey keeps me going. He keeps me on my toes!

"He's a teenager now, and he wants to go to all these concerts. We just went to one. He wants to *go,* you know . . . do what other teenagers do. I don't blame him—but I have to go with him!

"He knows if I don't go with him he won't go. . . . That's all there is to it, you know. But it don't bother him. . . . That's just the way it is . . . medically . . . you know. . . .

"And his social life . . . it's mostly over the phone. . . . But you should see my phone bills!"

Joey Collins: "I got a couple girlfriends. . . . No, let me get out of that category—my girlfriends! 'Cause I got a couple . . . maybe about ten or twelve. . . .

"But . . . there's this one lady that works at the Brown's Chicken by me. I go over there . . . she waits on me, you know. They got fish sandwiches. . . . She knows just how I like them.

"Sometimes I think to myself . . . is she married? But I've never asked her!"

"I had this one girlfriend that called me up. I was at my dad's. And everytime I had that phone call he would get on another line . . . listening!

"I said, 'You don't do that!' I said, 'Hey, if that's going to be the case, give me my own private line!' But they don't want to do it, so. . . .

"I'm thinkin' I shouldn't have given that girl my number, though. . . . Because she would call ten and twelve times a day—at night! So now we got this new number. . . . And I don't see her no more!

"Like I said, I got girlfriends. . . ."

Mrs. Collins: "It's so great, seeing him be a normal teenager . . . seeing him love his music . . . wanting to go to concerts . . . country western, you know. He likes doing all that stuff!

"And the phone . . . !

"But the low part . . . the low part is, there's never an end. You want the honest truth, right? *There's never an end to it.*

"Something is always coming up . . . something medical, you know what I mean. If it isn't one thing, then it's something else."

"The biggest hump early on . . . Well, you know, you were with us. . . . The biggest hump early on was the shunt revisions. All the time, shunt revisions.

"I figured once we got through that we'd have it made. But that's not true. . . .

"Because we got over that hump. We really did. And now everything else is popping up.

"He gets urinary tract infections all the time—that's the worst.

"Then, it seems like we never really had problems with seizures before. . . . But now it seems like every two years he's having a seizure on us. If it's going to stay—the seizures—I hope it's every two years. . . . But I don't want them anymore at all, really. So it seems like I'm watching him more so now than when he was younger.

"Maybe it's bothering me so because it wasn't that long ago, his last seizure. Maybe that's the reason. Because it happens so fast.

"There's no warning—no headaches, no nothing. They're totally unexpected and uncontrollable. Once they get him to the hospital they can control them, because they got the stuff there to do it with. But here, you're helpless.

"Don't get me wrong. Joey don't have a lot of seizures. But when he has them he has real winners! And you're just helpless.

"And to me, that's the most painful thing right now to see my child go through. I can't do nothing for him and he doesn't know what's happening. . . . It's just completely out of control."

Joey Collins: "When I have seizures, I don't even know what's happening! I don't know anything!

"All I know is I'm looking at where I'm at. Then I'm saying, 'What happened?' 'Cause one minute I'm at home and the next minute at the hospital. I'm like, 'What?' I'm like, 'Oh Boy!'

"You know what the scary part is? It's when you don't expect it."

Mrs. Collins: "He just doesn't have warning. Even the doctor asked him, 'Do you feel anything before?' he says, 'All I ever do is throw up, and then that's it.' No warning. To me, that's very painful to watch.

"And then, you know, with these urinary tract infections. We get his kidneys tested once a year. Everything's better than they used to be. . . . Yet he's getting urinary tract infections. Figure that one out! I asked for an explanation and I got, 'Because he's getting older.'

"Then there's dentists all the time. I don't know if I told you this one before. Joey went through this quite a few years ago . . . He's allergic to novocaine. We lost him in the dentist's chair! We had to do CPR on him.

"So now we're deathly afraid to go to the dentist. Everytime we go to the dentist I'm a nervous wreck. He's got to get a cavity filled, too. . . . We postponed it a while, though . . . because he'd gone into that seizure.

"But what I'm saying is, stupid things like that happen. To me it wasn't stupid—I almost lost him. One minute he was fine, sitting in the chair to get a filling. Next minute we're up in intensive care.

"So, you see . . . you don't know what to expect. There's never no end. . . . If it isn't one thing, something else comes up. . . ."

Joey Collins: "Somebody else asked me that once . . . like, when did I notice, kind of, that there was something different between me and other kids . . . I know, it was one of my doctors that asked me.

"I said, 'You got to ask my Ma; 'cause how you expect me to remember that far back. I can only remember so much!'

"It don't bother me . . . seeing guys walkin' around. Because . . . like my gym teacher . . . he's in a wheelchair, too. Like half my school, they got wheelchairs. Half the kids are kids in wheelchairs and half ain't.

"They're born like that . . . they got to live with it. And . . . when I go outside . . . I see other people with wheelchairs, you know. I'm not the only one. . . . So I'm gonna make the best of it."

Mrs. Collins: "I was really proud of Joey this one time . . . even though he blew it.

"He was running for an office at school, and I happened to be at school. This was the first time he ever got up on stage in front of a lot of people. And his face was turning red—because he forgot all of his lines!

"But I was *so proud* of him, because he had the courage to stay up there until . . . it took him at least five minutes . . . until he remembered his speech.

"He stayed there at least five minutes, repeating the first two or three words of his speech over and over and over until he remembered it. He kept doing them words over . . . and he stayed there and he finished it.

"I was proud . . . because he didn't run away. He stayed there and did the whole thing. . . . Even though he lost, he did it. I think that's one of my proudest moments of him . . . because he had to face something by himself, and he did it.

"He says, 'Ma, I blew it. I blew it. I blew it. I couldn't remember. . . .' I says, 'But you stayed there.'

"And I wasn't the only one proud of him. His counselor was very proud of him. Because when Joey first started high school he was a meek little thing. And now it's just the opposite! Isn't that something?!'"

Joey Collins: "The good things in my life . . . Well, going to school. And I go fishing with my dad if it's nice. Drive my hand bike . . . If it's nice out. If it's hot, like now . . . I'm in front of the TV from the minute I get up 'til the minute I go to bed.

"Once in a while I cook stuff or help clean up the house . . .

or answer the phone. . . . Help my mom if she wants help, you know. Sometimes that's just staying out of her way, mainly!

"But I like to get outside when I can. When I go out there I'm not, like, stuck in the house. You get stuck in, you go crazy. I just like to go outside, even just to sit. And it's close to my gran . . .

"Oh, and I make those napkin holders and cigarette cases . . . and I sell them. I do that around my house when I can't go outside.

"Not much makes me sad. Not that much . . . no. Just like if someone says . . . like if they are going to call you and they don't; then, yes.

"But my life has been okay."

Mrs. Collins: "I don't want my 'own life.' It's not that I can't have it. I don't want it. I'm very happy. I'm very content the way I am, as of right now. I don't know about tomorrow. But right now, I'm very happy the way I am.

"I don't want another man's problems! I got enough of my own! You know—think about it!

"I'm saying that today; but tomorrow, who knows. Tomorrow my whole outlook might look different. But as of today, I don't want an outside life.

"Oh, I go out shopping with my girlfriends and that. But menwise . . .

"Yeah, I go out shopping. I leave Joey with my parents. When he's in school . . . that's when I *should* go out. . . . But I'm afraid to leave the phone. At least when I leave Joey with my parents they know what to do if something happens. But at school . . . well . . . I'd just rather be here in case something happens at school. I guess I just don't trust the school system with my child . . . I've made an investment. . . .

"I want to know what's happening over there . . . I'm very active in the school. . . .

"I only have *one* child. . . ."

Joey Collins: "My mom is pretty important. Yes . . . she is. . . . She's pretty important.

"But, like I said, too . . . I got girlfriends!

"My mom can cook, though. She cooks good. And she makes

my bed. And she sews. She made that horse on there for me. . . . She seen it in some magazine. She made *all* that stuff over there.

"And we go bike riding sometimes . . . except if it's raining. I wouldn't. I remember getting stuck in the rain one time . . . my mom and me. Everything got wet!

"I like what my mom does. . . . I can't complain."

Mrs. Collins: "My son gives me a lot of pride. . . . Because he'll say, 'My mother did this,' or 'My mother did that.' It's all concerning what he says I do. That . . . that gives me pride."

"I don't really think about the future. Because if I do I get scared . . . I really do.

"I say to myself, 'Okay . . . now if something happens to me, who's going to take care of Joey? Because he still needs care, you know. He can't do some of the personal things himself. . . .

"Granted . . . his father will automatically get him. . . . But I'd probably come back and haunt the heck out of them!

"Or . . . if something happens to Joey . . . and I'm still here . . . because we're so close. . . .

"What the future will bring . . . I don't know. So I don't even think about it, to be perfectly honest with you. I kind of wipe that from my mind . . . and, like I said . . . we live as days go by. . . ."

"Joey doesn't talk much about the future either. . . . Not to me, anyway.

"Oh, he'll tell you he wants to get a job after high school, and all that stuff. His mother told him he has to go out and work!

"But other than that . . . no, he really doesn't talk about the future.

"I always tease him and say, 'With my luck, you'll probably get married . . . marry a handicapped girl . . . and bring her home to live!' I say, 'Go live with *her* mother!' "

Joey Collins: "My Ma wants me to get married . . . but . . . it's like, who do you want to marry? It's a hard choice. . . .

" 'Cause, like I said, I know a couple of ladies. . . . Like this one radio station I listen to; I got two from there. And then I got that one over at Brown's Chicken. . . .

"This guy I know . . . we were talking about this one girl,

him and me. . . . We were talking and I tell him I had two girlfriends. He said, 'Out of those two, who would you marry?'

"I said, 'Man, I don't know that.' Because at the time I didn't know. I still don't know. . . .

"Some people tell you, 'Get married.' Some say 'Don't get married.' You don't know what to believe. I don't anyway."

"I been thinking about what to do after high school. . . . This one guy I know, he's a disc jockey. Then there's this guy at the park district where I go play tennis. Then there's another guy who works at the post office. . . .

"So I got three jobs in mind: disc jockey; working at the post office; plus the ice skating rink at the park district. . . . So . . ."

Mrs. Collins: "My faith? It's there.

"I always did have faith. Sometimes you question it. . . . But I think that's only normal for everybody. . . .

"But on a scale of one to ten . . . Well, I don't go to church, so that puts me down a couple of notches. Does going to weddings count!

"From one to ten? I have to cut down a couple of notches because I don't go to church. . . . So I'd say about six or seven.

"If God were here right now . . . If he was sitting right there . . . I would just say, Why? 'Why?—Not just mine; all of them. Why? What's the reason?'

"I've never come to an answer in my head . . . not even a rationalization."

". . . . I didn't even take an *aspirin* when I was carrying Joey. If I took all kinds of medication . . . or if I was on an antibiotic . . . or if I drank . . . If I did them things I'd say, 'Well, gee, I'm at fault because I drank too much when I was carrying him, or I took too many antibiotics, or too many pills, or too many aspirins.' But I didn't. So I don't fault myself. I have no guilts at all.

"But I would like to know before I die. What causes it? It's important to me. What causes spinabifida?

"I'm still asking that question. I get no answer. . . ."

Joey Collins: "Like . . . I got a *Bible* I read . . . when I get the chance, you know. Because, like I said, I do these napkin

holders and cigarette cases in my spare time. . . . So, when I
get a chance I'll read *The Bible*.

"That's about it. But, I think about God. . . .

"Because one of my neighbors . . . she had a stroke. It was
like overnight!

"I saw the ambulance come from the window. . . . An ambulance and police came. They took her out the back way. . . .

"And the neighbors came over and told my Ma what happened. They said, 'Yeah, she *died*,'

"I'm like, 'What!' I said a little prayer for her.

". . . But like I always said . . . you gotta go once in a while.
Nobody stays forever.

"Because it's true."

Mrs. Collins: "What would I say to parents having a kid with
spinabifida? 'Hang in there.' That's about all you can say, is
hang in there. Because spinabifida goes in different degrees.
Some may be worse than Joey. Some may be better than him.

"The only message I can actually give is 'Hang in there. Live
day by day.'

"For me . . . I can see the outcome. Seeing Joey mature . . .
seeing him want to do things . . . seeing him happy . . . hoping
he stays happy . . . and finds life.

"It's worth it."

Joey Collins: "Well . . . I would tell any kid being handicapped . . . 'You got to live with it.' Not all kids . . . not all
people like to be handicapped. But that's your handicap.

"I would say to people, 'You got to live with it.'

" 'Try to do what you *can* do. Just try what you *can* do.' I
try to do stuff. If I can't get it, I ask either my mom or my dad
. . . whoever's around the house.

"But I always try stuff before I ask."

"I like my life. It's really better than what you've seen on TV
and that.

"Yeah. I really like my life."

The Felini Family

The Felinis and I have maintained infrequent but regular contact since Alex died.

In the late 1970s the Felinis had twin sons. Though no child ever replaces another, many who knew the Felinis and knew of Alex's death rejoiced in the sense of grace that seemed to encompass the event.

I interviewed Mr. and Mrs. Felini together in the summer of 1988, and 19-year-old Chrissy Felini* separately the same day (except for a brief period at the beginning when her father joined us).

Mr. Felini: "I was just thinking about the time when Dr. Praeder actually broke the news to me that the chances of Alex pulling through was very dim. It was like . . . the way he said it . . . the way it hit me . . . I was very mean. Nobody could have talked to me at that time. I just, like, walked away from it all."

"And then later . . . I think a day or two later . . . Dr. Verdi came and we were talking . . . and Alex got very sick . . . he got stiff like a board. I forget; they had a name for it. He got real rigid or something. I happened to be the one in the room . . . me and him. . . . And they all came and they gave him some kind of a sedative to relax him.

"And me and Dr. Verdi had a talk. And he did promise me one thing: He was not going to keep Alex on a machine. Because I'd said, 'I can't take him on the machine. But I don't want him to go.'

*For the purposes of privacy protection I added a daughter to the Felini family in *Go Out In Joy!* There is no second Felini daughter.

217

"And he said, 'We will not keep him on the machine.' He was going to let him go one way or go the other way. He said, 'He's either going to pull through or he ain't.'

"And that I'll never forget."

Mrs. Felini: "I remember when I was going to visit Alex . . . when he was in the coma . . . and you know, that end room, when you turn the corner . . . there was this boy in there that Dr. Verdi had told us about.

"I think by his condition he could have been in a home . . . but the parents preferred to keep him at home. But he happened to come in the hospital for something when Alex was there.

"And when I saw him . . . he must have been about fourteen or fifteen, 'cause he was tall and he looked about that age. . . . I said to myself, 'Oh God in heaven, I would never want to see Alex like this.'

"He couldn't do anything for himself, you know. And I thought, this is no way to be able to say, 'Oh, he's here, folks.' I really just felt *so bad* for that guy.

"I remember I talked to Dr. Verdi one night by myself about it . . . when Alex was in the coma. And I told him . . . the same thing my husband told him. I said, 'Please don't put him on machines to make him live. I mean, if he can't live on his own, just let it be. . . . Let him do what he can.'

"I'd gone to see him in his office . . . to tell him that. And then he called somebody, I think in Boston, to ask if he could give him any information on how to go further with Alex. And I thought, Boy, that was great. . . . He didn't have to do that. I mean, as far as I was concerned he was the *top* neurosurgeon. . . . And that wasn't even my thought, like to call Boston and further it, you know."

Mr. Felini: "All the men at work helped me . . . just being quiet no matter what I did . . . no matter what I said. . . . They just got quiet and they listened.

"I was wrong in a million different things, with what I was doing . . . I couldn't even concentrate. As soon as I'd finish doing something, I'd say, 'Uh, you finish it, Irv. . . .' or 'Pick it up' . . . or something. I would throw stuff around. I couldn't think right.

"They wouldn't say a word. . . . As soon as I'd walk away they'd go and patch it up. The boss would come by and look and say, 'Oh, he's doing a great job.' And he'd walk away, even though he seen me coming in late and seen me doing this. . . . He'd just turn his head and walk the other way.

"It was very funny . . . that's how they were with me. Because they didn't know what to say. They truly did not know what to say.

"Before Alex got in real bad shape, when he was just sick in the hospital and when he had a lot of visitors . . . a friend of mine came there with a gift. . . .

"He found out that Alex liked horses and he brought him a couple of horses up to the room, him and his girl. And I'll never forget him, this guy Danny. I see him every now and then, once in a great while. . . . And Alex really took a liking to him the first time . . . I guess because he gave him horses; because he did like horses.

"But they all shocked me when they all chipped in and brought him these here horses . . . they were very expensive. . . ."

Mrs. Felini: "I remember my sister was so much help. We lived a block away—my mother and her did. And every morning she would come over and we would sit and talk.

"I guess just her *time* was a big help.

"And my friends was always willing to sit down and talk about Alex, you know. . . . Because they knew him when he was first born.

"I guess just being able to talk about him as freely as I wanted was such a help. It wasn't like, 'Is this a good time to talk about him?' I mean, even if I was going to cry. So what? What I mean . . . it was still okay.' "

Mr. Felini: "At work . . . they had a lot of collections for me . . . because I ran through the insurance. And this one guy that *really* helped talked to the business manager and he told him the situation when I ran out of insurance. And he started a big collection. They had a lot of other people with similar problems at the same time. A ton of money was collected and it was divided up in three or four different ways, evenly. . . .

"So, that's just the way it worked out for us. I forget how much money they gave us.

"But then I'll never forget what Dr. Verdi did. He just tore up his doctor bill. He said, 'Don't worry about me.' He just says, 'I'll put it off to charity,' or something. He said it in a nice way. But he just said, 'Forget about my bill.'

"And then he introduced me to somebody at the insurance program at the hospital . . . for picking up some of the money. . . . He said, 'Just say that I sent you over there.'

"And I told her; and they did. She took care of all the bills. And they said, 'You don't owe nothing.'

"And then the money that we had collected from the guys that had the collection . . . I just figured . . . I just wanted to give it to Dr. Verdi, whatever the amount was. I was going to give it to Dr. Verdi. I don't know what his bill was or anything.

"He just wouldn't take it. He would not take a dime of it. He said, 'The only way I'll take it is one condition and one condition only.' It was to have some kind of fund for Alex . . . to keep his name going.

"And I just looked at him and I said, Doctor, it's your money; you do what you see fit.''

"And that's what Dr. Verdi did.''

Mrs. Felini: "I remember a lot of the doctors . . . how concerned they were. . . . And a lot of the nurses . . .

"And just seeing Alex and how well he performed . . . with all the surgeries . . . He was an inspiration. . . .

"And even all of the other kids on the floor . . . I mean, dear Jesus . . . I don't care how bad you felt that day . . . when you seen these kids you've got to feel inspired.

"I picture Riann a lot . . . when she used to walk around in her night clothes . . . so beautiful. And then Joey . . . and that little Gary . . . and Manuelito! You know, I used to have to laugh at him. He didn't even know he was funny, that kid. . . .''

Mr. Felini: "I'll never forget Alex used to say about Dr. McMahan, 'He's going to be the head doctor!' And, what is it . . . ? Alex always wanted Dr. McMahan to have a certain kind of shaving soap. Man, I'll never forget that! I told him, yeah, I'll bring it to him. . . .''

"Well, I gave it to him . . . a little bit late . . . . But I gave it to him. I'll never forget that.

"Now, I guess, Dr. McMahan *is* the big doctor there. And Alex already foresighted that. He told me. I said, 'Yeah, Alex . . . you're right. . . .' "

Mrs. Felini: "You know what upsets me, though . . . still to this day . . . and it's ridiculous. . . . Maybe because I feel so bad for the people. . . .

"You know Carl's* family . . . ? Now they, out of everybody, stick in my mind.

"Carl was able to go home for a pass . . . and watch TV . . . and go to the snack shop. . . . And they always looked like *he died*!

"Oh, that just, like, chokes my neck when I think of it. . . . It's like it's happening right now!

"I remember one day I—I probably told you this a hundred million times, Neen—but one day I remember . . . I was leaving on my way home . . . and I was going into the chapel . . . and two of them were sitting there in the snack shop. . . . And I said, 'Let me stop in and say hi to Carl.'

"And he was white because he just had cobalt. They were white because. . . .

"And I looked at them and I thought, My God in heaven, how *could* this kid survive?! If I had to live with people like that I'd want to die, too!

"I mean . . . *he's* going through the ropes. I mean, you're not . . . You're just there to help him . . . you know. And I'm trying to laugh with Carl. . . . And I'm thinking I wanted to ignite them. . . .

"I wanted to say, 'You idiots! *My* son's in a *coma*. I'd give anything to make him sit next to me!'

"But you can't talk like that because it's not right.

"And I thought, God, if I could say to Alex, 'Oh, Alex . . . let's go get a cola! We're gonna watch TV today! We're gonna go to the snack shop! Maybe you could go to school, even! How's that?!' I mean, 'Hey, this is *livin'*, hon. . . !'

*A twelve-year-old patient who survived brain surgery. He was a patient at the same time as Alex, but was not mentioned in *Go Out In Joy!*

"I just thought, I can't believe you people. I mean, Carl could die that night, but that didn't matter. It was *the time they were right there with him that was counting*. . . .

"I mean, to me Carl went through an awful lot. So just having him there, mobile . . . alive . . . you could talk to him . . . you could hug him . . . you could touch him . . . whatever. . . ."

"Grab ahold tight . . . real tight. Hold tight to the time that you've *got*. Don't worry about what's going to be. . . . Work with what you can work with . . . and don't feel *so sorry* . . . that . . . that you miss the importance of the moments you do have. . . .

"That really . . . like . . . like I said . . . I mean, it's fifteen years later . . . I shouldn't feel this anger in me. . . . It's terrible. . . . You know what I mean?

". . . Not that I'm angry . . . I guess it's just that . . . it's like an upsetting point. . . .

"They didn't . . . in other words . . . they didn't *grow* from where they started with him. You know . . . I think that's what it is. . . . The growth just didn't happen for them . . . which is sad. Much more sad than it is for me . . . because . . . that's their son. . . ."

Mr. Felini: "Yeah . . . I remember . . . I hate to use Carl as an example again . . . but I remember his mother . . . and especially his father. . . .

"His father didn't like something Dr. Verdi, or Praeder, or somebody said to him. So he made a phone call long distance to the Mayo Clinic. And when he got through talking to the Mayo Clinic . . . the same thing came right back at him.

"The doctor said, 'Well, what hospital are you at now?' And when he was told who Carl's doctor was he said, 'Don't leave. . . . You've got the best right there. You're wasting your time if you come up here.'

"And I kept thinking, Well, you couldn't spend *all of your money* to do something.

"Money is nothing. Nothing. It's just pure faith and how you believe. But he would use the words, '. . . spend more money on him. I'll spend more money.'

"I just looked at him and I says, 'Money ain't gonna make

it.' I don't care how you look at it! Like the doctor always told me, 'If you need blood I can't stick dollar bills in your arm. . . .'

"And I always thought of Carl's father that way. Stickin' in dollar bills and trying to make him live off of dollar bills. Just can't do it . . ."

Mrs. Felini: "Like Tony said earlier . . . people don't know what to say sometimes. . . . I remember I had just gotten home from the hospital seeing Alex . . . and I stopped by my mother because I had to pick up Chrissy. And some lady I knew went by and was asking me. . . . Like, if somebody asked me how Alex was, I would just tell him how he was.

"And she says, 'Oh my God, how could you be so calm?'

I said, 'Would I appear better to you if I carried on . . . and then I'd make *you* uncomfortable. You're asking me and I'm telling you, that's how he is.' I mean, that was rude on my part, but. . . ."

Mr. Felini: "I was always getting tired of hearing, 'Oh, it's got to be hard on you. It's got to be hard on you.' I looked at them and felt like saying, 'Yeah, what do you *think* it is? We both know it.'

"I hate to say it . . . but it's the same old malarkey. . . . Just to *say* something. They were better off saying nothing, I believe."

Mrs. Felini: "When somebody would say that to me, I'd tell them, 'It's not hard for *me*. . . . I'm not going through it. . . . My son's going through it. . . . He's laying in a coma; I'm not.'

"I mean, I don't even have to go to the hospital today if I don't want to go. He's not going to know if I'm there.

"I said, 'He can't get up and say, "Well, hey, I've had enough of this stuff . . ." '

"Really . . . how could I take their pity. . . . I mean, even for Alex . . . *We* didn't want to give him *pity* either . . . because that wasn't love. I didn't think of him in the sense of, 'Oh my God, I feel so bad for him.' I did. But not in the sense where it was a *pity* kind of thing.

"I mean, you don't want to see anybody suffer. If anything, you want to remove that pain. But, you know . . . there's a fine

line between being pitiful to somebody and, 'Yes, I do feel sorry
. . . but I'm gonna give them my best. . . .' ''

Mr. Felini: ''I was thinking . . . I remember I didn't want him
to go . . . I was, like, hanging on. . . . Then I come to realize
that it was the best thing for him to go. . . .

''It was the best thing to really let him go. . . .''

Mrs. Felini: ''. . . Just remembering what he endured . . . If
I think about him or talk about him I gain inner strength. . . .

''I always think back to the time . . . and I still feel bad about
when we were in the chapel . . . you know. . . . And I said,
'Let's pray that Alex dies.'

''And I think that was just a terrible thing to say to you . . .
because you can't do that.

''Just like somebody would say to me, 'Let's pray this person
dies.' I mean, my God, how can you do that? You can't. You're
not in control of that. You just don't have that power to do stuff
like that. . . .

''That was a door opening for me. . . .''

''Alex . . . the Wake . . . it was only five hours . . . I mean
I only had five hours left to see him . . . ever. So I sat in that
seat for those five hours *because I wanted to*. . . . Because I
knew that that was going to be it. And I wasn't going to let
anybody disturb me for these five hours. Because that's it. This
is *my* time.''

''And, you know, after Alex was brought to the mausoleum,
I was able to go on. Right after Alex was brought to the mausoleum my day started.

''. . . I guess I was able to start immediately because I was
preparing myself *as* he was ill. I kept always praying that God
would help me to deal with it in three ways: Taking Alex home.
Not taking Alex home. . . . And keeping me in reality, no matter what. I said, 'God, please place me in *reality* . . . no matter
how bad the realness is. *Please keep me in reality.*'

''Sometimes people would be upset when I'd talk about how
Alex really was . . . in the coma and all, you know. But I'd say,
'Don't be upset if I'm talking weird. You don't think I should
be . . . but you're going home to all your family members. . . .

I *don't know* if I am or not. So I can't step out of the reality. I have to do this. It's very important to me.

" 'Because if Alex does die, then not only will I be in bad shape, if I haven't had reality . . . but I have a four-year-old at home and I have a husband. So, I said, 'Even if it's cruel . . . I have to think like that . . . like Alex might die . . .' ' '

"I guess God must have just been giving me that inner strength. . . . And I had a good rapport with the doctors. I told them I didn't want them to pacify me.

"If I felt like somebody was trying to be too sympathetic with me I had to speak out. I mean, when I was talking to you—you and I could talk on the same chord because you knew where it stood.

"But I remember my father-in-law coming out to see Alex . . . He was in a coma, and my father-in-law was extremely upset—

"I said, 'Why don't you leave? It's not worth it for you to get this sick, because it's not going to help nobody.'

" 'Alex is not going to get better . . . and you're going to feel twenty times worse,' I said. 'If you could stay here and be this upset and Alex would sit up and be okay, I'd make you sit here forever. But it's not going to work . . . So what's the sense to it . . . ?'

"But I can understand how my father-in-law felt. If I was in his shoes I would have felt the same way. Only because I stood where I stood could I talk like this, you know."

"I would look at Alex lying there and think . . . 'I can never feel the pain you're feeling. My life, really, is still just about normal . . . in that I can go to the hospital and I can go home . . . I can go to the beach, if I want . . . or go shopping. I can sit down and eat three meals . . . I can watch television . . .'

"But Alex was *nowhere*. He was in limbo. I know they say normally if you're in a coma you don't feel pain. But regardless . . . I mean, Alex's world was over with. I knew that.

"But I still had the world. So I hung onto it. And I didn't want anybody to take it away from me. I was able to go on . . ."

Mr. Felini: "When Alex died . . . I really never wanted to let loose. It took me about two years. . . .

"When he was in the coma I always still wanted to hang on. . . . And after he really went I was bitter . . . not bitter with nobody special . . . just bitter with the world.

"I was always looking in the paper reading about all these killings . . . and goofy rapes. . . . And I'd say to myself, 'Somebody good and honest and clean . . . small . . . like Alex . . . All these young kids *go*. . . .' I'd say to myself, '*Why* them, and them . . . when it should be just the opposite.'

"One day I was talking to Fr. Garvey . . . We were going through a Bible class and we were just talking in general. . . . And Fr. Garvey said, '*All the good is never noticed. It's always the bad that's noticed.* Anybody could do a million different good things . . . but it's never noticed once. But there is more good done in this world than there is bad.'

"And when he said that it just hit me . . . and it stuck in my head. But it didn't really penetrate yet. I just looked at him when he said it.

"But then I started thinking . . . of what Dr. McMahan really did with my son, and how he was playing with him and joking with him. Dr. Praeder—how he really loved him. . . . And how Dr. Verdi was with him and what he actually *did* for him. And how he got me out of a big deficit. . . .

"And I said to myself, 'It's so true, what Fr. Garvey said.' It didn't really penetrate til six, eight months after that. . . . But when it did, that was my turning point."

Mr. Felini: "I don't think we had any marriage problems . . . real marriage problems . . . because of Alex. Carrie wanted to have more kids and I didn't. I truly did *not* want to have no more kids . . . because I could not see bringing something clean and pure into this world and destroying it.

"But as far as I'm concerned there was never no marriage problems or anything else. It's just, like I said, it took me two years . . . before I really got it out of my system.

"Carrie helped me out a lot more times than I ever helped her. . . . Because there was a lot of times, like I said, when I was bitter . . . aggravated.

". . . .Alex's death drew us close together, I believe. . . ."

* * *

Mrs. Felini: "That's what I would say, too.

"I guess the way I handled myself helped, and there must have been a good bond between us. . . . Because it didn't seem like our marriage got shaken much.

"There has to be a balance. I mean . . . a good example is: When Alex was in the coma and he had that bad episode . . . you know, that Tony was talking about. . . . We were leaving the hospital, driving through the park. Traffic was congested and cabs were going nuts and Tony was driving fast. . . .

"And I said, 'What's your gain . . . ?' I said, 'We'll *never* see him if we die. . . . And I don't want to die yet. That boy needs us . . . I mean, if he's going to die he's going to die . . . but at least. . . .' So I think that gave him some food for thought. But I was in control, so I was able to speak like that.

"And when we got home he said he was going to have a drink. . . . And he didn't drink at home, you know. So I said, 'If you think that's going to take away the pain then that's what you have to do.'

"So then he thought about it. . . . And he let it go. . . .

"I wasn't getting upset because I thought 'He's his own person. He has to find his own process to go through it. I can't expect him to go in my process.'

"So I guess, they might have been the major points. And then, I think too . . . Tony was Greek Orthodox, which he didn't practice. Then he became a Catholic because that was his choice.

"But since I've been born I've been a Catholic. I always *truly* believed that God was there to help you. So I think through my faith . . . it helped me, as hurting as it was, to see things in a different way. . . .

"My mother had a hard life. She *never stopped praying*. My mother made novenas. She went to mass all the time . . . even if she was sick. . . . I guess maybe that reinforced me. . . . My mother's faith . . . helped me do better with it.

"Whereas, I don't know how it was when Tony was growing up . . . So I would say to myself, 'You have to allow him to go through it his own way.' "

Mr. Felini: "I guess I'd just say to other people going through this. . . . You have to have faith in one another and support one another. My wife was the stronger one and she always was there when I needed her. . . . She helped me out. I think that's maybe what kept us going. . . .

"Just love and trust . . . hope for the best and pray for the best. . . .

"It's hard to tell people certain things because they don't always understand . . . or they want to hear something else. . . ."

Mrs. Felini: "I'd just want to say . . . really *appreciate* how precious life is. . . . Really appreciate and realize how precious we are to each other; how great it is to be alive. *Take* every little chance you get . . . not just with your sick child, but with all your kids . . . and all the other kids in the hospital. Because when they have a good day—it's great! It's a treasure. It's a memory.

"Know that God is really love . . . that He's not out to hurt anybody. Trust him.

"You can't stand alone. It's totally impossible. If you swallow up in yourself you miss it all. Because life is short. . . . If you get depressed or angry or whatever you lose something of your life . . . of being alive.

"You know, it's okay to be depressed or angry for a certain length of time . . . but there's a limit on it. Otherwise you just lose too much.

"When you let that self-pity go away you can broaden yourself . . . get involved . . . start stepping out of yourself. Tony and I . . . we got into this program working with the handicapped. . . .

"After a while that's what I think you have to do. You can't just let yourself dwell on it. . . . You've got to stretch out and see how broad the world really is, you know. Every time you feel the bad coming you gotta turn good in with it in order to help you.

"Then, too, I think you have to get with people who are willing to help you grow. I'm not saying people are out to hurt you. But there are a lot of people who are narrow . . . who just don't see beyond what has happened.

"But the more different things you get involved in the more different people you come into contact with. . . . And you're hearing new things from them and you're able to start seeing and hearing again. And someday you begin to think, 'It's okay, I can make it. I know it was bad. . . . But I'm going to be able to make it.'

" . . . And we did. Tony and I did.

"Since Alex died we've had twin boys. Chrissy graduated high school and has a job. She's had some hard times, too . . . but still, she's going on in her life. My parents are still alive. We've taken family vacations.

"But just watching the kids . . . seeing how well Chrissy and Anthony and James have grown . . . We did make it.

" . . . When the twins were born a lot of people . . . people who knew about Alex, you know, said, 'Oh, look at that—God blessed you twice. . . .'

"But I didn't think of him as, like, sending me a double prize or something . . . you know. Because, I mean, Alex was unique. . . . So maybe there was something . . . but I just didn't think of it in that kind of way."

Mr. Felini: "I guess it's the only way I know how to really put it. . . . He took something that I really loved; but then he paid back double.

"I was always wondering how Alex would be . . . and then I look at what I have now; two for the price of one. . . . That's the only way I know how to put it. . . . He took Alex . . . but we got two beautiful boys. . . ."

Chrissy Felini: "It's really weird when I listen to everybody talk about Alex. . . . Because I have only *one* memory of my brother.

"I remember my dad's old Chevy and I remember sitting in the back seat. It was just a two-door. . . . So you know how if you're in the back seat you can lean up against the door, but it's not really a door. . . . And I remember seeing my brother leaning up against there and smiling. . . . And we were on the way to the racetrack. . . .

"And that's all I remember. That's just all . . . and it upsets me that that's all I have.

"I sit and listen to everybody talk about him and I feel like I was left out.

"It upsets me now since I've gotten older that he's not here. . . . I wish at least I'd had the chance to know him before he died. It bothers me. . . .

"When I was in grammar school I did a science project on brain tumors and I went and talked to the doctors that were with Alex. I'm glad I did that because I learned a bit about it.

"But then when I got into high school . . . I think my junior year . . . I started going through a lot of things with myself . . . I really didn't know where I was going in my life . . . I didn't know what I wanted to do.

"And all my girlfriends just happened to have brothers the age of Alex . . . and they talked about them. And I started thinking when I heard them, God . . . God . . .

"A lot of people didn't even know I had an older brother. And then I'd talk about him. . . . And they'd say to me, 'Oh, I didn't know you had a brother.'

"And then it just started playing in my mind. But I let it go . . . because that's what I do when . . . when I can't deal with something . . . I just run away from it or I don't deal with it.

"But it kind of lingered in my mind. I thought how nice it would have been if he'd been here . . . if we'd been close.

"It upsets me I only have one memory. . . ."

"There's a part of me that's angry. There's a part of me that's hurt . . . you know. And I think, *why*? Why didn't I just get a chance like everybody else? Because everybody else got to know him except for me.

"And then there's part of me that sometimes wishes I was at the funeral . . . or at the wake. And then I realize that the reason why my parents did that was because if I'd have gone, I would have had *that* memory instead of the memory I have now. So I'm glad they didn't let me go to the funeral. I guess in the long run it worked out.

"But that's all I have, is him smiling. . . . I'm glad I have that memory. . . . That's good. . . . And horses . . . was him. That's about all. . . ."

"I think it was only about two years ago that I started talking about how I feel about Alex. There was this point I went through where I was alienating myself from everybody. . . . It was just a lot going on with me personally . . . and I was holding myself from everybody. I even stopped talking to my mom so much . . . and at times we were fighting and stuff. And my mom and I are real close.

"So we started talking again and I think that's when everything came out . . . when I started telling her how I felt about it . . . about Alex. . . .

"Even just knowing you were coming here . . . I kept saying, 'I don't know if I want to talk about this . . .' and then there's a part of me that wants to talk about it.

"I even was talking to mom about it on the phone yesterday. I was telling her, 'Mom, you know, I don't see why you want to talk about this.' And then she's telling me that she *wants* to talk about it.

"I think it's easier for them to talk about it . . . because I didn't understand, you know. I remember my father telling me that Alex died. I remember him standing up against the stove in our old apartment . . . and I remember him telling me . . . and I remember seeing everybody cry. And I'm thinking, 'Why is everyone so upset?' Because I guess it didn't make sense to me that Alex wasn't here anymore and I was never going to see him again.

"It's just never *all* made sense to me. . . . And then, when I started knowing what all this meant, is when I started getting upset about it.''

"But I'm really *glad* that I can talk about it when I want to talk about it. It isn't like, 'Hush, hush . . . you can't talk about this.'

"I just hope that in the future I learn to deal with it better. It's just going to take time, I guess, for me to accept it. See, I guess I just haven't accepted it yet. When I accept it . . . I'll probably be able to deal with it better.''

"When my parents go to the mausoleum . . . I can't walk in there with them. I don't know why. . . . I guess I just haven't come to grips with myself for walking in there yet.

"But there will be times that I'll sit with mom and I'll just bring it up out of the blue and tell her how upset I am. . . . And then we'll start talking about it . . . and we'll both start crying. . . .

"But what's good is that I can talk to her about it and she'll get upset . . . but she can deal with it . . . and she *wants* to talk about him.

". . . And his picture . . . it hurts . . . Seeing it . . . When I walk past the hall I see Alex's picture. . . . I think, 'Oh, God'. . . .

"I always say to my mom, 'I don't know how you dealt with it. I don't know how you could accept something like that.' I kind of find it hard to believe that she could just accept that. I mean, that's just got to be the most . . . I can't even imagine what it feels like. . . .

"And then she tells me how she held Alex after he died. I don't know how she does it. . . . That's a lot to absorb."

"My mom and I . . . I don't think of her as a mother only. . . . She's more of a friend to me. And now, just this year . . . I was finally able to open up to my father and talk about things that were bothering me. Now I don't feel so much like my father's only my father . . . he's my friend that I can talk to.

"And I was never able to open up to him . . . I'm glad that after all this time I can go up to him and tell him what I feel . . . and it's okay.

"It's real hard for me to open up to people, you know . . . to really say how I feel about them and stuff. It's real hard.

"Or to tell people I love them . . . that's *so* hard for me. Maybe it's because I'm afraid someone's going to be taken away if I put myself on the line . . . I'm afraid.

"I guess recently . . . it just feels like every time I start to get close to somebody the next thing I know, they're saying goodbye. My best friend just moved to Arizona. My other girl-friend who worked with me downtown—she's leaving today to go to school. I just got out of a real long relationship with some-body. I really put my whole self into this relationship . . . and it all fell apart really bad.

"So right now it feels like everybody I care about is just leaving . . . and it's really bothering me. . . . I was telling my Ma last night. . . . I said, 'Ma, I'm so sick of saying goodbye to everybody. I don't want to say goodbye anymore. . . .'

"There's a little part of me that just wants to not get close to anybody. So I don't get hurt anymore . . . And that's terrible. You can't just hold yourself back and never care about anybody again.

"So right now I . . . right now I'm really going through a hard time with myself. It's like . . . if I don't care about you then I won't have to say goodbye if you leave. . . .

"I don't know if it's because . . . I don't think it's because of Alex. . . . I don't know why I feel like that. . . . I wish I knew. . . .

"I don't know why I feel so afraid to get close to people. . . . I just feel real lost right now."

"I hate feeling like this. . . . I hate the way I feel about Alex's death. . . .

"I can't go on being angry for the rest of my life. . . . I guess I just have to talk about it more, maybe ask more questions about him. . . .

"I think whenever I'm able to go to see him at the mausoleum . . . I think then that will be the time I'll accept it. . . .

"But right now . . . I just hate the thought of him being in a drawer . . . and just being never seen. It really bothers me.

"I want him to be *real* for just five minutes."

Mrs. Felini: "I've told Chrissy . . . it gets less . . . the pain . . . if you talk about Alex more. The more you *express* yourself the better you're going to feel. That anger is going to start lifting from you.

"The sad part is . . . She says, 'You have so much to say about him.' The memories . . . She wishes she had him to grow with. That was *so* important to her.

"And then, they were so young. . . . So she really didn't get a chance to know him like we know him. She wasn't at the hospital much. . . .

"As a matter of fact, you know Alex better than Chrissy does, Neen. . . ."

Mr. Felini: "At first I used to always say to God, 'Why him and why not me? Why not me? Why him? Why not my wife . . . but Alex needs my wife more . . . so take me instead. Or take something that's rotten.

" 'Take your choice. . . . But not the innocent—'

"But then I knew he did the best thing. Because after a while I actually told him to take Alex . . . because I couldn't see him. . . . When I seen him get real stiff or whatever . . . that one time . . . Then I knew I could never see that happen again to him. And then, that's when I really said, 'Take him away.'

'I was just always wishing he would live through . . . I always still go . . . I'd like to see how he would be today. There's always the curiosity. . . .

"But then, like I said, he took him . . . when I prayed.

"I have no grudge or nothing. . . . I believe my faith is strong. . . ."

"If God were here right now I'd . . . it's always been on my mind to ask. . . . Why does he take the good so young? It's always stuck with me. I mean, why? Can you show me a good reason?

"But he's up . . . and can't be asked that question. . . ."

"I know one thing I'd probably say to Alex if he was here now. I'd say he's probably a million times better off where he's at. . . . Because I believe he's an angel up there.

"He's better off up there than down here. . . . Because there is a lot of vicious play down here. . . ."

Chrissy Felini: "My faith hasn't been too good lately. . . . I used to go to church all the time, because of my family.

"But after senior year I really didn't know what I believed any more. So I haven't been going to church for a while. It feels like repetitive readings . . . and I'm not getting anything out of it.

"I mean, I pray to God all the time and I talk to him. I just don't know why I don't feel God in church. . . . It just seems like it's all a show. No one answers to the prayers anymore. . . .

"I believe in God. I believe in all the Catholic things I've been raised on. That hasn't changed. It's just that I don't get anything out of Mass."

"When Alex died . . . in the beginning when I thought about it . . . I thought God was punishing me. I always felt like God does everything for a reason. . . .

"But then I'd think to myself, 'Why? Why would he be punishing me? That doesn't make any sense. When I'm four years old he's going to punish me? I mean, he knows what I'm going to be like when I'm older so he might as well punish me now!' "

"I guess if God were here now there's a part of me that wants to say, why did he do it? But then I don't think I'd say that. . . .

"Maybe I'd ask him, *why didn't he just give me a little more time*? But then, time is what everybody wants.

"I don't know what I'd say to him.

"I guess I just want a chance to say something to Alex. . . . I guess I would ask God if there was any way I could speak to Alex. . . ."

"I'd tell him I miss him. . . . It's really hard. . . . I don't know what I'd say to him. . . .

". . . My cousin, Mary, was telling me that Alex . . .

"I'm sorry I'm crying. . . .

". . . that night before his last operation Alex said he didn't want to have it . . . his last operation. . . .

"I'm sorry . . .

"He was always going through all these operations, you know. . . . And then this last one . . . it was like he knew. . . .

"And I wish I could have gone to the hospital and seen him then . . . because . . .

"There's one picture my parents have of him that really, really bothers me. . . . It's Alex sitting in a hospital bed and his head is shaved . . . and it really . . .

"I just feel so *bad* for him . . . because he was so young . . . and he was in the hospital. . . . And it just seems unfair. . . .

"It just really upsets me that I didn't get to know him . . . and that he suffered. That bothers me really bad. . . ."

"For some reason I've always felt like nothing I've ever done has been good enough. . . .

"And my parents have never made me feel like that. Like in school . . . I always got on the honor roll. But no one was telling me, 'Chrissy, you have to.'

"But I always felt like I wasn't doing good enough. I don't know who I'm competing with . . . or why I feel like I do. . . .

"I don't know. There's a part of me that's really angry that I don't understand why it happened. . . . I always say, 'God, why did you do this?'

"I just haven't accepted it at all. . . .''

Mrs. Felini: "I think just *seeing* Alex and *seeing* God . . . that would be the ultimate.

"As much as I always tease, 'Oh, wait 'til I get up there I'm gonna . . . this and this. . . .' I think their presence would just speak for itself. Just *seeing* them would make it okay.

"I think that would be the greatest feeling in the world."

Mr. Felini: "Just talking about Alex makes me feel good. . . . It's really going back in time. Like, when Chrissy was talking to you . . . I always thought of Alex when we took him to the racetrack that time. . . . And all of a sudden she said it. She brought it all up. I *wanted* to think about it.

"To me it's good memories. That's what it is to me now . . . really good memories.

"Don't ask me how . . . but I feel like he's right here now with us."

Mrs. Felini: "As deep as the pain is . . . it makes me feel so good to talk about Alex. I mean, my son *lived* for seven years. . . .

"When you love somebody that deep, why wouldn't you want to talk about him? He's somebody who lived, who you shared your life with . . . so you don't want to forget about him.

"I think it would be horrible not to be able to talk about Alex."

"Alex has helped me grow. As difficult as life has been for me it is not so devastating that I don't feel I can go on."

The Miles Family

Catharine and Eric Miles and I have remained in frequent and regular contact since Riann died. We have become close friends and see and talk with each other often. I also have gotten to know Eric, Jr. (28), Kevin (27) and especially Allison (22) increasingly better over the years. (Allison and my stepson even have dated from time to time, though I've tried to protect her!)

Soon after my husband and I were married, the Miles family gave us a lovely garden party to which all our "old friends" from University Children's came. It was an afternoon that reminded us all of our unique bond, that neither time nor separation could erase.

I interviewed Mr. and Mrs. Miles and Allison Miles each separately on the same day in late summer 1988. I interviewed Kevin Miles alone two weeks earlier, and Eric Miles, Jr. alone about six weeks later. I also briefly interviewed Allison Miles again in early January, 1989.

Mr. Miles: "I think the one thing I never really will forget was the day when Riann complained of having a headache and Catharine called our local doctor and he looked at her and tested her and sent her off to Morristown to a neurologist. This neurologist made a very alarming statement to Catharine: that he thought she had a brain tumor and wasn't going to survive.

"Catharine called me at the office—she was absolutely hysterical—and gave me the news. It was a terrible shock for Catharine; she should have been led into it more gently. But that's the way it was done, and it really rocked her. That is my most vivid memory."

Mrs. Miles: "I was just totally, totally devastated. I was so out of control that the doctor had to call our pediatrician and get him to calm me down so that I could go out and face Riann. I remember the pediatrician saying, 'You've got to pull yourself together. You've got to be able to cope. You're going down to University Children's in the morning and she's going to be examined by a neurosurgeon. But you can't let it totally devastate you.'

"And, of course, I didn't even know at that point what 'it' was. . . . But all those symptoms to me looked pretty severe. So that was the beginning."

Mr. Miles: "The first thing I wanted to do—thinking logistically as I took the train out—was to get her out of Morristown and get her to University Children's . . . some place I thought had better ability than somebody local or somebody up in Morristown.

"How do we get to the next step? Who do we find that is a really good doctor and get her into some, hopefully, better hands?—I think that was kind of what was in my mind.

"You know my feeling always was that there's a solution to this thing. I sort of live that way. And it took me a long time to realize the end, or the inevitability of what she had. I always thought that there was a solution around the corner, and I always tried to keep fighting for it."

Mrs. Miles: "I remember the next morning . . . leaving early to go into University Children's. And driving into the city . . . and the complete and utter fear and panic that I had about what we were going to hear. . . . I was absolutely numb and I could hardly talk. Riann was in the back and she was lying down and she was getting more and more lethargic and quiet . . . and all she wanted to do was rest.

"I remember the ride was just like I was walking into hell.

"We had to sit in the waiting room for a while before Dr. Verdi could see us. I kept running back and forth to the bathroom. . . . I was just so nervous and anxious. And I really had these negative feelings about meeting the doctor. I was determined I wasn't going to like him.

"When we got in there I remember I was so afraid I was

going to cry the whole time that I kept my sunglasses on and I sat there. Eric did all the talking; I couldn't even talk.

"Dr. Verdi didn't give us any diagnosis at all. He didn't even guess. He just said he wanted to admit her right away and do some tests and examine her and observe her. So she was admitted and we went up to the room and they started the testing. And Eric left to go to the office and said he'd come back that evening.

"But in the middle of the testing . . . an EEG, I think . . . I just got panicked all over again and I just couldn't be alone. I was so *afraid to be alone*, talking to the doctors . . . and I was *so scared*.

"I was also very scared of Dr. Jenssen! She scared me to death.

"So I called Eric and asked him to come to the hospital to be with me. I said, 'This doctor scares me to death and I can't answer all those questions and you just have to come.'

"So then we got through that day."

"The next morning we arrived at the hospital . . . it was Saturday, I think . . . and they had just finished doing an angiogram and were wheeling her back into the room. Then Dr. Verdi came in and spoke to us about the angiogram and said he felt it was one of three things: a tumor, a blood clot, or a cyst.

"I remember standing on one side of the bed and Eric was on the other side and I thought I was going to faint. All I wanted to do was to get to Eric on the other side of the bed. But I couldn't get to him and I just started to burst into tears. Riann was asleep and I was so grateful that she didn't see me crying like that because I was so out of control.

"Then she had a shunt put in that same day so they could drain the excess fluid so they could do a milogram later next week. . . . I think that's it. Anyway, she had a shunt put in and she was out of it for the rest of the day.

"I remember going down to the Chapel several times. I'd go down there and come back, go down and come back, go down and come back.

"And then I began wondering 'Who is this doctor? Is he any good? Is he qualified enough?' I remember I called my cousin, who's a doctor at University Adult, and asked him about Dr. Verdi and he said he was great and excellent.

"Then I remember spending the rest of the day just sitting in her room not being able to move, just sitting in the chair. And Eric and I just sort of just sat there . . . and I didn't know what I was going to say to Riann. . . .

"They didn't tell us . . . but I'm sure they knew it was a tumor by then. . . ."

"Then we left her that day and I remember we went to church that night and I remember Eric asking the priest to pray for Riann at Mass, that they were diagnosing her or trying to diagnose her and that she was in University Children's. I remember the priest saying at Mass that we should pray for Riann and that she was very ill; seriously, seriously ill. And it all just hit me, you know, the reality of the fact that she was really, seriously ill. . . . It was a huge awakening to me. . . ."

"We spent the whole next week waiting. They finally did the milogram on Thursday . . . or Friday. . . . It was the worst week. Just horrendous. I was worse that week than I was after the surgery or during the surgery, just because I didn't *know* what was wrong and the not knowing and waiting was so horrendous.

"So they did the milogram and told us, yes, in fact, it was a tumor. And obviously they wanted to operate on her as soon as possible. But they didn't operate until Monday."

Mr. Miles: "The first surgery . . . I think I was in a real state of shock. Neither Catharine nor I really understood a lot of what was going on. It wasn't that we were unwilling to accept it. . . . It was just, I think, that the doctors were trying to be gentle and they were sort of tippy-toeing around the facts. . . .

"We'd found ourselves in a world we'd never been in before. I'd never heard about a brain tumor . . . I mean, I've heard of it but I didn't really know what it meant. But the shunt operation; I didn't know what that was.

"Looking back on it, I think that we were probably, in our outlook at it all, very, very naïve and unprepared. . . . But no question, I was in a state of shock. . . . And I think we were all sort of in a state of shock . . . not knowing enough. . . .

"I think as we have gone on to other things and other problems . . . I think we have been much better prepared than we were for this."

Mrs. Miles: "They sort of broke it all to us very slowly and gently. We were *so unaware* of what you do with brain tumors and how you treat them and what the ramifications are. . . . We were so naïve that we didn't even know what questions to ask. So I think they just didn't tell us much at all . . . because we weren't asking. But we didn't even know what to ask.

"And I think it was very hard for them to tell us the real truth. I think it was very hard for Dr. Verdi. . . .

"After the surgery—which was probably the longest day of my life—he took us aside and told us that he'd gone in and decided not to remove any of it right then. . . . He said he wanted to wait and watch, and wanted Riann to get a little older before he would go in and remove any. And he was just going to leave things the way they were.

"And we thought that was great. Ha! Little did we know. . . . We thought it was great that they didn't have to remove any tumor and that she wasn't going to be maimed or paralyzed or in any way altered. So it was kind of a relief in a way. But Dr. Verdi was not sharing a lot with us. . . ."

"But . . . I was so unconscious . . . so preoccupied with my own worst fears at that point . . . I probably wouldn't have heard it anyway. And Eric and I never did say to him, 'Tell us everything.' We never did say that to him . . . not until after her second tumor surgery."

Allison Miles: "I didn't really understand. . . . I was five or six. . . . I mean, I understood to a certain extent, but I didn't really know what was going on. I knew she was sick and I kind of understood the brain tumor thing, but I was just really uncertain what was going on. And she was never home. . . ."

Eric Miles, Jr.: "It's a real vivid memory. I was about twelve or thirteen and Kevin and I were together at camp in Colorado and we had no inkling before we left for camp. . . . Riann had

had some headaches but it was after we left that they really became severe enough to have it checked.

"All of a sudden my counselor came into my cabin very concerned and said, 'Your family is going to call you after dinner tonight and I want you and your brother to go to the head of the camp's office.' So we were obviously concerned.

"And after dinner Mom and Dad called and said that Riann was sick and that she'd been getting headaches and she went to the hospital and had it diagnosed and what she had was a brain tumor. It was just completely out of the blue. I was really shocked.

"The first reaction, I think, was just real confusion, of not knowing what this was all about. I never faced any kind of medical problem like that or any illness in our family. So I remember being very confused and asking a lot of questions; trying to get a handle on it.

"And I remember Kevin just got very angry immediately, and was crying, and was confused and angry, and was asking a lot of questions, too.

"Mom and Dad were trying to explain as best they could, but we really didn't understand it. . . . We didn't really know what was happening. . . ."

Kevin Miles: "I remember my reaction when I first found out she had a brain tumor. My brother and I were at camp in Colorado. I was eleven, I think. We were told to call Mom and Dad. We called them up and Mom said that Riann had a brain tumor.

"The first thing that went through my mind immediately was death—'She's going to die.' That's the first thing I thought of. And I got extremely upset. Very emotional. I just . . . for some reason, I think maybe from television, who knows . . . When you hear the words 'brain tumor' . . . Death; that's the first thing. I thought she was going to die.

"But I didn't ask anybody . . . and I didn't talk to anyone at camp about it. I kept it inside. And when I got back home I was told immediately that everything is okay, you know; they were working on it and all that sort of stuff. And I don't think I ever asked if she was going to die or not.

"But I think that at some level, unconsciously or something, that that first thought staying with me in some way. That was my first reaction—I thought it meant death.''

Mrs. Miles: ''She was operated on in August, the first time. . . . And I knew by the end of October . . . inside myself . . . I knew she would die.

''When we finally got home and got our life back to normal—I mean, our life was *never* normal again—but got our routine going and she got back to school and things were sort of calm for a while . . . they weren't very calm for long. . . .

''I began to think. The reality of it was really hitting me . . . what was really happening. . . . And I was crying all the time and saying to Eric that I felt she was not going to live . . . that this was extremely serious.

''And he kept saying to me, 'Well no, that's *not* what the doctors say; that's not what the doctors told us.' And I would be crying and he would say, 'Now stop crying, stop crying. Everything is going to be fine.' He believed it. But that's what he wanted to believe.''

Mrs. Miles: ''It was in February . . . just after we met you . . . and Dr. Verdi was going to try again. He operated again . . . thinking he was going to be able to do something . . . remove some parts of it or all of it or whatever. . . .

''Anyway, he took us into his office after the surgery and told us he couldn't remove any of it. If he had she would have been paralyzed. She wouldn't even have just been paralyzed . . . she would have been severely damaged. . . . And that our recourse now was radiation.

''And we said to him, 'Well . . . does that mean she's not going to live?'

''And he said, 'That means that she's going to get off the bus sooner.' I remember that comment.

''But he said, 'You know, I have a man with this type of tumor who is still alive. . . .' He said she can live maybe ten years if she responds to radiation. . . .

''Then we realized, you know, that this was terminal. He didn't use the word 'terminal'; but we realized that she wasn't going to live.

"But we didn't know how long. We though she was going to live longer because that was what he intimated."

Mr. Miles: "It was very different from after the first surgery . . . the talk we had with Dr. Verdi. Again he was trying to be gentle and nice and thoughtful. . . . But he used the parallel about getting off the bus. . . . It was that she's going to get off the bus sooner than the rest of us. . . . And nobody knows exactly when. . . .

"But that was really the time that I knew that this was it. He was very clear about it.

"I remember feeling very upset . . . very disturbed. . . . I can't say depressed . . . I guess numb is the best way to describe it. Sort of numb and unable to fully accept it.

"I didn't want to believe it."

Eric Miles, Jr.: "I knew when mom and dad walked through the door . . . after her second surgery . . . I could just tell by looking at their faces . . . I could just tell by mom's face . . . that she was dead . . . that she was going to die.

"I just put my head down and walked out of the room. . . ."

Allison Miles: "I remember when mom told me that she was going to die. . . . I remember she told me before. . . . I don't really remember when it was. . . .

"When she told me I was just like, 'No, no it . . . it can't happen. . . . I don't believe it. It can't happen to my sister.'

"I didn't say 'No, it won't happen; forget about it.' It just didn't seem like it was going to happen.

"I remember wanting to talk to Riann about it . . . and just to see how she felt. . . . But then I knew I couldn't talk to her about it.

"I remember sitting down and trying to tell my friends. . . . I remember one of my friends . . . she was like one of my best friends and Mom said maybe you should tell her. . . . And I told her and she just kind of said, 'Oh' and never said anything else. I'll never forget that. She didn't mean to be mean. . . . But I just thought it was the meanest thing she could do."

Kevin Miles: "I was walking through the dining room . . . and Mom or Dad told me that she's not going to live.

"But the sentence that was always repeated was, 'It could be tomorrow; it could be three weeks from now or it could be three years. We didn't know.' That was what was always sort of said. But, that she was going to die.

"I don't think I was aware of any response inside myself. Because I think that once she got sick and this whole thing started I slowly but surely just started repressing more and more and more. Long before they told me she was going to die. I think I was already in some sort of way preparing myself.

"By that point I was . . . by the time I heard that, I was already finding new ways. . . . I had already started drinking and drugging, which I hadn't started doing when I found out that she had the tumor. But I had started it by then. . . . I guess I was in a lot of pain and didn't want to feel it.

"So I think I just heard it.

"When I got drunk I would try to talk to this girl in my class who I liked quite a bit. But I don't think I talked to anyone about it.

"I guess, I wish . . . I wish I could have talked to Riann about it. Even though I wouldn't have talked to her in a way of saying, like, 'You're dying.' I wouldn't have said that.

"But I wish I could have talked to her about how much trouble I was having with her being sick."

"I remember it . . . everybody in my family, my mother, the cleaning lady remembers it . . . that for a while after Riann was born . . . for a very long time . . . I was about three or four then . . . for a very long time I wanted her *out of there*. Get rid of her. Take her home. I wanted her dead. Which is a normal reaction. But most kids who have a reaction like that to a younger child being born . . . their wishes don't come true.

"A lot of people scoff at that. . . . But, I don't know, I think there was something there. So I had a lot of trouble with her dying, in that sense, in the first place."

"The closest I ever came to expressing anything to her about how I was feeling was . . . there were a couple different occasions when I brought her into my room for some reason and showed her drugs that I had bought. She didn't really understand what was going on. I showed her these things.

"And looking back on it I'd say it was sort of like saying, 'Do you see what I have to do? Do you see what I have to do?'

"I guess I wish I could have talked to my family about how I felt. But the person who I learned from was my father and he wasn't expressive about it at all. So I sort of took his cue. Even though inside I was literally being torn apart, as I know now. But back then I didn't even know I was angry.

"When I drank on the weekends during this whole thing I did all sorts of vandalism. I was very destructive to myself . . . getting into all sorts of trouble at school. . . .

"I was absolutely furious at her for dying. But that's something I've only come to realize lately. To me, at that point, anger was a totally unacceptable emotion to have toward somebody who was dying. To be angry at them was totally unacceptable.

"So I was bouncing off the walls inside myself. I was furious at her. I was in a rage at her for dying."

Eric Miles, Jr.: "I talked about it with Mom and Dad, and to a certain extent with friends, and with Kevin and Allison. But I was not much of a communicator and held a lot of those deep anxieties in.

"Like after her first surgery . . . seeing the scars on her head . . . I began to realize how terrible it was. And after her second or third shunt replacement . . . I began to realize, just myself, that this is an unsolvable problem . . . that this isn't going away. But I don't think I shared that with anybody. I just internalized most of it.

"My example, and I felt what was expected out of me, was to be strong and hold the family together. It was my own interpretation of things; but I think I had a lot of cues from Mom and Dad . . . That's something in retrospect that I see a little more clearly.

"I think I was expected to be strong; to not cause problems; to act as glue to help keep the family together. . . . But not to ever have problems myself.

"It was kind of like, 'Listen, we have some big problems over here; and by the way, Kevin's not coming along too well either. . . . So listen, Eric, please don't cause us any problems.

You're'—I hate to use the word perfect—'You're good, and just stay that way and don't rock the boat, because, God knows, we can't afford to have that happen right now.' It was implicit in their behavior. . . .

"I didn't know I even had an option. I knew I had a purpose; and my purpose was to be strong and to help my family and my sisters and Kevin. And I had a kind of very romantic and glorified notion about that; that this was a *great* purpose, and I was serving a very valuable and useful purpose by doing this. I think this notion was strengthened further by a lot of my father's reaction of not wanting to explicitly deal with it. And, of course, I wasn't either. All I was doing was stroking and soothing.

"Kevin would act out, and I would say, 'Kevin, don't worry; it's okay. It will be all right.' And when anybody would get upset or when anyone would start attacking someone else in the family I was always just Bang! right there, defending whoever was being attacked and trying to smooth the waters and making sure the feathers didn't get ruffled. . . . Trying to keep everything together.

"I think it did serve a purpose at the time. When you're going through something like that it is so traumatic that a level of that is good.

"But in retrospect, I wish I had been able to . . . had tried . . . had been given more of the tools to express myself . . . to allow myself to hurt. . . . To allow myself to *communicate* my hurt, to understand my hurt . . . To be able to understand it's okay to hurt, and to have problems, and to be wrong.

"But I didn't.

"The reason I'm seeing a therapist now is because I am feeling some of this in my later life. . . ."

Mr. Miles: "Well, Allison was so young that . . . that she wasn't fully conscious of what was going on. And Eric and Kevin, I think, were supportive. I don't have any memory of them being a problem then.

"But my coping was a problem . . . because I cope differently than Catharine copes. And this is something we've gotten help on after Riann died.

"What I do to cope is that I'm able to build a wall around myself and build a wall around my emotions. Or, as this one doctor put it, I have the ability—or the problem—of 'compartmentalizing.' I can put a problem into a compartment and then choose to live around it—ignore it if I choose to.

"And so I think my coping at that time was to face it when I had to, but not face it all the time. . . .

"And during that time I also had the problem that I couldn't become as emotionally involved as Catharine because I had to keep making a living, and I had to keep a job and keep the rest of the family in one piece. So I think my way of coping was sort of to compartmentalize and kind of put it over there."

"My training as a child, from my father, is that you never show emotions. I remember I was about nine . . . I think it was, when my brother died. He was three or four. . . .

"I remember very distinctly that morning my father coming into my bedroom and telling me my brother died the night before. . . . And that we—meaning we men—'have to be strong and not cry and not show any emotion.'

"And once my brother was dead and once the funeral took place . . . it was almost like he had never been. . . . I mean his name was never mentioned. It was never discussed. It was never rehashed."

"So I think that my compartmentalizing was really a self-protective device, and also sort of allowed me not to face it; which I think is also probably part of it.

"But it's kind of an inherited thing. . . ."

Mrs. Miles: "Mostly I felt lonely and empty and afraid. Afraid of what the *loss* was going to be like. . . . Fear that I might never survive it . . . that I would be an emotional cripple and not be able to function properly as a mother and wife . . . as a person.

"I wasn't afraid of how she was going to die. I was afraid of what would happen after . . . and how we were going to survive it. . . .

"But I really didn't talk to anybody but you and my sisters about that fear. . . . Eric just couldn't hear it; because he was just coping with today. . . .

"And I knew that when Riann died he would just say, 'Well,

we're going to get on with our lives'. . . . Because that's the way he coped.

"So I didn't get into those deep, deep inner struggles until later. Then, I was just trying to get through every day. I was looking for people who could tell me that it was going to be all right . . . and that I was going to make it . . . and that we all were going to make it.

"I finally realized that nobody could . . . nobody could give me the answers and nobody could take the pain away. Nobody had the answers."

"Then that next April . . . about one year from when her radiation ended . . . she was admitted for the last time. I remembered the terrible waiting and watching. . . . And coming everyday to see her, and getting off the elevator, and walking down the hall, and coming to her room, and looking at her, and saying to myself, 'What am I going to see today? What terrible thing is going to be surfacing today?'

"Seeing her waste away was just . . . awful. I was so afraid to come. I was really just anxious for it to be over. . . . Because it was *so* painful to watch.

". . . But, there were so many wonderful things she showed us in her dying . . . how one can die so beautifully . . . that I was just awed by her strength and her selflessness and her ability to cope with it. I just kept saying to myself . . . 'I just know I could never do that myself. . . .'

"That part was very, very inspiring."

"I wish I had involved the other children more in her dying. And I wish now, retrospectively, that we had kept her home to die. But we were so helpless in how to cope. . . . We were so afraid we wouldn't do the right thing for her. . . .

"My big fear was that she would be in terrible pain and we wouldn't be able to deal with it. . . . And she'd have terrible convulsions and we wouldn't know what to do. . . . So it was really out of fear that we took her to the hospital.

"We'd been so honest and involved the other children in her life. . . . And then all of a sudden we just whisk her off at the time of death. It was really unfair to them . . . and unfair to their coping and their grief. And I think we cut off a part of what shouldn't have been cut off for them. I think it would have been much better for them if she'd been home.

"And I also regret not having told her she was going to die. Now . . . years later . . . I think it would have been very good for her and us to share that . . . in helping her. I think she would have felt more comfortable talking about what was real and what was going on.

"I think probably she was trying to protect us; and I think if we had been more honest with her she wouldn't have had to maybe put on a lot of super strength that she didn't need to.

"If someone had told me that was in her best interest I would have done it . . . because I would have done *anything* in her best interest. . . .

"I look back on that now. . . . But, you know, it's mainly hindsight. . . ."

"The day before she died was really beautiful, though. We decided that it had just gone on too long for her . . . for the other children . . . and that they should see her. She wanted to see them.

"Allison and Eric went in the morning, I think, and Eric took them in. . . . And Riann got up and was laid on the couch.

"I wasn't there when they first got there . . . but Allison just wanted to play with her and take care of her. . . . They were so excited about going. . . . But they were scared, too."

Allison Miles: "I remember really well when I went to see her just a couple of days before she died. . . .

"I came in and I didn't want to cry in front of her and I just started talking to her. . . . And when she asked me to feed her and—that was when her head was all bent back—and I wanted to try to feed her jello. . . . And, I guess I didn't really know how to do it. . . .

"And I remember Mom asked me to go somewhere. And then she said to Mom, 'Don't tell Allison, but I don't want her to feed me . . . because it hurts when she does it. . . .' And I remember just sitting and talking to her then. . . .

"It was just so . . . hopeless . . . you know . . . I just . . . I mean, here she was, like trying so hard . . . you know . . . to not let it show that she hurt. . . . And I was trying so hard to not let it show that I was bothered by the whole thing. . . .

"It just . . . it just seemed . . . so . . . wrong.

"And I remember being so scared that I was never going to see her again. . . .

". . . . and I didn't."

Mrs. Miles: "I came later because I was bringing Kevin in . . . because he didn't want to come and we had to talk him into coming. Finally Meg talked him into going with me and helping me and driving with me. He went and said, 'Oh, I'll go and I'll sit in the car and I won't go in.'

"But I got him there . . . and we were all there in the room . . . *all of us.* And Riann just was so excited. And we were all taking care of her and hovering over her and playing all the jokes and games. . . .

"Then Kevin and I stayed longer. . . . But it was just, I don't know, a very mixed day. . . . It was great that we did that when we did it . . . because she died the next day. . . ."

Kevin Miles: "I had stopped going to the hospital for a long time when she would be in. I think, if I remember correctly, I just wouldn't go. I didn't want to go because I didn't like seeing her. . . . And it's so strange because it's not something I was even aware of at the time. I think I just said, 'I don't want to go.'

"So somebody—Dr. Verdi talked me into it on the phone or something—that I should come to the hospital with the family. And so I went to the hospital, I think it was a day or two before she died. . . .

"Dr. Verdi talked to me out in the hallway . . . and explained what was going on . . . or something. . . . Sort of gave me a man-to-man talk type of thing. . . . And then I went into the room and saw her.

"She was laying on the bed with her head all bent back and really thin, and mom was right next to her and sort of almost like translating for her or something. . . . Real skinny . . . and pale . . . and white . . .

"Sort of looked like a little concentration camp victim. . . .

"She would have these little seizures every once in a while

and Mom would just say in this real friendly voice, you know, 'Do you want to explain to Kevin what happens with your little seizures?' Because I'd try to make her laugh or something and that was painful for her, but she'd try. . . . And then she'd have these little seizures . . . and I'd watch that.

"The worst thing for me about the last time I saw her . . . was that she was *such a good sport about it*. Sitting there *dying* . . . her body all twisted out of shape . . . having these little seizures. . . . She was *so good* about dying. . . . She was such a good sport about it.

"And that's what just killed me, you know. . . . Makes me furious. I don't understand why.

"I didn't show a thing. I didn't experience any emotion. I must have. But it was all so . . . so far contained inside me . . . you know.

"It's all there now. It's just as real now as it was then in some ways.

"But I didn't feel anything. I wouldn't let myself feel anything. But I remember every little detail. I know what the room looks like, the floor. . . . What it smelled like . . . What it sounded like . . . Where the window was. Everything. But I didn't feel anything at the time.

"That's the last time I saw her. And I remember."

"I'm glad I went. Especially since I had so much trouble with her dying in the first place . . . because of how I felt about her when she was born.

"If I hadn't gone and seen her on the last day I think I'd probably have beaten myself up that much more in the years after her death. . . . And I beat the living hell out of myself anyway.

"I don't think I would have forgiven myself . . ."

Mrs. Miles: "I drove Kevin home in the car and he told me he was really glad he went. But I think he was angry at what he saw . . . He was still very angry about this whole thing. So angry . . ."

"The day she died . . . I remember getting up that morning and saying to Meg, 'I just can't do this one more day. I just can't go in there and watch it. I just wish it was all over.' That was about seven in the morning. . . . And about nine, just as we were getting ready to leave, one of the nurses called and said they thought I should get in there because . . . because things weren't very good—but they obviously didn't tell me what: that she was in a coma.

"So I remember, my cousin drove Meg and me in . . . because we were both, obviously, very anxious. And Eric had just gone to the office; so I called him and told him that they wanted us to come.

"He went right over and got there before I did. . . . And she was dead by the time he got to the room. And I got there maybe five minutes after he did. . . . And he was trying to find me outside in the parking lot or somewhere . . . to take me up there and warn me. . . . But he couldn't find me.

"So Meg and I went to the room. I walked in the door. . . . Oh, she looked wonderful. . . . She looked so peaceful. . . .

"The nurses were standing there next to her . . . two of the nurses. And I stood at the end of the bed and I thought, 'Oh, she looks so wonderful . . . and so happy . . . and so peaceful.'

"I didn't know she was dead.

"And then I looked . . . and I said, 'Oh . . .' And I looked at her . . . and I said to the nurses, 'Is she dead?' And they said yes.

"And I was really, really relieved . . . I was so relieved to see her look so peaceful being dead. . . . And it was really very calming for me.

"Then, of course, I didn't want to leave her. . . . And Eric kept saying, 'We have to go now. We have to go. . . .' And finally we left after about an hour.

"I remember people coming in. It was really beautiful. Everybody was saying goodbye to her . . . except you . . . and Dr. Jenssen . . . and Dr. Verdi. . . . After all those hours and nights you had spent with her . . . and you were deprived. . . . That wasn't fair either. . . .''

Mr. Miles: "I remember being at the bank . . . at a meeting . . . when they called that things were really bad. And I just remember calling Catharine. Somehow, I can't remember exactly, but somehow there was some difficulty getting through to her. . . . And I called and I think someone was driving her into town. . . . I can't remember exactly. . . . But just trying to get in touch with her. . . .

"And then jumping in a cab and going to the hospital. And by the time I got there . . . just almost at the same time, I think, Catharine's sister drove her in.

"And she was dead by the time I got to the room. . . . But had just died. I remember that very clearly.

"Then I remember Catharine being sort of, you know, emotional . . . as she should have been. Then I remember you being great, being very helpful. . . . I think Dr. Jenssen was there too. . . . I'm pretty sure she was . . . just being very supportive and being very helpful. . . .

"But . . . I was in shock. . . . Definitely I was in shock. No question. I mean, I think much more in shock than . . . looking back on it . . . than I really have ever been on any other occasion . . . even with some of our problems with Kevin. I was never as much in shock. . . .

"When I saw her I knew she was dead. There was no question. There were no hopes left."

Eric Miles, Jr.: "I was at school . . . and we knew the end was close. . . . And I remember a teacher, who's also a close friend of ours and my parents, stopped me in the hallway and said, 'Go right home after classes today. Don't go to sports. Go right home!' And he said, 'You understand what I'm talking about?' And I said, 'Yeah.'

"So I got Kevin and we went right home and Aunt Meg was there . . . and she didn't want to be the person that told us. . . . And so she kind of dodged and weaved all day, and was very uncomfortable doing it.

"It wasn't a big event. I wasn't shocked and upset. Like I said, when I saw Mom and Dad come through that door after her second operation . . . and I saw the look on their faces . . . I knew she was dead. In a way, I had already begun burying her . . . the pain is so great I have to bury her now. . . . I have to push it away. . . .

"So actually knowing it had happened was not as big of an event."

* * *

Kevin Miles: "The day she died I was at school and my brother was at school, too. And a man who worked at the school in the development office . . . was friends of my parents . . . was told . . . because he knew us pretty well. And he found me. It was about two o'clock in the afternoon and I was about to go to sports, which was something I never missed.

"And Mr. Brown said, 'Don't go to sports today; you need to go home right now. You have to go home right now.'

"I said, 'Why?'

"He said, 'Just . . . you need to go home right now.'

"And I just said, 'She's dead, right? She's dead. Isn't that right?'

"He said, 'I think you should just go home right now.'

"And I rode my bike home. And my parents weren't back yet from the hospital. And my aunt was there and I did the same thing with her, you know.

" 'She's dead, right? She's dead. Just tell me. She's dead' . . . you know. But she couldn't say anything.

"We waited for Mom and Dad to come home and we were in the den and we all sat down and they told us—Mom told us— that she died at ten o'clock in the morning . . . or something. But I didn't respond at all except with a smile and a little laugh . . . which is pretty indicative of where I was at that point.

"I just had this, like, sort of disgusting feeling or something, you know. I didn't experience any tears or emotion. . . . I mean any emotion of what you might consider usual grief. I just sort of laughed and got up and left the room."

Mrs. Miles: "It was very hard to tell the children. . . . I remember we came home. . . . They were in school and somehow we didn't want them to find out via the grapevine at school. . . . But it was just about time when school got out and Meg went over and picked them up and brought them home. . . . They said afterwards they knew Riann was dead.

"We called them into the den . . . they came in and sat down. . . . Eric told them.

"That was so pitiful . . . to watch them. . . . The boys were so angry and Allison was so lost and lonely. . . .

"The boys just kind of removed themselves. . . . It was real hard for them to cry and express it.

"Allison was just so lost . . . just needed so much to be loved. . . . That was the beginning of her and my being so attached to each other. We just clung to each other for a long, long time. . . . We still do. . . .

"But she was very open about it . . . which was wonderful. But the boys were not. . . . But that was to be expected. . . .

"Young Eric would try, on the surface, to discuss it. But Kevin wouldn't at all. He'd just remove himself. . . . He'd leave the room. When anyone would talk about her or ask questions about her he'd just remove himself. . . ."

Kevin Miles: "I got on my minibike and drove down to the place I would always go. When you asked me if I had a person I talked to during the time she was dying, you know . . . I think if there was anything that I did talk to it was this place that I would always go to . . . where I would sit by myself and sort of isolate a lot. . . . Or, I'd talk to my dog. . . .

"But I went down to that place. I do remember going down to that place and looking up in the sky and saying, 'God. *Ha. Ha. Right!* God? Right. God . . . sure.'

"And I went down there to the little ravine and smoked a cigarette or something. I did break a couple of logs against the trees. I don't really remember breaking them over Riann . . . I remember like breaking them over God . . . what my concept of what God was at that point. . . . Pretty warped.

"That's what I remember about the day. And then I probably drank or got high that night sometime. . . ."

Mrs. Miles: "It was so important to me that the funeral would be so beautiful—as beautiful as it was. . . . And that everything ran smoothly and that all plans had been carried out. . . . And that the children really thought of her. . . . And that we were able to talk about it."

Eric Miles, Jr.: "The funeral was hard, but I had my mission, which was to be strong and help everybody else and look good for family and friends. I remember my friends just being kind of in shock, with their mouths hanging open. And a lot of them came to the funeral, which was wonderful. . . . But they just didn't really understand all of it; and they couldn't. . . . But they looked at us and you could see in their eyes there was a great degree of concern.

"It was not, in an emotional sense, a big event. I think the biggest event was realizing that she was going to die as I saw Mom and Dad. . . . And then eight years later . . . when I first began to grieve. . . ."

Allison Miles: "I remember how many people went to the funeral and how many people cared . . . and a lot of things. I remember Dad getting mad because he didn't want me to wear what Riann was wearing. Because I remember Riann and I used to always dress alike. . . . And I asked them what she was wearing in the casket, and she had on this skirt that we used to wear at Christmas, and I wanted to wear that to the funeral, you know. . . . And Dad got all upset and said he didn't want me to wear it. . . . And that's just normal . . . But I remember wanting to have the same thing on that she did.

"I remember the pictures of friends' faces as I was walking out, you know . . . pictures. . . . I just looked and I saw my friend Mary looking at me. . . . It was like it was a dream, you know. . . .

"I remember I didn't really cry that much until walking down the aisle at the end. . . . As we left the funeral and Mom and I were walking out and her coffin was in front of us . . . and I was just like, 'She's in it. . . .' And I remember that being really final."

Mr. Miles: "I think . . . I guess I was in sort of shock . . . in a way. I certainly think I was emotionally in shock.

"I remember very distinctly . . . I remember leaving the church and getting into the limo to go over to the cemetery. . . .

"I've got to say . . . in a way . . . I think my feeling was one of relief . . . that I just wanted to get it over with, to get it over and done with. . . . Although I was touched by the service I was very impressed with what the Jesuit priest had to say—he was neat.

"But I suppose more than anything I was just glad it was over."

* * *

Kevin Miles: "I remember the funeral, the day of the funeral
. . . almost like the day before the funeral and the day after the
funeral . . . almost like one big party. There were so many
people at our house, so much food being brought over, and so
many relatives all over the place. . . . And everybody—us being
Irish; but not just the Irish—everybody drinking constantly.
There were so many people around that it was very easy for me
to sneak around there drinking. And I drank a lot. . . .

"I went to the funeral. I was very concerned that I sit in the
front seat of the limo. I remember that. . . . I guess I didn't
want to be back there with my family because I would probably
have had to feel more . . . even though that was something I
was totally unaware of. . . . But my body knew what to do.

"I remember, I think I put up a fight about what kind of
clothes we were supposed to wear. . . .

"I remember when we showed up there in a limosine and my
friends walked by. . . . I remember my friends walking by and
looking in the window, you know. I was just sort of looking at
them and I didn't know what to do.

"So we went in, and I think my brother and I insisted on
pushing the coffin up . . . I think so. . . . I remember at some
level I wanted to just carry the thing myself on my back. But we
went up there and sat down and I just listened to the funeral.
You know, over the years part of me sort of blocked out what
went on at the funeral. . . . I mean, what the day was like and
what was said and things like that.

"But I do remember being at the funeral and looking over at
the coffin, you know, and thinking that, okay, okay, I guess I
was supposed to be sad here or something.

"And then this weird thing happened where I was looking at
the casket, this little white casket, and I said to myself, 'Imagine
if your brother was in there . . .' you know. . . . And that started
choking me up a little. Looking back on that it just absolutely
amazes me. 'Imagine if your brother was in there. . . .'

"I couldn't face this thing. . . . So badly I couldn't face this
thing that I couldn't even think of *her*. . . . I mean, it was just
like, you know. . . . It was like I had to think of somebody else.

"We went to the grave . . . I just remember being numb . . .
for the burial. . . .

"I remember those things and then the burial and then going

back to the house for the parties. . . . Go back to the house for the big parties, you know. . . . And everybody got blasted.''

Allison Miles: "I remember going back to my grandmother's house after and everyone was, you know, drinking and talking. . . . And I got really mad : . . I was. . . . I don't know who I said it to . . . but I just said I was so mad that they were all laughing and having a good time and drinking and eating. . . .

"I was like . . . 'How can they *do* this?' I thought, 'This is horrible!' I was thinking 'This is such a horrible thing to do. . . .'

"I remember that really well."

Mrs. Miles: "I remember one of the most beautiful things that happened. . . . The night she was buried we were all back here . . . and Eric took the boys in the room and had them sit down and told them how proud he was of them . . . and the wonderful job they'd done in helping. . . . What wonderful brothers they'd been to Riann . . .

"He was crying. And I don't think they'd ever seen him cry. . . .

"So after they finished talking the boys went up to their room and they wrote us a letter and put it on our pillow . . . telling us what wonderful, loving, giving, strong parents we've been through all of this. . . . That was the greatest gift we could have ever gotten . . . short of having Riann back.

"I have it framed. . . . It's very, very special. . . .''

Kevin Miles: "One sort of significant thing I remember is that my dad took my brother and I into the bedroom and sat us both down on this little stool, you know . . . little stool in their bedroom. And he shut the door and stood in front of us and said . . . this is after, you know, he was half in the bag, and everybody else was. . . . And he said, 'I just want to tell you boys that I'm very proud of you and how you've dealt with this whole thing.'

"And he tried to go on, and then he just . . . *broke* . . . down. . . . He *broke down.* And I just remember watching him *fight like hell* to not let it come out. . . .

"And he broke down. And as soon as he broke down—I mean, it came out almost like a powerful sneeze. . . . If you've ever seen somebody who sneezes really hard; your whole body just goes—and he ran out of the room into the bathroom. And he kept saying, 'I'm sorry. I'm sorry. I'm sorry.'

"And Eric and I just looked at each other and Eric went, 'Wow.' And I think he came back out and we went on with the party.

"I had never ever seen him cry in my entire life before. My brother said he did cry on his father's grave, which I wasn't there for. . . . But I had never . . . I'd never seen him cry at all."

Mr. Miles: "I don't think I cried the day of the funeral. . . . I think . . . you know, I never let myself become sort of hysterically crying because, again, that was what I was trained never to do.

"I really can't remember crying. . . . I think maybe Catharine and I did it together . . . but I think that was after the funeral. . . .

"I really can't remember crying. . . ."

Mrs. Miles: "It took about a year for it to hit me . . . really hit me . . . that Riann was dead. It was in April . . . the following April of the year she died. . . . And I started having depression and anxiety . . . breathing problems . . . and crying a lot. I remember getting up in the morning and being so depressed and just crying all the time.

"It took quite a while to hit, I think, because I was mostly so relieved she was out of her agony and pain and we weren't having to live with that time bomb all the time.

"And I think that when that all wore off I was really, really depressed. . . .

"And I was scared, too. I'd never felt depression before . . . never felt *that* kind of depression before. . . . And it scared me to death.

"And I was afraid to be alone. . . .

"And I thought about suicide . . . and all those horrible, helpless feelings.

"I remember Meg recognized this depression and she told

me I should go to a psychiatrist, which I did. But I think that second year was really as bad as the first year, maybe worse. . . .

"The first year all the anniversaries were difficult . . . Christmas, the big moments of anniversaries of her life, and what we'd done together that last year or two. . . .

"Then the second year it was that awful loneliness and devastation that she was *never* going to be back. . . .

"It was hard to find a psychiatrist or a psychologist who counseled bereaved people back then. I just happened to luck onto someone through a Jesuit priest I knew who recommended him. And he was perfect for me.

"He was so understanding and gentle, and affirmed me a lot . . . because I was really afraid of myself . . . and I really was becoming so insecure. I just didn't know what was right and what was wrong anymore . . . what I was feeling. . . . And he was very helpful and I went to him for a year and a half. . . ."

"I think that if I were to do it over maybe I would have gotten more family counseling. . . . And learned more in communication skills. That's one thing I would have done differently.

"But there wasn't much emphasis then on family counseling . . . fourteen, fifteen, sixteen years ago. But I think that would have been very important."

Mr. Miles: "The mourning process is one of the things that I had trouble with . . . coming from this tradition of not mourning . . . of when it was over, it was over and put away. And this is when Catharine and I got help in talking about mourning and talking about the need to mourn and the need to face it.

"It took Catharine and me a long time to really be able to communicate about it and sort of mourn together. . . . But we did.

"It took a long period of time. . . . It wasn't just done in the next couple of weeks or months. . . . It took a long time to do that.

"I do remember crying . . . really later . . . and I think it was with Catharine. . . . But I didn't feel relief. I think I felt guilty . . . because the whole mourning process was foreign to me. No, I really can't say guilty. . . . I just didn't let it last too long."

"I think the thing we totally lacked—*totally* lacked—was anybody who had been on the same boat, that we could talk to.

"To me, one of the greatest things Catharine is doing now is her work with families of children with brain tumors at University Children's. I've sat in on a few of those sessions, and I think they're *very* helpful.

"The biggest help that I could have gotten . . . looking back . . . was to talk to somebody who I could communicate with who could tell me what was going on at the time. . . .

"Just as an example . . . the hospital where Kevin was later has a team approach. And Catharine and I spent a lot of time before, during and after our various sessions with the social worker. And so we were really able to know what was going on, what the process was. All of our questions were answered.

"The thing that I think was the most difficult for me was really *not knowing*. It's, in a way, sort of like anything else . . . the more you know about it the more you can come to grips with it.''

Mrs. Miles: "I would really have benefited from other people's experiences . . . I think I relied too much on the doctors' advice and not someone who really had been through it. And that's why I feel so strongly about the volunteer work I do with brain tumor families . . . because I feel I would have loved to have had someone who'd been through it there for me . . . to help guide me. . . .''

Allison Miles: "Thank God Mom and I had each other through it because . . . I would always come down and her and I would sit in that blue and white chair in her bedroom and I would just sit and cry. . . . I cried a lot, you know. . . . I didn't keep it in. I don't think I was old enough where I could have built up a defense system at that point.

"But I remember after she died. . . . I mean I knew she was dead . . . but I had dreams all the time that she was in the closet and I'd run and open the closet. . . .

"Before she died she was doing this needlepoint thing for me in the hospital, and then I got it on my birthday and I was like, 'Oh my God, she didn't die. . . . She didn't die. . . .' And I ran upstairs.

"I guess I just didn't really think she had died, you know. . . . I mean I *knew* she had but. . . . It was all just a little too over-whelming. . . .

"I had Riann's baby pillow and this doll, Wendy . . . it's still in my room. . . . And when I wanted to cry I would just grab those two. . . .

"It comes . . . it came at different times . . . I remember. I'd cry and cry. It was . . . probably a couple years after she died and I used to ride my bike to the grave all the time. . . . And every time I went I sat and talked with her for a while. . . . And I sat and I. . . . You know when you just cry and you just cry until you feel like a lung is going to come out or something . . . you just have to cry something right out. . . .

"I remember doing that and realizing. . . . She's really dead."

Kevin Miles: "From when she got sick . . . from when she was dying, life always seemed to me like a very sad, tragic sort of dreamy thing. And I sort of hung onto that sadness.

"But it wasn't until I was nineteen years old that I was able to ever admit to myself, 'Okay, my life is screwed up. . . .' And though I was nineteen when I first thought I had some problems, it wasn't until I was twenty-six that I fully faced a lot of these problems.

"And I did some insane things, increasingly severe, between the ages of thirteen and twenty-six. I did everything in my power, without being blatant about it, you know—putting a gun to my head—I did everything in my power to be self-destructive. There was total insanity.

"Usually it had to do with alcohol and drugs. Car crashes . . . Trouble with the law . . . Beaten up by policemen . . .

"Incredibly self-destructive behavior where anytime anything good happened to me. . . . Like, I was an actor; and when I was in the movie . . . the night before the big scene I was sup-posed to do . . . I went out and got blasted and got beat up by police. Things like that constantly.

"Then, by the time I was nineteen, basically between nine-teen and twenty-one, I was in and then out and then back into drug/alcohol rehab programs. . . . And then in a psychiatric hospital for a whole year. . . . And I got out of there and still struggled.

"The sort of funny thing is that I was so afraid of *facing* a lot of these feelings that I had . . . especially about Riann and things related to that . . . and so much of it has to do with Riann.

"I learned a lot in the psychiatric hospital. And then I got into psychoanalysis for four days a week for almost five years. And I learned so much. . . . And I learned all these words. . . . I learned why I did things. . . . I learned what I was feeling. . . .

"But I didn't change. I still didn't *express* my feelings. There's a big difference between verbalizing your feelings and expressing your feelings.

"People talk about working something out and working through the pain. From my experience, which I have a lot of, I don't think words do it. I think words can lead you to expression, but the words don't do it. It was only when I started to *express* the pain and anger and everything that my life started to change at all.

"I got sober through a program where you're with other people. I tried to do it by myself for a while and nothing happened. . . . And I started to find out just how big my rage was, and is . . . and it's huge. I struggle with that so much. I have so much anger. . . . I'm an extremely angry person. But I'm not a mean person. . . .

"So I learned how to *express* my fears and my anger and my rage. For years, despite alcoholism, even when I wasn't drinking, I had severe problems with depression, where I'd be in bed, for two days and the doctors would put me on anti-depressants. It was just horrible. . . .

"But directly correlating with finally learning how to be open and express my anger, I don't have to sleep like I used to."

Eric Miles, Jr.: "I would have probably tried to be the 'White Knight' even if Riann hadn't died, because I saw the behavior in myself even before she got sick. And I saw that I was being given the cues even before that. But I believe it was certainly exaggerated by Riann's death.

"I think that a lot of the problems . . . the struggles that Kevin has with himself were also there before Riann's death. . . . But I think they, also, were exaggerated because of it.

"I have a kind of reflexive image of myself as what I call a 'White Knight.' I'll seek love and attention and respect and confidence through the eyes of my family and friends by being a White Knight and by trying to do what they think is right.

"I really started doing this somewhere in high school. Kevin would act out and I would be the peacemaker. We'd both get drunk; but Kevin would get caught, and I'd just breeze in unscathed.

"But being a perfectionist like that and demanding that of yourself . . . and letting others demand it of you . . . is honestly not realistic. All it's going to do in the end is make me frustrated and bitter and depressed.

"The first time I began to realize this was about the end of my college, senior year. I began to ask a lot of questions within myself . . . 'What am I going to do? Where am I going to do it? What's my career? How do I want to lead my life?' Big questions . . . questions that Allison is going through and struggling with right now.

"I can remember talking with some friends and talking with this social worker at school. I knew then that there was a problem there beyond just the mere growing up and coming out of college anxiety. . . . I knew there was something more, but I didn't want to get to it.

"Then I fell in love with this girl. . . . It was a courtship process which must have lasted a year and a half before we were really recognized as 'going out together.' It's been a big fear of mine . . . fear of loss in my relationships with women. I tend to kind of shy away from a lot of emotional involvement in that sense. In dating women it takes me a really long time to make a decision to ask a woman to go out on a date . . . to start developing some kind of relationship. . . .

"But I fell in love with this woman. . . . And after we had been going out together for about six months, I guess, I told her about Riann. But when I did it I exposed myself in such an emotional way. . . . I loved and trusted this woman enough . . . there was obviously such powerful emotion that came out when I told her . . . that it scared me. . . . It was like . . . for the first time like I really knew . . . really *felt* Riann was dead. And the power of the emotion . . . it scared me. I broke down and cried.

"I think I realized then that Riann's death had had a deeper effect on me than I'd ever let out. . . .

"But from then on I was very absorbed in graduate school and moving my career along and new experiences and new friends. . . . And so I didn't deal with it.

"After graduate school I came back here and was wrapped up in getting my social life going and doing well in my career. But at some point earlier this year I began to notice some depression that just seemed different . . . or longer . . . or worse. . . . And I couldn't understand it. I was getting depressions that were kind of broad . . . in questioning myself. . . .

"And I think a lot of it was this White Knight and perfection thing beginning to hit the barriers. . . .

"So I went to this therapist who has been helping me try to sort through it. And that's how we developed this idea of the perfectionist and the White Knight. . . . How it evolved, through Riann's death in part, as my role in the family. . . . And how it has affected my behavior in life.

"I've only relatively recently been able to understand it in that sense . . . and begun to see how understanding it can help me help myself to be a more happy and satisfied person.

"But *changing* those tendencies . . . those White Knight . . . perfectionist tendencies . . . is obviously harder. The depth to which these reflexes are built into me is incredible. After all, a White Knight wears shining armor and rides a big white horse. He's on a big white horse above everybody else . . . and his armor keeps him from being hurt. . . .

"But I've been hurt anyway. . . . The woman I loved . . . the one I trusted enough to grieve with about Riann . . . she essentially dumped me later. That was a *big* loss for me . . . because I still loved her. . . .

"And I lost my relationship with Kevin . . . Kevin and Eric as mutual supporters . . . Kevin and Eric almost as one. We identified so closely with each other in our emotional lives, in our social lives . . . in everything we did. And then, as his sickness began to develop . . . we began to lose each other.

"I, as the 'White Knight' was trying to carry his load—always trying to defend him in the family; always trying to create peace between he, Mom and Dad. . . . And eventually it became such an enormous burden on me that I shed my White Knight role, probably for the first time ever.

"I confronted Kevin and I said, 'I don't know you anymore. I can't deal with you anymore. Part of my frustration is *my* problem because I've been trying to help you but you don't want my help . . . you don't acknowledge it. I'm frustrated to hell with you, and I don't want you anymore. . . . Get out of my life. . . . You just hurt me too much.'

"And I just kind of threw that away. And that was a very big moment in my life. It was a loss almost as painful as Riann . . . maybe more so. Losing Kevin seemed to completely legitimize the fear of loss I had as a result of Riann . . . and said to me this is pain I cannot bear.

"Because losing Kevin was, in a way, like a death, too. . . . Because what we knew of each other and had with each other was gone. It was like the old Kevin was dead. . . . And it's probably going to be a long time before the new Kevin emerges. And I don't know what the new Kevin is . . . or if I'll even like it or want it.

"He and I were so close . . . far closer than I was with Riann. . . . So, in that sense that loss was very great for me."

Allison Miles: "After my sophomore year in college I remember I was really upset. . . . But I didn't realize, 'til around my senior year, that it wasn't the other stuff that was going on that needed to be talked about. . . . It was things related to Riann that needed to be talked about. But I had always been too scared. . . .

"I saw the psychologist Mom and Dad had seen once or twice when I was younger. But I always felt like he was, sort of, their guy and I never really opened up to him.

"Then I saw this lady in the city the summer after my sophomore year. But she kind of reminded me of . . . I don't know . . . of a Rock Shores housewife. That sounds really harsh. I'm not trying to sound mean. But I just felt like I couldn't open up to her either.

"But then I saw this guy at college . . . this psychologist. And he was totally removed . . . like it wasn't a friend of Mom's who recommended him or anything. He's an incredible guy. He really helped me out with a lot of things . . . things I've never talked with my parents about.

"I said to myself when I went to see him, 'You've got to work this out about Riann. It's thirteen years ago. . . . You're twenty-one. . . . You've got to get over this. . . . You've got to deal with it as an adult.' But it was kind of hard . . . because I'd really never talked to my parents about anything I talked to this guy about. . . .

"Eric and I talked about it earlier this year. . . . I remember thinking consciously after Riann died, 'You'll never do anything to worry your parents. You always have to be perfect; have *great* grades; be everything Riann ever would have been plus tons more to make up for the pain.'

"And that . . . putting up this, like, perfect front . . . that's really hard to live up to and it's something I didn't even realize I did until this year.

"I did it because I wanted to make my parents happy. And I think I'll always want to please them in that way. But it makes me never look at myself.

"I'm always saying, 'Well, I can do better at that' . . . or, 'You can get better grades.' Then I get the best grades I could and I'm like, 'but I could have done better.'

"I can remember doing that starting about seventh grade. I think that's probably normal . . . but just trying to live up to . . . I don't know how to explain it . . . but. . . .

"Riann died . . . I just said, 'Well, she was such a great person that I have to fill that void within Mom and Dad's life,' you know . . . and I think in some cases in Kevin and Eric's lives, too. . . . Plus being the only girl left. I said, 'Well I just better take that over . . . and just be everything . . . and . . .

"I think things would have been a lot different if Riann hadn't died. I try not to think about it . . . because you just don't know. . . . I think Mom and Dad would have always had high expectations of their children . . . which is fine . . . there's nothing wrong with that.

"But Riann's death . . . it was a complete loss of control in their lives . . . and I think my Mom likes to be in control and be organized. I think because of that she just wanted to have everybody . . . just, 'Okay, everything's going to be *right* from now on.'

"'Cause, I mean when you look at pictures of our family . . . we were just the perfect little family and nothing was wrong. And then you take a piece out . . . take Riann out . . . and . . .

"I think Mom and Dad haven't meant to . . . it's been subtle . . . but maybe they put pressure on us. . . . I don't know if they have on Kevin because he was kind of the mess-up. That was his role. But Eric's, like, you know, the 'White Knight'. . . .

"I don't really know where my role is but I think . . . if Riann had never gotten sick and she . . . I just can't even fathom that. . . . But I think maybe I would have felt like it was more equal . . . like we were the two girls and we could kind of do our thing. . . .

"But it's all hard to know. . . . I mean, my parents are absolutely the most incredible parents I could ever ask for . . . and I'm not trying to sound like they're not caring, because they are. But . . . I guess there are just certain parts of me that . . . in the back of my head . . . I mean . . . I just don't want my parents to think, 'There's nothing wrong with Allison.' But I'm probably not ready to tell them what is wrong. . . . I don't know if I'll ever. . . . I probably should some day . . . but it's things that involve Riann . . . and it's just too . . . it's still too hard. . . .''

"On my twenty-second birthday this year I was with a bunch of my friends. . . . We were at the shore . . . it was right before graduation. . . . And I just completely fell apart on my birthday . . .

"I was having a great time with all my friends . . . and I just totally fell apart. . . . I felt so much *guilt* . . . like, 'Why didn't *I* die?'. . . . 'Why did she die?' and 'Why couldn't she have lived this?'

"I just felt, you know, 'Here I am with all my friends . . . I'm in college. I love this school and I've had so many great experiences . . . and *she* . . . *never* . . . *got* . . . *any* . . . *of that*. . . .' Just, all the things that lots of people take for granted . . . and she never got to do any of it.

"You can carry that around as baggage for a long time . . . and I think it's affected a lot of things I've done.

"Not that I don't think I'll be able to ever throw it away. . . . I don't know if I'll ever be *totally* free of it. . . . But, I mean, I think if I just said to myself, 'Well, she *did* die, and you *didn't* die . . . and you have to stop feeling guilty because you didn't. . . .'

"That therapist I saw at school helped me a lot with that. I don't know if I could have dealt with that at an earlier age unless somebody had really dragged it out of me. . . . Because I couldn't even admit until last year that I felt really guilty."

Kevin Miles: "I think today I feel a lot more comfortable about the anger I had while Riann was dying . . . and for her while she was dying. I think maybe some of it seems to have dissipated.

"I went to her grave yesterday. . . . You know, I used to go to her grave a lot with a six-pack and sit there. . . . I was already drunk before I had the six-pack . . . but I'd wind up there at the grave at six o'clock in the morning . . . be weaving and everything, you know. . . . But then I realized that it doesn't count . . . it sort of doesn't count when you do it that way.

"So then for years I'd go back to the grave when I wasn't drinking . . . at various times . . . and nothing would happen.

"Now I go back to the grave *sober* . . . you know, things are going well. . . . And yesterday I was very comfortable with just . . . just crying like a baby. . . . And I didn't feel any anger yesterday. . . . I just felt a lot of sadness and a lot of hurt . . . . pain . . . this sort of empty feeling

"I always had the feeling, when I think about it, that I just wanted to hold her once more . . . like touch her once more before she died. . . . Like I wanted to just talk to her once more . . .

"But I think I'm a lot more comfortable with it. . . . It almost seems like the anger I had for her dying is a memory now more so than a feeling.

"I don't want to have to go through anything like Riann's death again . . . and I wouldn't wish it on anybody. . . . But I don't think I'd be the person I am today if it weren't for that . . . and for being a recovering alcoholic—though I know a lot of people won't know what I'm talking about. But most people haven't gone through as much as I've gone through.

"There are some moments where I've been able to really help some people who have had friends and relatives die. The thing that's so amazing . . . because of this 'education' I've gotten through my own hell. . . . I know what they're feeling even when they don't. I'm able to say, 'I think I know what's going on.' I give them examples.

"And because it's so true to what they're feeling . . . it just punches a chord in them and they open up. . . . And I'm able to help them get rid of some of their baggage. . . .

"And also be a *fine* example of how *not* to deal with death."

Eric Miles, Jr.: "Today I guess I'm kind of a classic yuppie . . . very ambitious . . . very motivated. I have a pretty broad array of interests along professional lines and social concerns. I spend very much of my time working . . . and I do some volunteer work.

"I'm a pretty intense person . . . I'm still a pretty private person. . . . Also lonely in some ways . . . in wanting to share more of my feelings and my emotions and still struggling in trying to do that. That does create some loneliness. . . .

"I think I'm bitter in some ways about what our whole family has gone through . . . what Kevin has gone through. . . . Feeling something good has come out of it . . . but still searching in ways to understand it better . . . because it's so much a part of my life . . . so much of it's based in my life. . . .

"I see so much in what I'm doing right now . . . so many interesting possibilities . . . that I like being Eric Miles, Jr., doing what he's doing right now. But right now I'm also trying to find a way not to have to answer to the old idea of doing everything perfect in order to give myself self-worth. . . . To not have to develop my self-worth through the eyes of others . . . or through my role in the family as the protector . . . the person who smoothes out the problems and keeps them together and never has a problem himself . . . because there are so many other problems there that I don't want to be another problem. . . .

"The pressure I feel on that from my Mom sometimes is very big. 'I need you to be perfect. I need that for myself and we need that for the family; so please be perfect.'

"My Mom is so loving and feeds me so much reinforcement . . . and I get a lot out of that. But I'm trying now to find a way to not be so susceptible . . . to not be a slave to her need for me to be perfect. . . . Which translated throughout my life into my need for me to be perfect . . . in order to get love and attention . . . to get a better idea of self-worth.

"So it's funny . . . I depend quite a bit on Mom for reinforcement and for boosting my confidence and self-image. . . . But that type of dependence isn't healthy . . . because it's just kind of building a wall against the incoming tide . . . which is just going to run over it anyway. . . .

"I can remember when Kevin left for the hospital—that was hard for Mom . . . she cried at the table. . . . I can remember she said, 'I swore to God that none of my children would ever end up in a psychiatric institution. . . .' That was just so painful for her.

"And, of course, my immediate reaction was, 'God, I could never do something like that. . . .'

"So I understand her need. . . . I respect her need. . . . But I can't fill it. I don't want to fill it. She's got to give up something. . . . and I have to give up something."

"My father is a wonderful person and a very giving person . . . a very warm person. He was my ultimate role model growing up . . . where I took a lot of my cues from. I love him. I respect him.

"But I remember I was in high school . . . or early college. . . . I remember kind of coming to better understand the weaknesses my parents have as humans. . . . And one was Dad. . . . And I remember getting very frustrated at one point . . . and I still do to a certain extent.

"In my perception . . . Dad has a very naïve view of the world. . . . And maybe I harbor some resentment . . . in that it was through a lot of his example that I internalized that I should be a very independent, strong person who would not be susceptible to all emotional issues which are more, kind of, the 'province of women.'

"And as I got to know Dad better as a human being and Mom better as a human being I began to understand myself better in these two different parts and ways.

"My Dad and I have very enjoyable times together because we have a lot of common interests . . . and I think we both get a lot out of that. . . . But in terms of fully deep emotional sharing . . . it's much harder to do that with my father than my mother. In some ways Dad doesn't seem to want to get into that.''

Mr. Miles: "I think my problem with showing any emotions is something that came, in general, out of the 1920s. But it's also something, I think, that came out of my father's very troubled childhood.

"When Kevin was hospitalized we spent a lot of time going back. . . . And we realized that my father was certainly affected by . . . and his sister certainly was affected by . . . the particular world they grew up in.

"My father never knew his father, because he died when he was very young. And his mother remarried . . . and then when he was still very young his mother died. So he never knew his parents . . . and had been brought up by stepparents. . . . And so there was not the openness of emotions. . . .

"So . . . I've gone totally the other way. . . . I really believe now in openness and showing your emotions. . . . Really as much through the whole experience with Kevin and being counseled there . . . my whole look at that has changed. . . . I know it's so much healthier for people to be able to get the emotions out and get the feelings out. . . .

"For me . . . I find it's much less difficult for me to display emotion now than it was at the time Riann was sick and when she died. . . . But every now and then I've got to catch myself . . . and say, 'Hey, that's not the way to go, you know. Look what we've learned. . . . Open yourself up. . . .' ''

"There was a time after Riann died that I really thought we ought to bury her and let her go and not keep hanging on and bringing it back up year after year. . . . But having lived through that now for fourteen years I think that it has been good for Catharine . . . and, in retrospect, good for our family.

"I guess the only question I have is, doing it as much as we did, was it good for Kevin?

"But looking back on it all . . . and we've thought quite a bit about it. . . . I really don't think we could have done anything differently. I think we were as open and honest and realistic as we could have been with all the kids, certainly more so with Eric and Kevin than with Allison. . . .

"I think Kevin's problems, which are complex problems, really are more than Riann's death. I'm personally convinced that whether Riann died or not, Kevin would probably have still had some of the same problems and have gone through the same phases that he's gone through.

"I think that Riann's death was, in a way, kind of . . . maybe . . . that 'extra load' that brought it forth when it did. But I think that it would have come anyway.

"And I also have to believe that he a little bit used her death as a crutch for excusing some of his actions and some of his behaviors. I don't know . . . I don't know if I'll ever know. But I think we both handle it well in our own ways . . . and respect each other's judgment on it."

Mrs. Miles: "I think one of the most difficult things that kept coming back in the last fourteen years was that our family wasn't complete . . . that there was somebody missing . . . there was something missing. . . . And that person's missing brought about a lot of other side issues that surfaced in our family . . . side issues that became important issues that had to be worked through, be dealt with and overcome.

"We had to deal with a lot of pain and sorrow, and everybody did it differently. . . . It was very individual with each person . . . and they dealt with it at different times. . . . We didn't get over with it all at once. . . . It dragged out for a long, long time. And there will always be scars.

"There are times when I think that if Riann had *just lived* . . . we wouldn't have had this, or this, or this to deal with. . . . Then I think, 'Well, we wouldn't be what we are now . . . and we all seem to like what we are now. . . .' So that's the good with the bad. . . ."

"Riann's dying was a disaster to our marriage. We had always been so communicative, we thought, and shared things and been honest with each other. We had really good communication skills, I thought.

"But the minute Riann was diagnosed, that communication

barrier just went up . . . and we really had trouble being honest with each other.

"We didn't want to hurt each other. . . . We wanted to protect each other. . . . So we wouldn't really share what was going on inside us because we thought it was too painful for the other.

"If I was experiencing one period in my grief Eric wouldn't be experiencing it at the same time. . . . It was just like a merry-go-round . . . a roller coaster. . . .

"And I was resentful because he didn't verbalize it. . . . And I verbalized it so much that he probably got so tired of listening . . . I know he did. We just really had trouble for a long time, and it was based on communication . . . and both of our different ways of grieving . . . our different ways of handling it. . . .

"I thought about separation . . . but, well, we had so much. . . . We both had the ability to make our marriage work. It was just a matter of being diligent about it and *working* at it . . . and not giving up on it. I just knew that if we were to separate it wasn't going to make our life any better.

"I thought, in fact, it would make it worse . . . Because we would have to deal with the problems entailed with children . . . And I knew what that would do to the children on top of losing Riann . . . and having us separate. . . . Our problems would be compounded as far as the children were concerned, which would only add more to our misery. So all the more reason to try to make it work. . . .

"And it did work. Communication . . . honesty—being honest and saying what we felt. . . . We had to learn new communication skills. . . . But it did work.

"It took a long time. . . . As we both emerged from our different grief periods we were able to regroup again . . . but in a different way. . . . Because we were both very different people.

"The story about 'never being the same again . . .' You never are.

"But the big fear I had was that we would grow out of this and we would grow worlds apart. . . . Because as you grow out of it . . . you're always searching for that new person, that different person who's evolved. . . . It's almost like starting to build a whole new personality. . . . And that's kind of scary.

"Before Riann's death . . . and before our anguish over Kevin's period of difficulties . . . our marriage was very different. I was a different person. . . . I was a much more dependent wife—really a little girl in a sense. And now we both are much more individuals in the marriage . . . and able to not be so dependent on each other.

"Yet we love each other and respect each other and . . . well, we're both more mature. I think we've grown through the problems and the difficulties and struggles . . . We worked at it *so hard* that we've emerged more mature and able to understand each other as individuals and respect each other's individuality.

"Before, we were intertwined in our dependency . . . but it was an immature dependency. Now we have a different type of dependence.

"I think when you've been through a lot of struggles together . . . you grow through them together, but yet you become individually strong."

Mr. Miles: "There is no question that our marriage has changed a lot because of Riann's death. It was very shortly after that Kevin got into all of his problems . . . And facing that and struggling with that and going through the psychiatric hospital scene and the ups and downs of that. . . .

"The bottom line is that what has happened, through *an awful lot of help* and through an awful lot of different sources, is that our marriage has strengthened considerably.

"I fully realize that it will never be what it was before. . . . Because when we first got married everything was sort of idyllic. . . . We had four great kids . . . and everything going great. . . .

"Our marriage has become much more realistic. Our expectations are more realistic.

"But there's no question that our relationship has strengthened. . . . so that when we have other serious problems, whether they be with Catharine's family or my family or whatever, we're much better able to cope. I think you have to say it's a much more mature relationship.

"But it will never be what it was before . . . because those days are just gone. . . ."

Allison Miles: "I wish I remembered more about Riann. I mean, I remember little things here and there . . . like she and I probably had one fight in the eight years of being buddies, being sisters. . . . But I remember when she died I was like, 'I'm so sorry . . . so sorry we had that fight. . . .' I just remember dumb things like that. . . . Not that it was dumb . . . but I do wish I remembered more.

"I always think, you know . . . like even when I read *Go Out In Joy!* . . . I always think those are such important memories . . . even helping me to deal with Riann's death at age twenty-two.

"I wish I had more memories. I wish I *knew* how I felt through the whole thing. . . . I wish I knew how I acted. . . . I wish I could remember more. . . . I mean remember really significant things."

"I think I would tell any kid going through the death of a brother or sister . . . the most important thing to do is grieve it. Thank God I did as much as I did . . . and thank God I had Mom who let everything out, you know . . . rather than like Kevin who didn't grieve . . . he just buried it all. . . .

"I think I buried a lot of things too . . . but I think grieving it is probably the most important advice . . . crying. . . .

"And I think talking helps . . . talking to your brother or sister who had died. . . . I still say goodnight to Riann every night. . . .

"I wish there was something . . . something like a formula . . . or some prayer . . . for dealing with it. I mean certain books and things help . . . like Mom sends people prayers and stuff . . . but you really don't know what to say. I just wish there was a formula. . . .

"You just need to stay close to your family, I guess. . . . that's probably the most important thing. . . . To just stay open and keep talking about it and don't block it out . . . because it's going to come out another way if you do. Just grieve it . . . with your family. . . .

"Don't do like I've tried to do, you know . . . and also what Eric's tried to do—try to be perfect and make everything go right in your life. Don't do that. And don't rebound and go the other way . . . like Kevin . . . either. . . .

"But if you're always trying to please and you're always trying to make everything perfect in your life to take away pain from others . . . The pain that's inside you is just going to keep growing . . . and it's just going to keep stuffing you and stuffing you. . . .

"And it starts to . . . it starts to show, and—I mean, maybe it will never start to show. . . . Maybe it'll always just stay down there—"

"I mean . . . I found . . . I just don't let it out. I'm like, 'You just keep doing what you're doing then everything will be fine. You've dealt with Riann and you don't have to deal with it any more.'

"But, I really hadn't. . . .

"And the more you try to make everything look like it's fine . . . the more you start hurting inside.

"I think I've always been pretty open about my mourning . . . always open about how much I miss Riann . . . because I always miss her. . . .

"But there are certain . . . certain parts I just . . . it's too hard to open up."

"As you're going through it . . . you just think it's never, ever going to get any better. . . . You're never going to be able to cope . . .

"And some days you just never know when it's going to hit you . . . and you're a wreck. I remember . . . at times I wouldn't think of Riann for a day . . . and I would be like, 'I'm sorry Riann.' I'm sorry I didn't think of you today.'

"And one April 29th . . . the day she died . . . you know, I always go to church and I always talk to her and kind of have my own little private grieving or whatever. . . . And then one year . . . one April 29th . . . I felt so bad that night . . . because I had almost forgotten the day. . . .

"But you just have to accept it and learn that you have to go on. . . . You're never going to forget. But though the pain is still there . . . it's different in some ways . . . because time has gone by and you've learned to accept it. . . ."

"The resenting part is hard, you know . . . resenting God . . . the anger. . . . It's normal, but . . . you just have to try to think of the good things. . . . It sounds so cliché, but try to remember all the good things about the person . . . the good times you had together. . . .

"Like I always think, 'Oh, she's better off, or she's happier now. . . .' I don't know if I buy all that, but . . . it's just so hard. . . .

"There are so many people I talk to and that I want to help . . . if I know somebody's just died. . . . And I just say, 'I don't want to say this . . . but it's going to get worse . . . you know. . . . You're going to have more pain . . . in the next. . . .' "

Kevin Miles: "I would tell kids who had a brother or sister dying . . . first I would say, 'Allow yourself the freedom, as difficult as it is. . . . Give yourself permission to *feel whatever is there inside of you* about the situation. However the situation makes you feel . . . no matter how crazy it might seem to you . . . give yourself the freedom to feel it and be aware of it and *express it.*

"Be careful about who you listen to. A lot of people will tell you, 'No, no, don't feel that way about it. You shouldn't feel that way about it.'

"There is no *correct* way of feeling. Find out *yourself* how you actually feel about it . . . whether it makes you furious or sad or happy . . . it doesn't matter. There are no rules at all.

"The second piece of advice is: If you can find out how you feel about that, then find somebody that you feel comfortable expressing it to. Then tell them how you feel about the person in your family who is dying.

"Really take care of yourself by *expressing* it to someone that you trust. Talk about it as much as you can; and express it. There are no rules in that area either. . . . Sure, in the middle of a restaurant you're not going to turn the table over. But if you have to break things where it's okay, do it. . . . Or, a room where you can go and just scream, do it.

"The third thing I would say is . . . be there for the person who is dying . . . *as painful as it is.* Just try to stick it out and be there for them . . . because, I think . . . if you're there with them a lot . . . maybe you'll start to learn some of the acceptance of their dying from them. Because it seems a lot of people who die . . . it seems they start to accept it sometimes. . . .

"And also, by being there you'd be watching what's happening and you'd have to face it and have to deal with it. . . . Though that's a tricky thing . . . because I was around it. . . .

"You can still not deal with it when you're around it. . . . So you have to just keep checking with yourself . . . sort of with your own heart and thoughts and feelings about what's going on inside of you.

"Be there for that person as much as you can. And don't beat yourself up. Those are the things I'd tell some little kid who was my age."

Eric Miles, Jr.: "I think you have to pay attention to your own needs. That sounds selfish . . . But in the long run, for everybody involved, if you can pay attention to your own needs and understand them and not feel selfish or guilty about them, and communicate them in a constructive way . . . then you're only helping.

"You talk with kids who have terminal illnesses, or people with terminal illnesses . . . and one of the greatest reliefs for them is to hear one of their close friends or family get mad at them or share their feelings with them . . . to say, 'God dammit, I *hate* what you're doing to me.' For them it's a relief.

"I wish I could have done that better right from the start.

"I think sibling groups help . . . *if* you can start right from the beginning. It's hard with young people who are sibs . . . especially teenagers . . . because they say, 'Hey, I'm too cool. I can handle this. No problem.' For any teen to express deep feelings like that . . . it's completely foreign. . . . They're just of a different mindset.

"But if you can start something right off the bat to encourage communication and to relieve any kind of inhibition or guilt. . . .

"Teach them to pay attention to their own needs. Say that it's okay. . . . Just keep repeating to them, 'It's okay to express your own feelings . . . the frustrations. . . . It's better for you and it's better for the person who's sick and it's better for your family.'

"At University Children's . . . what the group Mom does . . . Twice I've sat with a group of from five to fifteen-year-old sibs . . . and I talked about those issues. . . . I tried to make that my message without getting on a stump.

"I tried to hear them. . . . And I tried to pull out some feelings and emotions and reactions . . . recognizing that that's a release. I told them, 'Tell your parents that—don't forget. Don't forget. It's okay to be angry at your sister who is sick. It's okay to be angry at your parents who aren't paying attention to you. . . . Because, dammit, you're human.''

Allison Miles: "I guess I'd say to parents, be honest with your kids when you're going through the whole thing. . . . Don't whitewash it or lie to them in hopes you can help them. I know it's only meant to do good . . . because you're so worried about them. . . . But I think it's the worst thing you can do. . . . Which, you know, happened to me a lot . . . but I was little and they were trying to protect me.

"But you have to be honest with them and you have to just be there for them and communicate as well as you can . . . which Mom really did. Mom really wanted to grieve . . . and as I said . . . we have each other and that was really important. . . . But Dad . . . you know—He's gotten a lot better communicating now but he didn't . . . he was having trouble just dealing with . . . We were all having trouble. . . .

"It's just important to be open about it."

Kevin Miles: "I think, first of all, parents should set an example for their children by being open and expressive about their feelings about the child who is dying, no matter what those feelings are. . . . Set an example for their kids, difficult as that may be, to be open and really express what is going on.

"Fear—even if they think that fear may make the brothers and sisters afraid—be open with the fear; be open with the pain. . . . Set an example.

"The second thing is that if there are young kids involved . . . you know, sometimes it's very difficult for them . . . They don't know which way is up. . . . Sometimes they need help. They can't help themselves and they need to be helped. If that's the situation, watch the kids' behavior, don't listen to their words. Do listen to their words; *but watch their behavior*. I was always saying I was fine . . . fine. . . . But watch my behavior and I was saying that I was dying. Listen, but watch. Actions do speak louder then words.

"I guess the other thing I'd say is . . . after the child died . . . or is dying . . . I think that the kids who are alive have to be allowed to make mistakes, because your life is getting all shaken up. Your grades might drop, your work might suffer, whatever. . . . Let them know that it's okay to make mistakes. They don't have to be perfect throughout the situation, because if they do, it's like white-knuckling it.

"Be forgiving . . . give them their range. . . ."

Eric Miles, Jr.: "I'd say to parents, 'Listen to your kids. Listen not to what they are saying, but to what they are *doing*. . . .'

"And pay attention to your own needs, no matter how bad or selfish you think they are . . . because you're going to have to pay attention to them sooner or later. . . . And it's going to be tough to pay attention to them later.

"You have to do this by communicating as much as you can of your thoughts and feelings and angers and frustrations to everyone, including the source . . . especially the source.

"And see someone who can help you do that on your own . . . who will counsel you to help you through those steps.

"What I can't believe, though, is—and this is something else I would say to kids and parents—is just what an *incredible* effect Riann's death has had on our family, from the day she got sick. It completely changed all of our lives . . . forever.

"And no sense resisting the change, because it has happened. And you can go with it, or fight it and lose. Loss can be escape. . . .

"But it's amazing to see how it happens . . . just ripples through your lives and everybody else's. . . .

"There is good and there is bad that comes out of it. If you don't understand the bad, work with the bad . . . like through communication . . . and sharing.

"It's going to be a tough life. . . ."

Mrs. Miles: "I guess I'd say to anyone going through this . . . Find someone or some people you can trust, that you know can help you, really understand you. . . . And find someone who will listen. . . . And, hopefully, find someone or some people who have experienced what you're experiencing and can kind of tell you what is going on . . . what you might expect. That's why I'm so glad I've been able to go back to University Children's and work with other families who have . . . or have had . . . children with brain tumors. Eric and I both think that's so important.

"Also, learn how to communicate with your spouse and your family. *And be open and honest with your family.*

"Try to find your God in your period of grief . . . because you're so alone. And remember that you *are* alone in your grief, and that nobody can make it better for you. . . . It's really up to you and to your relationship with God to work through it.

"But remember that whatever you're feeling is normal for someone who is grieving and who has had such a devastating loss. Perhaps you can find groups that can help you know that . . . perhaps bereavement groups like Compassionate Friends . . . groups that can affirm you in your darkness. . . .

"And find someone that can tell you that you're going to make it. You're going to survive it."

Allison Miles: "Faith is a tough subject for me right now. . . . Mine's changed a lot. . . . I don't know if I want to try to talk about that right now. . . .

"I mean, it helped me when I was younger. . . . I always used to pray to God and pray to Riann as if, kind of, they were the same person. . . .

"I think it's important for everyone to have a faith . . . because I believe there's a God. . . . But you go through the anger part, as I said, and you think it's God's fault . . . or you don't know where to place the blame . . . but you can't blame it on him . . . you know. . . .

"It's not anyone's fault. . . . But, I mean, it's tough because when you're going through a bad time you want to have your faith . . . because you want to have something that is a mainstay. . . . But sometimes you feel like it let you down.

"I think faith is very important, but right now mine's . . . just in the past four years it's . . . I don't really know where it is. I mean, I'll always have one, but right now I'm just really confused about it. . . .

"When I was little I had to go to church every Sunday. I didn't know really what I was believing in. . . . You know . . . the

Catholic faith . . . I mean it's great . . . but it's kind of strange in some ways. . . .

"I try, but . . . I mean maybe if I'd grown up in another religion I would have said to God: 'I'm angry. What do I do?' . . . without feeling this incredible sense of guilt. . . .

"I guess that was tough . . . in trying to deal with my anger . . . I'd be angry at God; but feel *so* guilty for thinking that that I couldn't be . . .

"I still pray a lot . . . but I've had a little church-going problem of late. . . . But I think that will work out in time. I think I need to find, sort of, my own religion. . . . I've said guilt so many times it's not even funny. . . . But I guess I'd rather kind of go to church alone. . . . I'd feel like it's more my faith that way. . . ."

Kevin Miles: "My spirituality is huge now. I have a higher power. I pray a minimum of twice a day. My heart, my faith, my spirituality was reversed for me after I came so close to death so many times through my self-destructiveness. . . .

"Near the last time I ever had a drink I came so close to death that it was apparent to me that I shouldn't have lived . . . that I should have died.

"But some of those things that happened to me made me realize . . . I was able to see very clearly that, you know, 'I'm sure not keeping myself alive.'

"I *wasn't* keeping myself alive. Now I am. I'm fighting for it. But somebody else had kept me alive . . . because I had friends in high school who weren't as crazy as I was . . . and a couple of them are dead.

"So my spirituality is very big. But I don't really go to church because . . . I don't like the church and I don't like all the rules. My faith is very much along the lines of Christianity—I'm not a Buddhist or anything.

"But the truth is, I think a lot of the problems I had with my sister's death . . . some of the behavior patterns I learned about dealing with things . . . come from Catholicism. . . . Irish Roman Catholic church stuff.

"Today I don't believe in . . . a punishing, guilty God . . . I believe in somebody who is not like that at all. I'm still defining what I believe. . . .

"I pray a lot and I believe in a higher power, but it's not in the *church* sense . . . because I had it crammed down my throat when I was growing up and it had a really bad effect on me."

Eric Miles Jr.: "I always had this strong Catholic upbringing of course, and went through all the normal religious education. . . . But I never really took religious practice very seriously. I felt the act of going to church was a good thing for yourself and your community . . . for family. But I guess I always believed in a kind of very private God you can communicate to . . . you know, with the lights off in bed. . . .

"I used to communicate with that God more than I do now. . . . And my 'White Knight' image is very much one of self determination and the ability to do it by myself. . . . So it was an admission of weakness to pray to God when I hurt. But that seems to have faded some from my life.

"I still consider myself a Christian because of my concerns, and the things that I do, and the love I share with people, and the moral fabric of my life. But I don't have an active dialogue with God . . . or with Riann. . . .

"Maybe it's because I have this . . . some anger. . . . I've only gone to him when it hurts. . . . And when I go to him and say *please* make it stop hurting . . . and it doesn't . . . then I say, 'Well, what good is this?'

"I don't fathom 'having it out with God.' I seem to fathom more having it out with myself. . . .

"God's there. I imagine God is kind of benignly looking down and saying, 'Uh . . . right with you Chas. But, you know, you're on this earth and these are human struggles . . . and everybody's got to struggle . . . and good luck . . . and remember, think of me and work by my rules, and things will work out.' "

Mr. Miles: "I have a vision of what Riann might look like now. . . . Tonight we were looking at some pictures of her back a long time ago . . . when she was in camp. . . . She looked so much like Allison. . . . I never really had fantasized kind of what she might look like at age twenty-three. . . .

"If she was here right now . . . Wow! I'd say I was *glad* to see her . . . how *glad* I was to see her. . . .' "

Mrs. Miles: "When I go to Riann's grave I tell her I miss her . . . I feel her presence in my life. . . .

"I ask her to give me strength and guidance to do what she would want me to do. And I ask her to help me with my problems . . . with life problems. . . .

"And then there are a lot of times when I tell her I don't think it's fair. . . . And I know that she's happy and peaceful and that's the most important thing . . . but that I miss her terribly. . . ."

Allison Miles: "If Riann were here now . . . I'd just want to hug her . . . you know. . . .

"I don't know what I would say . . . just tell her I love her. . . . I'd just want to sit and talk with her for a minute. . . .

"I think a lot . . . like, what would she look like and what would we do? But you just can't think about it. . . ."

"In a way I feel like she's always with me . . . wherever I am . . . wherever I live. . . . I always have her picture right next to me and like she's always kind of at my side. . . . I think I'll always talk to her. . . .

"I just want her to meet people like my friends . . . and like the man I'll marry someday—like, 'Isn't he great and don't you love him!?'

"I'll always just talk to her. . . . Like when I go to her grave I just kind of talk to her and tell her what's going on in my life. . .

"I say, 'Riann, I really miss you.' I say, 'I hope things are okay up there' . . . you know, like their weather is going to be bad or something.

"But when I talk to her I always kind of envision her with all the people she loves around her. . . . I don't know if she's here or I don't know if it's 'up there.' I don't know where 'it' is . . . but I just have a feeling she's with the people she loves. . . .

"I want to keep her a part of my life. . . . I think no matter when it is in my life I'll always talk to her and . . . like . . . ask her to help me. . . .

"Now I ask her to help me try to complete the mourning process I started when she died. . . . Not that it's ever going to be over . . . but . . .

"It's so funny . . . anything that I ask her to do now . . . is to help me with *her*. . . .

"I ask her to help me try to get through the guilt I feel. . . . Because, I know she looks down, you know, and says, 'What are you feeling so guilty about . . . and what are you doing this for and what are you doing that for?'

"I know she wouldn't want me to feel that way . . . but it's hard. . . . It's hard to get rid of it. . . .

"I ask her to help keep our family close and keep Kevin on track . . . and Mom and Eric, you know . . . getting through their tough times. . . .

"I usually feel better when I go and talk to her . . . and have a good cry. . . ."

Kevin Miles: "When I went to Riann's grave yesterday . . . I remember the feelings. . . . I told her that I want to live.

"I said, 'You know, I've been doing so much the past years since . . . since you died . . . to try to die.' I was behaving like, 'OK, I can still walk around dead while I'm on the planet. That's what I did: walked around dead, under the blanket of alcoholism and drugs.'

"But, I told her, 'Believe it or not, I am actually *living* right now. . . . This summer I celebrated one year of being sober . . . of being sober *the right way*. I've made a lot of changes; I said, 'You know, I actually was able to have some time this summer when I felt *so free* . . . completely free and alive. . . . And I know that that will come back.'

"But I was just basically telling her that I want to live . . . and I want to have a full life. And I just was, like sort of asking her to help me . . . if she . . . if she could, you know.

"I also talked to her about the pain I feel about coming back to this place . . . because I haven't been home in over a year. Because when I used to come home I'd usually wind up having a slip with my drinking and drugging sometime soon afterwards. Or else I'd get a massive depression.

"But it was completely different this time. It's very painful to be at home and to be in the town this time. I think one reason it's painful is because, for the first time in my life, I've let go of my home. Because even when I wasn't living in Rock Shores and somebody would ask me where my home was I'd say, 'Rock

Shores, that's my home. That is always my home.' I was adamant about it. It's like I was hanging onto the place. And if I was hanging onto the place I was hanging onto Riann, because memories of her are throughout the place.

"Maybe that's why it hurt so much to go home yesterday, because I realized for the first time that it wasn't my home anymore. It's where I am *from*. But it's not my home. It's not my place. I have a new place. I think that's why it hurt so much . . . letting go of something I've been hanging onto for a long time. . . .

"I know it's a good step . . . it's a step that's going to free me up. . . . I'm going to be able to grow . . . to grow up finally—I'm twenty-seven going on thirteen right now. . . .

"But even though letting go is a good thing, a positive step . . . helping me grow . . . It doesn't feel like I would think letting go would feel. It hurts even though I'm giving up a thing that wasn't good for me in the long run. . . .

"So I think I sort of went to Riann's grave yesterday to tell her . . . about letting go . . . and to ask her permission . . . sort of. . . .

"I just wanted to ask her if everything was okay. . . . 'If everything's okay, then I'll be okay. But I have to know if everything's okay?' I think that's what I was doing yesterday. Trying to see if everything's okay. . . .''

Eric Miles Jr.: "I guess I'd say to God the same thing I'd say to my Dad . . . if I thought he'd understand. . . . 'Why . . . why didn't you tell me that it could *hurt so much*? Why didn't you prepare me for that?'

"I guess my dad had his way of doing it. He did what he thought was best. So would he even understand it . . . really?

"Then I'd ask God, 'What can I do to help *me* . . . because the pain is there . . . it's always going to be there . . . and I want to be able to deal with it, to handle it, to not let it push my life—or the fear of it push my life—in ways I don't like it to.'

"So, I'd say, 'Please God, tell me what I can do . . . to understand it, to be able to deal with it.' "

Allison Miles: "You know . . . like after all these years . . .

"I'd say, 'God, why did you take her?'

"It hurts. . . .

"You always think you can handle it, and sometimes you can forget . . . but . . . I know it's the first thing I'd ask him.

"I know it's not his fault . . . but there're just so many incongruities in this world and so many things . . . and I guess you're not meant to . . . But I'd ask him why he took her. . . .

" 'And you better be treating her well!' "

Kevin Miles: "I would just say, 'Thank, thank you . . .'

"And I'd say, 'Please help me to help myself to have a very good, full life.' That doesn't mean walk around with a smile on my face all the time. . . .

"A full life . . . a good life.

"And thanks for keeping me alive long enough to be able to live. . . .

"It's like having two lives . . . one I've learned with and the one I'm living now. . . ."

"That's what I would say."

Mr. Miles: "I'm really . . . I'm not mad at God . . . as Catharine has said she is on occasions. . . . Because, I don't know . . . I'm just too much of . . . I don't know the word— not necessarily 'realist'. . . .

"I just know that these things happen, just the way accidents happen. . . . I have lived in a world where bad things happen to people. . . . And I really can't say I'm angry at God, you know, for this particular thing. . . .

"I'd ask why . . . why the bad things happen in the world . . . and go back to the theoretical problem of why is there evil in the world? I'd like to ask him that question.

"But, you know, I've got a lot of things I'd like to ask him about the future . . . the plans and secrets of the universe . . . all that kind of thing . . ."

Mrs. Miles: " 'Why?' Fourteen years later. 'Why?' That's my *first* question I'd ask God. 'Why?' "

Allison Miles: "Riann was just a sweetie . . . you know. . . . She was so . . . she was just so good and always cared about everybody. . . . Just so good and gentle deep down . . .

"She always worried about everyone . . . and wanting them to not be worried about her. . . . When she was so sick . . . she was always so accepting of it. . . .

"She loved all her friends and she loved going to school. . . .

"She was just *my best friend*.

"Sometimes when I try to describe her to people . . . you know . . . they'll say maybe it's just 'hindsight'. . . . A lot of times people are sort of 'overglorified' after they die. . . .

"It's just hard to understand unless you knew her. . . ."

Eric Miles, Jr.: "Riann's death has greatly affected the people around her. A good example is this book. . . . Hopefully it will help many others. . . .

"And I think it made our family face some of the things we're facing now. It took a while, but it made us do that.

"It gave me a deeper emotional sense of perspective in my life and in other things. . . . Little things just aren't as important. . . . You understand your priorities in life a little better. When you've faced a brutal situation you've got to put the real priorities first to survive. And we had to.

"Our family has grown incredibly strong. I don't know whether it's good or bad to be that strong at times. We're very dependent upon each other in a lot of ways, and that creates difficulties.

"It will be hard, I think, for the poor people Kevin, Allison and I marry. They'll have quite a burden to carry. I mean, they're going to get to know us and go, 'Wow, this is a handful!'

"A big handful . . . But a lot of *good* in that handful. . . ."

Allison Miles: "I've learned so much. . . . You just see people get so trivialized about their lives . . . and upset because of just some dumb thing like they actually forgot something at the grocery store. . . .

"You just look at people and want to say, 'There are so many more important things.'

"Even though we lost Riann . . . there's always, 'Out of darkness comes light. . . .'

"We're *so* close. I mean, granted, we're having our troubles, and we go through our ups and downs—I was going to say, 'Rocky Shores!'